THE
SHORT
STORY

THE

SHORT

STORY

KENNETH PAYSON KEMPTON

HARVARD UNIVERSITY PRESS
CAMBRIDGE, MASSACHUSETTS

To
Willis Kingsley Wing

FOREWORD

THIS BOOK WAS WRITTEN for all those good people, old or young, who feel sure they could write stories if only they knew how to begin. I have no patience with formulas and fiction factories, but neither do I believe that fiction cannot be taught. I have taught it at Harvard and Radcliffe, using the methods outlined here, for upwards of thirty years. But it was not, primarily, to inspire a flood of new stories that I finally set down these methods in print. Many who feel sure that they could write stories if only they knew how to begin may be helped merely by the discovery that knowing how to begin is not quite enough. This book was written in the hope that better, if perhaps fewer, stories will be written.

It is the result of long experience in writing stories as well as in teaching. Its ideas have been discussed with other writers, with readers, with editors and agents, and above all with students—and have often been modified in the process. But the principle upon which my teaching and my writing have been based—that a good story entails an unwritten contract between its writer, the editor, and its readers, and that good story writing must reconcile these often conflicting points of view—has never been altered.

I have taught creative writing so far without benefit of any textbook, for I have never been able to find one which was neither an abstract study of high art nor a practical handbook, but a little of both. Though driven at length to write something that might fill this need, I promise *not* to prescribe my book for my classes. It is too late to begin that now. And my book, in any event, is not one to be studied. There are few footnotes, there is no index; the only appendix is a list showing the whereabouts in print of the various stories used for illustration and an acknowledgment of permissions to quote. I hope that the reader who runs may read with no loss, and with some pleasure as well as some profit.

K. P. K.

1 January, 1947

CONTENTS

PART I

TECHNIQUE

PART II

CONTENT

CONTENTS

PART I
TECHNIQUE

PREVIEW

Fiction interprets human experience in dramatic terms. A story may be as factual as what happened to its author yesterday. More often the facts are modified, varying amounts of imagined experience are added, and the characters, the scene, the action—though real-appearing and true to life—cannot be identified as living persons, any particular place, or the literal details of human history. If it might have happened somewhere to somebody, that is enough. But that is a good deal. A story may reach into the past behind its immediate action, which itself may be a distant past to the reader; it may concentrate on a moment of its present, or of his; it may disclose a future that neither its characters nor the reader can really know. The short story particularly, with a premium on space, for emotional weight must try, at least by implication, to do all three. The more successful it is, the further it removes itself from history and the closer it comes to universal truth.

Whatever the approach, whatever the material and method, every story begins with a tacit profession of authenticity, as if simulating the factual authority of written history, which amounts to a promise by the author to the reader. "Once upon a time," the storyteller used comfortably to say. Nowadays the trend is more informal and explicit: "There was this girl," or "I possess a capital of thirty thousand pounds," or "It happened like this." Behind these words the author is opening his plea for conviction: "Believe me, you'll get it straight." And the promise carries an artful compliment. "All I have to do is tell it. *You* will understand." Every conscientious writer must have felt this obligation. Charles Lamb knew of it when he wrote to Wordsworth: "There is an implied and unwritten compact between author and reader; I will tell you a story and I suppose you will understand it." Lamb did not define the reader's side of the bargain, perhaps because it is obvious. The reader reciprocates merely by continuing to read. "Keep me interested and I'm with you," expresses his willingness at least to suspend disbelief. A somewhat one-sided agreement, perhaps, but so it should be. For the author began this affair; a seller must be prepared to go more than halfway. There are plenty of other things to read, other things to do besides read. No author has a right—though the younger and undisciplined sometimes think they have—to ask more.

If this direct, individual relationship between writer and reader were all, we are inclined to think that fiction would be easy. But one reader is of no use to an author. He cannot even gather a group around him and tell his story to them in person, as the ancient storyteller did. Nowadays an editor's help is needed, and his presence, though necessary and in the main profitable to both other parties, creates problems. For the editor *thinks* he knows better what will interest a reader than the reader himself knows. He is often wrong, and his mistakes injure authors as well as himself. Dominating his desire to please the reader, moreover, is the necessity of making his magazine, one of several supplying substantially the same product to potentially the same customers, show a profit. The editor has read countless manuscripts, he knows all the tricks of the trade, and is tired of reading; much of the eager zest for stories, invaluable to an author in a reader, has been drained out of him by hard work. He is sure, perhaps, only of what went well last month or last week, of the relentless efforts of his competitors, and of the sales resistance of his super-customers, the advertisers. With this surfeited, hard-boiled businessman the author must undertake some sort of compact before he can hope to reach a reader. There are grave risks in such a transaction, but authors—and good stories—continually survive them.

4

This book will study the writing of short stories from all three of these conflicting but compatible points of view: writer's, editor's, and reader's. Its purpose is to outline and recommend a clearer conception of the writer's obligations to the other two contracting parties than has usually existed, in young writers' minds or in books on writing; and this in the hope that better, if possibly fewer, stories will be written.

The smart amateur or apprentice takes a clear look at his chances, at the forces beyond or only partly within his control that will operate for and against permanent success in a contemplated vocation. Let us take the dark side of authorship first.

For over a hundred years the trade has been increasingly overcrowded. True, markets and readers have multiplied enormously, but rumors of big profits and the widely held notion that anybody with a pencil and paper can write a story have pushed the number of aspirants far ahead of the number of possible outlets for their work. Editorial readers of a national weekly receive hundreds of unsolicited manuscripts daily; they accept one or two. Magazines announce a crying need for new writers and boast of their discoveries, when the real need may have been only for economy: more stories at the lower rates new writers are glad to get. Correspondence schools, some schools of journalism, and many second-rate literary agents echo such ballyhoo, counting on the tuition or reading fees that will pour in from hopeful people who may never sell a story. A vague feeling, encouraged by lecturers and memoirs, that the writer's life is pleasant and relatively easy has swelled the ranks of would-be writers out of all proportion to their ability to write, as has the natural craving of an active and ingenious nation not yet far removed from pioneering for education, cultural benefits, and good living. Any honest author, no matter how successful, will testify that *his* life is incredibly hard—though he is likely to add, except at low moments, that it offers non-financial rewards that make it worth the trouble. Since few sensitive and imaginative people know themselves well, such testimony may be suspect; and one can hardly agree with William McFee's opinion that all would-be authors should be spanked and put to bed. Yet authorship is a serious business, not a hobby or pastime, *not* a result of inspiration or daydream. No one should take up writing for a living without at least temporary and partial other means of support. Nobody should undertake this work unless happiness seems inconceivable in any other. (Not that happiness may look attainable even in this.) An editor once said: "Two kinds of people come in here with manuscripts. A very large group who are all steamed up at the idea of making a million or of just seeing their names in print. And a very small one who only want to get something off their chests. The second kind are the writers. I wish to God there were more of them."

It is something, after all, like the difference between infatuation and marriage. "If you simply can't do without her," my dad once told me, "and if she'll have you, of course, *what* on earth are you *waiting* for, a sign from heaven?"

If that's the way with you and writing, push in, get going, keep up your courage, and God help us all!

Perhaps the greatest single difficulty confronting the would-be storyteller is the unlearning of his academic prose. This is the all-purpose rhetoric taught him from grade through graduate school or mistakenly acquired without help as an asset to authorship. It is the medium of themes, theses, reports, textbooks, and critical commentaries by the thousand. Traced back through such men as Macaulay, Gibbon, Samuel Johnson, Dryden, to Sir Thomas Browne and Francis Bacon, it has been the standard medium of written expression of expository or didactic thoughts during the centuries when such thoughts—for good fiction grew very slowly—were the chief reputable prose outlet of educated minds. For such purposes, at its worst it is still the best way we have of explaining or exhorting, short

6

of a diagram or a piece of lead pipe. Trouble is certain, however, if we allow practice in mere rhetoric to persuade us that this kind of prose is fit for storytelling. Trouble comes if we do not root academic prose clean out of ourselves, not only as a means of expression but as a habit of thinking. It is no better story medium than a dictionary; it is far worse than the directions printed on the label for opening a jar of pickles or a can of shoe polish.

For example:

In the exercise of supreme power, the first act of Justinian was to divide it with the woman whom he loved, the famous Theodora, whose strange elevation cannot be applauded as the triumph of female virtue. Under the reign of Anastasius, the care of the wild beasts maintained by the green faction at Constantinople was intrusted to Acacius, a native of the isle of Cyprus, who, from his employment, was surnamed the master of the bears . . . Acacius had . . . three daughters, Comito, Theodora, and Anastasia. . . . On a solemn festival these helpless orphans were sent by their distressed and indignant mother, in the garb of suppliants, into the midst of the theater; the green faction received them with contempt, the blues with compassion; and this difference, which sank deep into the mind of Theodora, was felt long afterward in the administration of the empire. As they improved in age and beauty, the three sisters were successively devoted to the public and private pleasures of the Byzantine people; and Theodora, after following Comito on the stage in the dress of a slave, with a stool on her head, was at length permitted to exercise her independent talents. She neither danced, nor sang, nor played on the flute; her skill was confined to the pantomime art; she excelled in buffoon characters; and as often as the comedian swelled her cheeks and complained with a ridiculous tone and gesture of the blows that were inflicted, the whole theater of Constantinople resounded with laughter and applause. The beauty of Theodora was the subject of more flattering praise and the source of more exquisite delight. . . . But this form was degraded by the facility with which it was exposed to the public eye and prostituted to licentious desire. Her venal charms were abandoned to a promiscuous crowd of citizens and strangers, of every rank and of every profession: the fortunate lover who had been promised a night of enjoyment was often driven from her bed by a stronger or more wealthy

7

favorite; and when she passed through the streets, her presence was avoided by all who wished to escape either the scandal or the temptation.

This passage from Gibbon's great history is academic prose at its very best: carefully organized, smooth flowing, comprehensible, interesting. Too, it is narrative. But imagine its approach to the subject, its tone, its stylistic devices employed in fiction. The first trouble would be the writer's persistent desire to cover the subject at every point, to tell all. He would be trying, against enormous odds, to be forcefully clear, which is none of the storyteller's business. Further obstacles would be his abstract generalities, his dignity, his long or latinate words, euphemisms of familiar phrases to avoid repetition, his strictly logical structure, and rhythmic sentence patterns—more often compound or complex than simple—which if necessary sacrifice space and even close meaning to the demands of rhetorical grace for well-rounded completion. A story manuscript weighed down by only two or three such attributes would find no readers today.

A piece of almost any capable short story will present a sharp contrast. Here are a few lines from William Faulkner's "That Evening Sun":

And then about half the time we'd have to go down the lane to Nancy's house and tell her to come on and get breakfast. We would stop at the ditch, because father told us not to have anything to do with Jubah—he was a short black man, with a razor scar down his face—and we would throw rocks at Nancy's house until she came to the door, leaning her head around it without any clothes on.

"What yawl mean, chunking my house?" Nancy said. "What you little devils mean?"

"Father says for you to come and get breakfast," Caddy said. "Father says it's over a half an hour now, and you've got to come this minute."

"I ain't studying no breakfast," Nancy said, "I going to get my sleep out."

8

"I bet you're drunk," Jason said. "Father says you're drunk. Are you drunk, Nancy?"

"Who says I is?" Nancy said. "I got to get my sleep out. I ain't studying no breakfast." [1]

The most noticeable difference is in paragraphing, marking the change from logical to chronological structure. But in this short story as elsewhere, Faulkner is not even consistently chronological: in mid-passage he shifts, for good reasons, from what often happened to what happened on some particular day. The presence of voices, a time sequence, and the attempt of fiction to refrain from full explanation but maintain intelligibility and interest by a thin but ceaseless stream of concrete details (breakfast, the ditch, the scar, rocks, the door, no clothes) have precluded any formal design. Something like a continuum of existence is what the storyteller is after, and he is willing to ignore vast areas susceptible of record that might be included, if only the little said is graphic and impelling. To tell all at any point would not only stop the story but take all the spice out of it, depriving the reader of his cherished right to infer (note how the implications that the children's father runs their house, that Jubah is Nancy's husband give the reader the chance), and to enjoy suspense. This demand for verisimilitude, moreover, has invaded sentence structure, phrasing, diction. Here is an adult recalling childhood. The words are not only characteristically short and simple but also exactly as heard in dialect (yawl) instead of exactly as listed in a dictionary or prescribed by grammar. Colloquial idiom has taken the place of academic good usage; repetition, instead of being avoided, is valued for its naturalness; and the sentences string along anyhow in the manner of childhood expression. In short, what the storyteller has to say must be clear by a wholly different and more difficult standard

[1] From *These 13*, by William Faulkner; Random House. Reprinted by permission of the publishers.

9

of clarity. Logic, abstractions, generalities, rhythmic sentence patterns, polished phrases will obscure his meaning. By other ways, less formal and less accurate but incomparably more vivid —often with no precedent—he must try to make a stream of sense impressions, *which he has felt,* live again in the reader's inner senses. Conrad put the problem well in his preface to *The Nigger of the Narcissus:* "My task which I am trying to achieve is, by the power of the written word to make you hear, to make you feel—it is, before all, to make you *see.*"

Another obstacle in the novice's path is a huge assortment of textbooks. The inquiring beginner faces a library of manuals and *vade mecums,* many of them overlapping, some of them flatly contradictory, and virtually all of them using diverse hypotheses and a jumble of loose terms. Were he to read anything like all of them, he might better go into something else, say insurance, as did a too-conscientious friend of mine. If he choose one, which shall it be? Something dignified and thoughtful that has withstood the test of time, such as Brander Matthews's essay "The Philosophy of the Short-Story" or Bliss Perry's *A Study of Prose Fiction,* risking the lack therein of contemporary material and technique? Something frankly commercial like John Gallishaw's *The Only Two Ways to Write a Story* or Trentwell Mason White's *How to Write for a Living,* relinquishing the possibility that he may be better than the pulp or slick fiction factory that such books promote? Or the latest in an endless stream got out by publishers with the regularity, and transience, of women's hats? Something formidable like *The Art of Fiction,* by Clayton Hamilton ("With a Foreword by Booth Tarkington, an Introduction by Brander Matthews, and Supplementary Suggestions and Laboratory Notes by Burges Johnson"); or something folksy by Dorothea Brande, telling him how to behave and what to eat and wear while *Becoming a Writer?* Or shall he shun the lot and go it alone?

The question is as hard, even for an unprejudiced person

(which I am not) to give advice on as it is for the individual to decide. Shunning the lot comes close to a solution but isn't quite that. Probably not one book in the impressive collection is really bad. Their chief fault in general is the fact that most of them were written not by storytellers or editors but by professors or critics: people who look at a story as an object to be analyzed, a dead thing, not a live one, not the sort of thing that can be done again. Scholars are painstaking and thorough; they love to dismount, disassemble, and dissect; but when a work of art has been broken down to its last conceivable footnote, their interest usually ends. Also, they are preoccupied with theory, tradition, perfection. They require and delight in terminology for manifold parts, never minding if their labels obscure the substance they set out to illuminate. Not one of these books but will increase in some measure an intelligent student's understanding of fiction. Yet hardly one can be guaranteed to increase by one sentence or one idea a potential author's ability to write a good story; and most of them will certainly decrease that ability. Notwithstanding the hard labor that made them and the shrewd publicity that launched them, to that end they are irrelevant.

If you need a handbook, choose one by somebody who has been actively connected with the writing or publishing of stories. Arthur Sullivant Hoffman, long editor of *Adventure,* is such a man; his *Fundamentals of Fiction Writing* is practical without commercialism, makes no scholarly fuss, and focuses strictly on a beginning writer's problems. I hope my book will be as good as his, and a little better since he wrote several years ago and short-story technique is expanding rapidly. Edith Merrilees and Frances Newman have written sensible books on this subject. If Bernard De Voto would put in book form the editorials he wrote for *The Saturday Review of Literature* called "English '37: The Novelist and the Reader," we should have another work that is both practical and high-minded. But don't waste time *studying* any book on writing: the things to study are not in print. Read a book once, perhaps let it lie handy for reference. Nothing more.

A third force often hostile to good work—and this one lies in the individual—is impatience to get into print. To be published is a natural desire in persons of the loftiest aims. After all, writing is a public performance, and the desire to be read, to feel that one is not merely starting but going on, is normal and wholesome—a far better frame of mind than its opposite, the diffidence of the incurable amateur who can't bear even the sympathetic eye of his dearest friend. But rushing to print has hurt many good writers before they could get well started. The saying that almost everybody has one book in him is quite possibly true; but does it follow that publishing, or even trying to publish, that one right away will be a good thing for all concerned? It may be the opposite. A well-known college teacher promised an A in his course to any students whose work passed any editorial gate before the year was out. His motive—to break down the barrier between academic theory and literary practice—was sound; but the results proved unfortunate. One canny sophomore received the highest grade for writing a letter to a newspaper praising one of its editorials. Another actually sold a story but suffered a bad case of swelled head, stopped writing, and after graduation went into business. Several students, one of them the most promising writer in the class, were permanently discouraged by a snowstorm of rejection slips.

The fact is that going on is not only no easier, but is usually harder than getting started. Selling my first story after several tries, I well remember thinking that the rest would be plain sailing. Ten years later, humped over the typewriter, I found myself thinking the same thing while struggling with Story Number 101. It took me the better part of two hundred manuscripts to realize that such dreams are illusory. Writing never grows easy. Facility increases with practice, but so do other qualities such as self-criticism which render facility itself suspect. Not an author I know but has encountered periods of failure, often years after being, as he thought, firmly established. Why not let such a period be early and voluntary, a period not of failure but of preparation? With temporary success a man's scale of living rises, his obligations increase; editors pay higher prices for his stories but become warier about buying, expecting a better and better product from him. Writers need time to fortify themselves against the slings and arrows, not only of impersonal misfortune, but of what is going to seem to them sheer editorial perfidy. They need time to build ability and confidence in ability that will survive any disaster. They need slow growth, a long period of mental gestation, opportunity to observe and objectify and rank various facets of life in perspective and proportion. And our literature could do with fewer flash-in-the-pan prodigies, fewer one-shots and fly-by-nights, more writing men and women girt for the long pull.

In 1934, after innumerable disappointments, William Saroyan sold a piece to *The American Mercury*. "Myself Upon the Earth" is a lamentably poor story but a remarkable document. Half-starved but tranquil, forced to pawn his typewriter, Saroyan had managed to get back this excellent machine, this symbol of the authorship he had not yet attained. Over the incident he poured out his sentimental soul:

I have said that I want to preserve my identity. Well, I mean it. If in doing this it is essential for me to remain unpublished, I am satisfied. I do not believe in fame. It is a form of fraudulence, and any famous man will tell you so. . . . But I will confess that you've got to be proud and religious to be the sort of writer I am. You've got to have an astounding amount of strength. And it takes years and years to become this sort of writer . . .

All this rambling may seem pointless and a waste of time, but it is not. There is absolutely no haste—I can walk the hundred-yard dash in a full day . . . I am not asking anyone to stand by. I am not promising golden apples to all who are patient . . .

I shall come soon to the matter of the typewriter, but there is no hurry. I am a story-teller, not an aviator. I am not carrying myself across the Atlantic in the cockpit of an airplane at the rate of two hundred and fifty miles per hour. . . . I am trying to gather as much of eternity into this story as possible . . .

In a moment a century may have elapsed, and I am doing what I can to keep this moment solid and alive.[2]

Would-be authors should not write like Saroyan (or like anybody else, for that matter), but they would do well to cultivate his patience, his indomitable belief in himself and the value of experience, his desire to preserve his identity even at the risk of never selling anything. They should apply this state of mind to their own development as craftsmen and adopt this statement as a creed. In the end it will prove more valuable than a pay check at a dollar a word.

More than counterbalancing the dangers of academic prose, irrelevant texts, and haste, several positive and helpful forces lie ready to hand.

Most accessible is the individual's own life. I mean not so much what has happened to him and what he has done, as the constant impact of merely being alive for a number of years on his mind and heart and all his senses. Few of us realize that on this subject we are the unique and incontrovertible authorities. It is only natural for an unknown, unpublished writer to discount his own experiences as negligible and unpromising. "*My* life?" he says. "Why, nothing has ever happened to *me.*" The material seems unpromising merely because it is so familiar. He gets from it none of the romantic excitement derived when he hears or reads of others' experiences. But he forgets that when he begins to write he and himself as reader have changed shoes. What is dull to him because familiar may be a source of wonder and delight to another simply because it is not. "The grass is always greener," an old song has it truly,

[2] From *The Daring Young Man on the Flying Trapeze and Other Stories,* by William Saroyan; Random House. Reprinted by permission of the publishers.

"in the other fellow s yard." This is the first occasion on which it is necessary for the inexperienced writer to differentiate between his needs and capacities as a writer and those of the man behind the printed page. There will be others. The great creative artists are the men and women possessed of unquenchable curiosity and something approaching total recall. Tolstoy's daughter, who served as his secretary and knew him well, says of him: "No person was outside his interest, or any subject . . . Nothing bored him—except artificiality. He loved all that was natural."

Forgetting things that have moved one emotionally is not easy. We think of total recall as a gift of genius, the mark of a Wordsworth or Proust. Maybe it is, but it can hardly exist without mental or emotional responsiveness, which themselves spring from alert senses. Without presuming to genius, a man can open his eyes.

Time goes by, as Saroyan says, "a century in a moment." No matter if months—years—of youthful impressions have slipped out of conscious memory. The subconscious is still well stocked with them, and you will use them without knowing you do so. And plenty more where they came from. Human experience is the most valuable and the cheapest commodity in the world. Anybody can begin acquiring it at any time, and one who wants to write had better begin now.

"It seems as if the day was not wholly profane," says Emerson, "in which we have given heed to some natural object." Close your eyes a moment, until the reflection of print on paper has faded from the finest camera ever made. In that partial darkness imagine yourself blind. How successfully could you reconstruct your surroundings, in a few words, for another pair of eyes which, never having seen the room, would have to translate your cold black letters into color, line, mass of the living image? Open your eyes and let them look straight ahead, resting anywhere they may, in the room or out a window. You will find something there that you never saw before. It may be no more than a shadow or highlight, the design of bark on a tree trunk, smoke rising, a human figure in motion. Probably your eyes have passed over it, your mind has become superficially aware of it, hundreds of times. But you may never have really seen it until this moment, because until this moment you may never have considered how you might through words make somebody else see it in his mind's eye. It may be something with which you are instantly familiar, know all about. It may not. If not, you might want to look into, as well as at it. Doing so would put you in good company, and librarians and people in general don't seem to mind how many questions these crazy writers ask.

Sense impressions, the philosophers say, cannot be defined. Words are slippery, and we are never positive that A's senses react to a given stimulus exactly as do B's. But what defies definition can be described in ways that transcend accuracy and defeat philosophers. It takes doing. The poets know how, as do the more sensitive novelists; and short-story writers have a special need for learning these ways because they are space-saving and emotionally evocative. Whitman knew how when he wrote of the carpenter's plane's "wild ascending lisp." Kipling did when his timid boy in the crib at night "felt as if everything was coming." There are no hard and fast rules; but make figures of speech short, familiar, if possible appropriate; and make mistakes and try again.

That experiment you tried with your sense of sight can be duplicated with smell and hearing. Non-smokers are in the habit of saying that the rest of mankind are killing their olfactory nerves and their taste buds, but the rest of mankind will continue to doubt this. My parents used to mention with disapproval Keats's covering his tongue with cayenne in order to experience the cool refreshment of wine. It is possible that the poet knew what he was doing. Certainly one can go too far along these lines, making sensation an end in itself; but does one have to? A broken hand, wrapped in a cast for a month or

16

two, will after healing have a completely new sense of touch. But the same effect can be imagined, with whole bones and a calloused palm. Giving thought to the exact nature of the touch of a hand, or of lips, may make one an absent-minded lover. At less risk feel of a book, replace it on the shelf among others, turn around several times, and with your eyes closed try to find it again by touch.

This is part of what I mean by the value of daily experience. A small part only. For most of our experience rises from contact with other human beings, and human beings constitute the primary source of material for stories. But alert, impressionable senses will make it easier for you to imagine and create the feelings of the people you are going to write about.

More help is to be found in the experiences and discoveries of writers. To the beginner, personal contact with an established author is often more useful than any textbook; literary history is full of such rewarding relationships: Hamlin Garland learning from William Dean Howells, Edith Wharton from Henry James, Kenneth Roberts from Booth Tarkington. Not all of us can catch the friendly eye of such an adviser. Indeed, not all writers are articulate about their work; the creative process is peculiarly cumulative and self-destroying— fire effacing its cause; and with the best will in the world sometimes a man is simply incapable of telling the steps through which his mind passed in achieving a known result. Yet enough good material has been published along these shadowy lines to make prefaces, letters, and journals of authors a very probable source of aid. Conrad's prefaces, for instance, to the uniform edition of his novels. Or Henry James's, which have been collected into a single volume called *The Art of the Novel*, or Ellen Glasgow's *A Certain Measure*, or Edith Wharton's preface to the 20th Anniversary Edition of *Ethan Frome*, or Frank Norris's *The Responsibilities of the Novelist, and Other Literary Essays*. No matter that these are chiefly novelists writing of concepts and technique in the novel; the unit is larger but the materials, often the methods, are the same; in each case we have an experienced creative artist telling us off-stage what he wanted to do and how he did it. And the short story itself has not been neglected. Katherine Mansfield's letters and journals are full of oblique and direct references to her work. In *Creating the Short Story,* an anthology edited by Henry Goodman in which each story is prefaced by the author's account of its composition, or the similarly contrived *Modern Writers at Work,* edited by Josephine K. Piercy, we have valuable help of this sort; for here is not one but a score of writers, a symposium on the subject, and even from the fact that the best of them, as judged from general output, are perhaps the least coherent and articulate some good may be drawn. Allowing for a margin of error in such work (for Sherwood Anderson's resentment that anybody should have the effrontery to inquire into *his* methods, for Ring Lardner's raillery and Hemingway's irony, and for the silly preoccupation of one or two third-raters with purely mechanical matters)— still there is great good to be gained from all sincere efforts of authors to say what they were up against, how they met the enemy and in how far they believe they defeated him. Besides technical and conceptual suggestions, in general the most helpful qualities to be found here are a quiet assurance (not to be mistaken for conceit) about the writer's ability to transmit experience in its simplest terms—such as Conrad's single question to the lay reader of his first manuscript: "Is it clear?"—and an honest, a very genuine humility. Such books by authors about authorship are the next best thing to having an author as friend.

Advice from editors, oral or written, lies in the same category. Relatively little has been published, for editors are habitually overworked and there is, after all, no good reason why they should take time out to generalize about how they want things done. But when the day comes, some help of this sort will appear periodically in the young writer's morning mail. It won't seem helpful, but as soon as the recipient recovers from his sense of outrage that anybody could find his piece less than perfect, it will be. To graduate from an era of rejection slips to one of refusal by personal letter, with reasons given, may be hopeful enough. If a mere hint about rewriting is vouchsafed some day —well, there is a text in itself.

But probably the greatest single source of aid lies in published stories.

I am not in favor of studying models by means of parallel columns or marginal notes which maintain a running commentary nudging the reader into comprehension of just how the masterpiece achieved perfection. Two vicious forces are thereby set up: an implied false generality, for the masterpiece would not be a masterpiece if its circumstances of creation were not exceptional; and an inferiority complex, or a complete muddle, in the mind of the student as soon as he confronts this flaw. Nobody actually knows how a great work of art such as Maupassant's "The Piece of String" came into being. It is there, a miracle, like a moss picture on a headstone. It can be gratefully admired, a marvelous thing out of reach, and should be. If analyzed and broken down, however, its unwavering suspense and aching pathos appear to be the direct result of several transgressions and some pretty slipshod writing. By all academic counts it should have been a failure! What then is the earnest analyzer to do?

Despair, which is bad enough. Or try to imitate, which is worse. Stevenson's remark about the "sedulous ape," uttered innocently with strict reference to stylistic exercises in academic prose, has been seized upon by teachers who never sold a manuscript, twisted out of shape, and made to serve as chief standard for story-writing. "Well, it gives them *something* to write about," a teacher told me lamely as her class wrestled with versions of the Book of Ruth, while the stories they knew something about and perhaps could tell lay buried in their hearts. This academic perversion has its parallel in commercial writing circles. Somehow word got about that the way to sell a story was to tabulate the offerings of some chosen magazine as to length, theme, setting, character types, plot; then to "slant" your product that way—that is, imitate as closely as possible without plagiarism the kind of story the magazine appeared to favor. In my experience no editor above the pulp level will concur in this theory. Over and over, directly and indirectly through agents and writing friends I have heard the editorial statement, almost the plea: "Write them as you see them. The good story is a natural, never slanted at anybody, and is bound to get published. If we don't take it, somebody else will."

But if imitation is unwise, why do I say published stories should be read?

We are apt to forget that even a short short story is an integration of many small elements which illustrate methods of work shared by some writers, ignored by others. It is in the comparative study of methods, not in imitating content or style, that reading is useful. The masterpiece will never appear again, but its triumphant substitution of, for instance, emotional tension for strict time sequence can, with luck, be emulated. In "The Killers" Hemingway heightens suspense by letting a clock be twenty minutes fast. Nobody can do that again and get away with it, nobody should try. But that clock can be held as a symbol of Hemingway's silent overtones, unsaid things working like yeast in the dark, and the result, a sort of functional prose that lives by suggesting far more than it states, will always be worth the effort. In short, it is methods and devices, common property of all, that by means of reading can be noted, compared, and used. Or shunned! Our analysts and imitators seem never to have considered that anything in print may be bad. But who can read Hawthorne's "The Birthmark" without getting an object lesson on the dangers of setting up a hypothetical situation of which the author has no first-hand knowledge? What thoughtful reader can go through even a small part of Hemingway without discarding his interminable "he saids" as sheer laziness, or vowing to avoid the obscurities in which, too often, his stark prose involves him?

Young writers should read widely, choosing authors according to their taste and not from a sense of duty. They should read humbly but alertly, noting improvements and failures, sound methods and mere affectations, exceptions that prove the rule and journeyman's work too slick and trite to prove itself. The short story is the youngest child of literature, but for half a century now it has been well aware of itself. From imitation of European models and mere groping in the dark for anything an editor would buy and a public would read, its American authors have come into a knowledge of what, technically and substantially, they themselves want to do and how they themselves want to do it. They can show us if we will read them, and by reading them, perhaps in some respects we can equal or better their best.

Having considered the pros and cons of his step into authorship, the novice would do well to look briefly at himself as, possibly, an author. For good fiction—I assume that he will not be content to write anything less than the best of which he is capable—is the result not of studying rules, or knowing writers, or even reading, but of being a particular kind of person. A person neither attractive nor unattractive, neither moral nor immoral—all popular belief and many scholarly findings about past authors to the contrary notwithstanding—but of mind, emotions, perceptions, and tastes particularly and abnormally constituted. The novice might well compare his present self with such a person, trying to see if he is or could conceivably be like him; and if so, whether he really wants to be.

To describe the genus is difficult and dangerous. Anything specific enough to have meaning is bound to invite exception. But Christopher Morley came close through self-portraiture when he remarked expansively (perhaps toward the end of a meeting of the Three Hours for Lunch Club?), "I have a notion that every day, from toothpaste to toothpaste, is an artistic whole." On the other side of the world a Japanese novelist, Lady Murasaki, was reaching for the same idea when she wrote that the storyteller's experience seems to him "so important that he cannot let it pass into oblivion." Donald Hough, without denying this, studies the profession more specifically and realistically in the following passage:

A writer must work alone; he must forego occupational gregariousness with others of his trade. His first job is to reflect something of the life by which he is surrounded and of which he is a part. This eliminates other writers as neighbors; a writer ought to be surrounded by normal people living a normal life, and writers are not normal people and they live a ridiculous life. They do not live, they pose; they walk on a perpetual stage, taking all parts but their own, working up a sort of protective coloring so they can worm their way into circles from which they hope to extract sustenance. . . . A writer . . . has an ungovernable impulse to participate in everything he sees.[3]

As a class, in my experience, writers are bridge, checkers, and chess players—not always good ones, but liking the relief from their thoughts brought by games of close concentration. (Hemingway somewhere tells how hard he tried, one evening in Madrid, with "The Killers" half written, "not to think about the story.") But writers are also walkers, golfers, sailors, farmers, woodcutters, fishermen, liking relatively untaxing pursuits that allow a mental accompaniment. They are light sleepers. They get the horrors for no communicable reason. They can work, and profitably, for hours doing nothing but look out a window. They cannot remember their own telephone numbers, but they never forget the most detailed and apparently inconsequential circumstances surrounding their receipt of a sight, sound, smell, taste, or touch of (to them) significance, and are willing to spend hours of odd moments

[3] From *Snow Above Town,* by Donald Hough; W. W. Norton & Co. Reprinted by permission of the publishers.

trying to recreate the image in such a way that the words will mean to some heedless reader precisely what the sense impression meant to them. Creative writers, too, find it difficult to take sides; for they are inclined to look for and find at least two sides to every question, as well as to every person: from such discoveries are stories made. And of course they blow hot and cold over matters in which nobody else can detect the slightest importance.

There will be wide variance in these superficial characteristics. But as regards three basic qualities, essential to competence in this kind of work, I believe there will be little or none.

The first is persistence.

Inexperienced writers are often bothered by their own change of heart about work in progress. Somewhere between conception and completion—frequently as early as page 3—reaction sets in and a piece that was to set the world afire goes cold. The natural assumption is, first, "If I can't believe in it long enough to finish the rough draft, it must be no good"; and then, "Or maybe *I'm* no good."

Now this reaction is perfectly normal. Experienced, established writers know it well; and they know (as the beginner does not) how to cope with it. Robert Sherwood admits that "between plays" he becomes regularly and utterly convinced that he will never finish another. Edith Wharton once mentioned, by the way and not complaining, the *"lacunae* of dullness and sterility" incident to the writing life. In the preface to *Nostromo* Conrad recalls a "disturbing mood that lasted some little time" when "it seemed somehow that there was nothing more in the world to write about." John Marquand tracks this doubt down to its last detail:

You were living in two worlds when you were writing. You were trying, very unsuccessfully, to be omnipotent in the region of the imagination. You had delusions not so very unlike those of some man in an asylum who thought he was Napoleon Bonaparte. The main difference was that you never possessed the inmate's sublime conviction. If you had any modesty at all—a very bad thing for a writer—you lived in a little hell of your own uncertainty. Without any help, and out of thin air, you were obliged to create an imaginary world and to people it with what were known as "Characters." . . . You had to live two lives at once at such a time, to exist with ordinary people and at the same time to adjust yourself to the people of your imagination. They were with you all the time and you could not get away from them. They were there when you were talking to someone else. They were there when you read the newspaper or paid the bills, or went out to dinner. . . . This process was not agreeable. . . . The thing had some of the elements of a nervous malady, except that you knew you would get over it eventually.[4]

And Thomas Mann, allowing Tonio Kröger to voice his own experience, would not even admit the comfort of that assurance:

"Literature is not a calling, it is a curse, believe me! . . . It begins by your feeling yourself apart, in a curious sort of opposition to the nice, regular people; there is a gulf of ironic sensibility, of knowledge, skepticism, disagreement, between you and the others; it grows deeper and deeper, you realize that you are alone, and from then on any rapprochement is simply hopeless. . . . When these worthy people are affected by a work of art, they say humbly that that sort of thing is a 'gift.' They never dream that the 'gift' in question is a very dubious affair and rests upon extremely sinister foundations."[5]

If widely known authors, with publishers and readers waiting, can feel like this and survive, there must be something in their attitude toward work, in their relationship with themselves, worth learning.

To come at it one must consider the difference between a trade and a profession, which I take to be independence of spirit: in a profession you take orders only from yourself. Richard Hughes made the implications of this difference clear.

[4] From *So Little Time*, by John P. Marquand; Little, Brown & Co. Reprinted by permission of the publishers.

[5] From *Tonio Kröger*, by Thomas Mann; Alfred A. Knopf, Inc. Reprinted by permission of the publishers.

"The laboring man," he wrote, in *In Hazard,* "sells his labor, at a rate of money. . . . His working day is the number of hours he is willing to waste, in order to have the wherewithal to live and to enjoy his leisure. The professional man also calls what he does 'work'; but his meaning is exactly opposite. . . . Whereas the laborer looks on work as the means to get money, the professional looks on money as the means to do work." Or, as Ellen Glasgow put it in *A Certain Measure,* "I liked money, but I liked other things more."

But writing, or any other artistic effort, is unique even among professions in having no external machinery of compulsion for continued production. (There is of course an inner urge, an impulsion, but we are not concerned with it now.) Office hours, clients, classes, patients set up such machinery approaching, for other professional workers, the external authority of the boss's orders or the factory whistle. Nobody else cares a hoot if the free-lance writer stops. He has only rarely a contract or deadline to meet. And since the pleasure a human being can derive from any kind of steady work is capricious, and his pride in that work evanescent, since results are slow and success is uneven, the invitation to stop may be constant in some form and at times almost unanswerable.

The chronology of composition itself, in fact, and in the hardiest professionals as in the greenest tyro, may be closely similar to the course of a manic-depressive psychosis. It can be roughly diagrammed as follows:

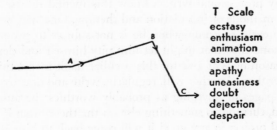

T Scale
ecstasy
enthusiasm
animation
assurance
apathy
uneasiness
doubt
dejection
despair

On the vertical scale representing psycho-emotional "temperature" (T) in relation to work at hand (and by natural association, all similar work, then all work), the barbed line records the rise and decline of this factor during composition. A is the point at which the author finds an idea feasible and begins to write. Everything looks good at first. T rises steadily, sharply or gradually according to temperament, with the fervor of creation and under the stimulus of physical accomplishment. B is the point at which reaction (which may of course have been caused by nothing to do with writing) begins to occur; and from B the drop in T may be almost perpendicular, extends usually as far below normal as B was above it, and is always to a level below A. It is at this level, C, in a state of mind and spirit somewhere between apathy and despair, that a lot of good work has been finished.

Finished despite doubts not alone of the worth of this job but of any future one. Finished in the salving knowledge that creative exercise has weakened or temporarily atrophied critical judgment so that there is no immediate way of knowing whether the thing is good or bad. There may be later, minor rises in T, but each is likely to be followed by a drop to a level lower than the beginning of the rise. The end of the work may find the author in an up trend, since after all the thing is *done;* but he will see this elation for what it is and discount it, hoping only that he has done the best he can. And when the story sells (if it does sell), he will be amazed.

I say professional writers know this mental disease and develop methods of inoculation and therapy. One will work only in the early morning when he is not subject to personal and telephone calls that might let him pity himself and desist; but the reason he will give for this peculiar habit is that things are quieter then. Another will, regularly, write and destroy the first three pages of anything as probably worthless because superheated, turning to something else on the theory that if the discarded project is any good it will come back to him and force itself to get written. Another will refuse to begin a piece until it has bothered his mind for long enough to give him assurance that he can stick with it. And another, as he begins and his spirits rise, will persistently cry down the idea to himself, not talk about it to others, keeping that initial rise lower and the subsequent fall less severe. All of them know what they are doing. Eventually a habit is formed, they are not happy unless they are writing, even if, writing, they seem to be getting nowhere; and independence of spirit, driven by that inner urge, has triumphed over the rest of the mind that sought to slay it. "I write," says William Faulkner, "when the spirit moves. And it moves every day."

The second basic quality is imagination. This word has been fought over so long that those on the battleground must use considerable energy even to recall what they are fighting about. Webster says imagination is "That power or function of the mind whereby we have ideal experience." With a slight addition to the word "mind" and a strict interpretation of the word "ideal," the definition is good enough for any storyteller. He will need an emotional stimulus for what Webster terms a mental process, something of the heart as well as of the mind for rich imaginative functioning. And he must take "ideal" in its first meaning, "existing as an archetypal (or original) idea," not with any sense of perfection or of unreality.

In a creative artist the imagination functions, I believe, in three ways. It is partly mere fancy, which moves happily into make-believe, the sort of innocent guesswork that tells stories to itself about princesses and dragons, that creates life unseen behind lighted but drawn window shades passed at night, inside people glimpsed but never known. Such life is probably all wrong factually, and it may prove all wrong in a story unless another function of the imagination is brought into use. Coleridge argued that the imagination has a restraining, a unifying, a synthesizing power; and so it must have here. For restraining, a healthy doubt as to whether dragons still exist.

27

For unifying, the inner eye capable of seeing that a dragon may still exist in, say, human form. For synthesizing, the deductive and associative alertness that sees much in a brief glimpse—evidence in a torn shade, a muddy shoe, or close-set eyes based on such details previously observed, with plausibly drawn inferences resulting. In short, this part of the imagination motivates and makes plausible, and thus significant, the guess of the fancy; and truth-to-history accuracy becomes irrelevant to storytelling so long as the motivation is sound by standards of probability and human understanding and universal truth. I mean, for instance, in the case of the torn window shade: actually, in the lives of those people behind it the shade may be a matter of not the smallest importance; if, however, the author's imagination sees it, let us say, as a symbol of a young wife's losing fight against poverty and slovenliness, and can build up from other observed and appropriately imagined experience further details of character and environment supporting this ideal hypothesis, to the end that it all *sounds* true and our hearts are torn between pity and rage that such a nice person should get into such a fix—then who cares about historical accuracy? In a state of heightened emotional tension, we know from our own lives, the smallest mishap (a torn window shade) can seem catastrophic. Universal truth has been tapped. The story has meaning transcending actual fact.

The creative imagination, indeed, is partly this very readiness and ability to seize upon symbols for their emotional value. It is in large part sympathy for, curiosity about, and love of people; not people as potential friends, of course, but simply as beings worthy of the most objective, excited, and compassionate scrutiny; people struggling, winning or losing in real life, therefore conceivably struggling, winning or losing in as yet unwritten stories. Tolstoy "loved all that was natural."

My third basic quality may go by several names. Rare in youth, its need is a sound reason for not rushing into print. In this affair, something is wanted to leaven the fact that a writer must draw from his own experience—something to keep him from writing only about himself. For any man's experience is shot through with caprice and prejudice applicable only to himself, insusceptible of dramatic interpretation because he is too close to see it clearly. Milton published his polemics on marriage and divorce as soon as his first wife left him, but he waited a long time before writing a story, *Samson Agonistes,* about a blind man deluded by a woman. His caution was that of the artist, who bides his time until all the evidence is in and all possible fallacy offered by his rage, chagrin, and loneliness is out. What personal facts of Shakespeare's life are discernible in his plays? Of Chaucer's in *The Canterbury Tales,* or of Conrad's in all his stories of the sea? These great storytellers, and many less gifted, had the third basic quality. The short stories of James Farrell and the novels of Thomas Wolfe, though brilliant enough in other respects to demand a reading, lack it. So, too, do dozens of first novels that lean hard on autobiography, "rushing out," as Ruth Suckow says, "with a highly personalized account of what [the authors have] learned from life so far . . . including [their] findings about women" —stories that substitute prejudiced fact for imaginative truth, appear to all but their authors and sensation-hunters mawkish and jejune, and may come to seem so even to them. The error may be less flagrant than sheer exhibitionism; life is exciting, one can't bear to let it go by unrecorded; but without the leavening force the record is bound to err nevertheless. What Wordsworth applied to poetry applies here, though not strictly in terms of time: the story should be inspired by "emotion recollected in tranquility."

Some people will call this quality detachment, others adaptability, still others merely a sense of humor; and I have heard it referred to as the author's third eye. They are all one. The trait I am after results in perspective and objectivity, creating, for instance, a state of mind that will admit a reader's or an editor's taste as not without importance, that will see any experience through which the author has passed as possibly unique in impact but not in occurrence—will see it, that is, in relation to countless other experiences of its kind that must have happened to other people.

By ironical implication Budd Schulberg makes very clear today's need of this quality, in *What Makes Sammy Run?*, the story of a copy boy from a New York daily who went to Hollywood and in a year rose to $2000 a week without ever writing a script. "And then there was," Schulberg says through his narrator, Mannheim, speaking of the great director Sammy Blick had become—

there was his colossal lack of perspective. This was one of his most valuable gifts, for perspective doesn't always pay. It can slow you down. I have sat in my office and said to myself, There are twelve millions of your fellow Americans unemployed this morning. Who the hell are you? If that kept me from writing a line all morning it might mean I had perspective. Or thinking how the world was fifty million years ago and all the men who had their chance at living in it and what that had to do with the big pay-off scene in *Nick Turner, Boy Detective* I was supposed to turn in by five o'clock. That's perspective too. Or just staring up into millions of stars at night until you become molecular. Perspective is a fine thing. It can make you very unhappy. . . .[6]

It *is* a fine thing; it is a basic quality in all great and most good work. If you have it and it makes you unhappy in conditions similar to those Schulberg describes, quite possibly the better you will write. Its possession can turn a weak writer into a strong one. Recognition of the need of it and admission of its lack, even, can prevent the appearance of another bad writer by preventing him from writing at all.

But why worry about whether or not you have these three qualities, persistence, imagination, detachment? If you really want to write, you will write by these means: you will keep on

[6] From *What Makes Sammy Run?* by Budd Schulberg; Random House. Reprinted by permission of the publishers.

being interested in people, being more interested in what you see happens to them than what you are apt to feel happens—or doesn't happen—to yourself; and you will keep eternally at it, rain or shine. Thus you will have and use those three qualities without having become self-conscious about them.

As for physical equipment, a few things are indispensable and the rest can be left to individual taste. Typescript is of course obligatory; far better to produce it than hire it done; for most writers the peck system is as good as any, and it can be acquired quickly and soon becomes as unobtrusive as hand-writing. Nearly as essential is a dictionary. Webster's is the best for general use, the big one if possible, otherwise the desk size. (*The New English Dictionary on Historical Principles,* 10 volumes, is of great value to anybody writing stories laid in the past.) The best paper, for everything but final draft, is the cheapest: namely, yellow manila copy at about .35 the ream. Any light white bond at less than $2 a ream is all right for the editor. Heavy kraft or manila envelopes with gummed flap, in two sizes, the larger big enough to hold the smaller and the smaller big enough to take typewriter paper (8½″×11″) without folding, are going to be useful sooner or later, too.

Other books worth owning or having accessible are:

> Langer, *Encyclopedia of World History*
> Roget, *Thesaurus*
> Rand McNally, *Commercial Atlas*
> Everyman *Encyclopedia,* 12 vols.
> Soule, *Synonyms*
> Bartlett, *Familiar Quotations*

To these I add two books that cost nothing: a telephone directory, the bigger the better, no matter how old, to suggest character names; and a mail-order house catalogue for its excellent descriptions and drawings of a thousand-and-one objects too familiar to have been closely observed. These books are best ranged on a shelf of their own or at the back of your desk or work table, within short reach.

The foregoing preview of authorship has no dramatic close. Except in critics' minds, a writing life has no climax; and these pages are but a glimpse of a beginning. If, having survived their candor, you still want to write, you might well stop reading and begin. You begin by thinking, for an hour or so, of something or somebody you have been in contact with recently and like to think about—anything or anybody on earth will do, so long as your knowledge and liking are the results of first-hand experience. After thinking, write down what you remember, deleting yourself from the experience unless you are sure that your part is no more than observer, that the something or somebody you want to write about comes out as of prime importance. Try to set down the subject exactly as it is, but without a line of academic prose. Let there be a time sequence, but never mind any plot. Get a thousand words, three or four pages. Read it over. If it comes anywhere near doing what you set out to do, tear it up and go and have some fun. If not, especially if it seems to do something else, tear it up and try again.

2

TALK

IT IS CUSTOMARY and useful to break down a work of art in any medium—sound, color, clay, or words—into two large areas, content and technique. For close study of the short story we must consider these areas separable, bearing in mind, however, that any such separation is arbitrary, that in operation the functions of the two areas are complementary and interdependent. A noble theme may sound merely pretentious under poor telling, and the popular magazines sometimes glitter with skillful technique masking wooden characters and outworn situations. Thus, investigation of either area implies and will necessitate frequent reference to the other.

Unchronologically, with respect to the creative process itself, let us consider technique first. Technique is a toolbox, an assortment of ways and means with all of which a writer should be familiar before he ponders the best way of telling a story. Its counterpart, content—approach to and management of story material, the experience behind it, the ideas it dramatizes—is never hurt by being let alone a while. Perhaps by first discussing how to write stories, this book will make the riskier job of suggesting what to write seem less dogmatic.

Technically, a story tries to set up and maintain an illusion of life by recording a sequence of facts about people. It has always tried to do this behind every other aim. We are not concerned here with precise origins, and even if we were, so deep-rooted is the narrative instinct that I am not sure the first short story ever told on earth would be discoverable. But of our modern form it is possible to identify two reverend ancestors, two archetypes that arose in the habits of different kinds of people, existed separately for a while, then branched and merged in a product that had attributes of both origins and yet was a distinct entity in itself.

The earlier ancestor, since speech preceded writing, was popular and secular; it was the told anecdote, the funny story that still circulates in living and locker rooms today. When first a commercial traveler or tired husbandman, meeting an acquaintance, said in effect, "Stop me if you've heard this one," and went on about a mother-in-law or two newlyweds, he told something that in structure, method, and intent has strong similarities to some of the work of O. Henry, for instance, or the short stories we read week after week in *The New Yorker* or the *Saturday Evening Post*. This ancestral told story could be clean or lewd, but it must be light if not really funny and it must have a point at the end—a point unexpressed but carefully prepared for and suggested, then left to the hearer's inference.

The other, later beginning was literary; it was written down to be read by those who could read, and it was serious-minded. Aesop's *Fables* are perhaps the earliest examples, and there are many later and less known ones in the *Gesta Romanorum* and the bestiaries of the Middle Ages. Here, too, was a representation of human beings in action—or of animals possessing human qualities—but for a different purpose: instead of entertainment, for satire or moral instruction. Churchmen encouraged this prose, seeing the possibility of moral teaching by means of story; and down the centuries pious people have clung to the belief that stories must be moral. As late as the mid-eighteenth century in England and the beginning of the nineteenth in America, it was felt that without this provision daydreaming by reading stories (the drama, with similar origins, struggled under a similar handicap) must be sinful—it was too much fun. Much earlier, of course, it was only natural for writers to suppose that a sure way to avoid such a charge was to use characters, such as animals, or personified

34

abstractions, with which no reader would be apt to identify himself emotionally; and then to build up each tale to some elevating thought, "signification," "application," or, frankly, moral. Thus this literary source also had a kind of point at the end; but its point was either openly stated as an appendix to the story, or made so explicit in the text that no inference was required to grasp it. Take Aesop's "The Fox and the Grapes":

A hungry Fox one day saw some tempting Grapes hanging at a good height from the ground. He made many attempts to reach them, but all in vain. Tired out by his failures, he walked off, grumbling to himself, "Nasty, sour things, I know you are, and not at all fit for a gentleman's eating."
It is easy to despise what you cannot get.

This tendency to moralize or philosophize about human nature by dramatic exemplification, this desire to make a serious point of the story, has also come down as an aim of the short story today, although its original crude explicitness has fortunately been discarded as readers' wits sharpened and technique developed. By skilled craftsmen it is used fittingly and subtly to increase our knowledge of life; but we see it also in the work of such men as the socially-conscious proletarians, who write stories to get political action, and in that of many popular hacks who know their readers long to feel a warm moral glow.

If these archetypes had radical differences, they shared one element vital to narrative: quoted speech. In both, speech was used for verisimilitude and to demonstrate the type and temperament of the speaker (as the Fox's assumption of gentlemanly tastes demonstrates his low character). Down the long history of storytelling to the present day of movies and radio, whose direct impact on the senses challenges the written story, it becomes increasingly apparent that one of the prime technical requisites for the storyteller is an ability to make characters talk like living people. Least illusory, even potentially misleading, is the character who never or seldom opens his

35

mouth. Better, often useful for space-saving and transition, but not really vivid, is one whose speech is paraphrased in indirect discourse composed and uttered for him by the author. The people on paper who seem to live and breathe are those whose very words are voiced. For almost all human beings are more or less vocal. As readers we have come to recognize quotation marks as a symbol of the sound of a human voice. When they and the words they enclose can be transmitted naturally, the author's task of maintaining illusion is lightened by half. Convincing dialogue is one simple and plausible way of revealing and contrasting character; and certainly the juxtaposition of dissimilar characters, with conflict first implied and then demonstrated, is a wellspring of storytelling.

The question is how to make the talk of people in stories sound real and convincing. We can come at an answer best by a comparative study of examples of dialogue, deciding what qualities help to create illusion and what prevent it by an effect of unreality or of obvious artifice.

Years ago a serious but untalented student in Harvard College wrote a story about army life called "Jim Bent, Deserter." As the story opens, its protagonist, having learned of a love affair between his friend and fellow officer Kane, and the wife of their commander, a Major Lane, goes to the lady and tries to shame her into breaking it off. They talk:

"This outrageous proceeding must stop," Bent said as he opened the door.

"And who are you to dictate to me?"

"You know it is ruining Kane, and God knows it is awful for your husband. If he should find out he'd kill you. And by God he ought to know! It is the most shameless thing I've ever heard of for a woman of your age to make love to a boy behind your husband's back. Why some day he will do something that—er—can't be patched up. And who will be to blame? I tell you, it must stop!"

"Will you kindly leave my house and mind your own business?" stormed Mrs. Lane, stamping her foot down on the floor.

36

Hoighty-toighty! But ignore the silly situation, consider merely the words by which these two people are made to express their feelings. The unreality here is plainly the result of imaginative deafness. Bent and Mrs. Lane don't talk, they rant; they spout run-of-the-mill phrases that popped into the writer's head. Perhaps he had read stories in which people carried on like this; perhaps he had seen movies (it was back in the days of silent pictures) whose captions and titles got him into the way of thinking such speech natural; certainly he never once listened, for writing purposes, to two human beings talking under stress. If he had ever listened, Bent's opening speech would have been less abrupt, his approach more diplomatic and less sanctimonious, he would surely not have argued for the Major's best good or threatened Mrs. Lane with death at her husband's hands; on her part the Major's wife would probably have interrupted that long and impudent sermon, and her indignation would have found some less incongruous expression than the stamp of her foot ("down") on the floor. The passage is brilliantly bad, approaching inadvertent burlesque. Its failure to characterize individuals is proved by the feasibility of swapping the spoken lines, in a hypothetical opposite situation giving Bent's remarks to Mrs. Lane and hers to him, without loss of what little sense here resides. Such talk is only dimly and remotely human. Nothing more real, however, can be expected from second-hand material and hand-me-down diction. You have to have life models. You have to come out of the library and listen to living people.

But listening is not enough, for stories are not biographies. Listening gives the language, the groundwork—but far too much of it. Adaptation, shaping, excising become necessary. To what extent, without loss of reality that springs from life modeling, we must now decide.

In a short story wittily called "Safe in the Arms of Croesus," Owen Wister assembled four contrasted characters, tablemates on an ocean liner homeward bound from Europe in the twen-

37

ties, and recorded their reactions to each other in order to demonstrate that money can dominate brains.

"This your first trip?" [the big businessman, manufacturer of a nerve tonic called Muscatol, asks the brainy young law-school graduate].

"My seventh," said the boy.

"Well, their hotels are falling over each other putting in bathrooms. We're telling Europe where to get off."

"Isn't it glorious to lead the world in plumbing!" exclaimed the boy.

"Oh!" protested the gentle lady. "We lead it in kindness and generosity to all in misfortune."

"And in Art and Letters," said the boy. She looked at him reproachfully.

"And in enterprise," said the editor. "And energy. And resourcefulness."

She looked at him gratefully.

Muscatol had not been attentive to any of this. "This your first trip?" he asked the boy.

"My fifteenth," said the boy.

"Take a card," said Muscatol, handing him one. "I'm head of our publicity department. Name is Cartwell Ross Cartwell."

"Call me Home Sweet Home," said the boy.[1]

In sharp contrast with the first example, this is plainly the work of a mature and practiced writer. Probability has been weakened, perhaps, by prevalently short speeches that quicken the tempo of the scene beyond strict verisimilitude, but the interplay of voices is so engaging that only a captious reader would object. Here talk and accompanying action do reveal character. We catch the boy's irony, the spinster's sentimentality, the editor's 100 per-cent Americanism, the tycoon's stupid conceit, merely through the words they speak and their behavior while speaking—catch these traits via a continued overtone of meaning that keeps us chuckling. Valid objection can be made, how-

[1] From *Harper's Magazine,* October, 1927. Reprinted by permission of Owen J. Wister and Mrs. Walter Stokes, executors of the estate of Owen Wister.

ever, on the kind and depth of characterization effected. These are not individuals but broad types, two-dimensional beings hardly more substantial than the personified abstractions of morality plays or the incarnations of Ben Jonson's "humours." Once each demonstrates his dominant characteristic we can predicate his speech and acts to the end of the story. Upon close examination, moreover, the forms of dialogue here used seem to accentuate the slight artificiality of uniformly short speeches already noted. If you underline the verbs of saying, their monotony becomes quickly apparent: each follows something said, and with one exception (*he asked the boy,* sixth line up) all are inverted, preceding instead of following the subject. Remarking these mannerisms, one begins to wonder whether anybody could actually be as dumb as Wister's tycoon, as instantly witty as his youthful lawyer; and with the doubt illusion breaks. A consistently funny story might conceal this unreality, but "Safe in the Arms of Croesus" turns on a serious theme: the surrender of the boy's high principles to big-business quackery. This talk is a long-shot better than the ludicrous blunders of "Jim Bent." As useful aids we can note here the readability of short speeches, if not carried too far, and of dramatic character portrayal. But there must be more to dialogue than this minstrel-show technique.

Near the beginning of "The Killers," just after the two gunmen have entered the lunchroom, Hemingway wrote this passage:

"I'll have a roast pork tenderloin with apple sauce and mashed potatoes," the first man said.

"It isn't ready yet."

"What the hell do you put it on the card for?"

"That's the dinner," George explained. "You can get that at six o'clock." George looked at the clock on the wall behind the counter.

"It's five o'clock."

"The clock says twenty minutes past five," the second man said.

"It's twenty minutes fast."

"Oh, to hell with the clock," the first man said. "What have you got to eat?"

"I can give you any kind of sandwiches," George said. "You can have ham and eggs, bacon and eggs, liver and bacon, or a steak."

"Give me chicken croquettes with green peas and cream sauce and mashed potatoes."

"That's the dinner."

"Everything we want's the dinner, eh? That's the way you work it. . . . This is a hot town. What do they call it?"

"Summit."

"Ever hear of it?" Al asked his friend.

"No," said the friend.

"What do you do here nights?" Al asked.

"They eat the dinner," his friend said. "They all come here and eat the big dinner."

"That's right," George said.[2]

I think the best thing about this talk is its naturalness, its apparently untouched veracity. These short lines are far more appropriate to the speakers than were Wister's; their machine-gun rhythm exerts a powerfully suggestive effect. Again a skillful overtone of meaning pervades the passage as we are allowed to infer from speech and behavior the restlessness, arrogance, and bullying humor of the gunmen opposed to George's simple-minded, patient loyalty to his business and his town. We cannot help noticing, moreover, that character revealed by this talk is that not only of types but of individuals: that is, of persons identifiable first as members of known groups, but—secondly and more importantly—rising each out of his group with the possession of unique characteristics. Among such are George's fidelity to time and his daily specials, coupled with his clock that is incongruously and perhaps habitually twenty minutes fast; the ability of the gunmen to crack wise over George's head despite their evident nervousness; and George's pathetic eagerness to acknowledge what he stupidly takes to be praise of the town and the prestige of his

[2] From *Men without Women*, By Ernest Hemingway; Charles Scribner's Sons. Reprinted by permission of the publishers.

diner. All this rich insight into personality do these few words afford us. And yet, if Wister's dialogue was too much managed, surely this passage is managed too little. The scorn of the realist for dressing up prose, sound in moderation, has here produced talk too accurate to be anything but dull for long; as this talk in the lunchroom becomes dull the minute we realize that the Swede is not coming to be killed. It is talk that puts too great a strain on the reader's powers of quick comprehension. There are five men hereabouts (Nick Adams is watching, and Sam the cook is in the adjoining kitchen), yet Hemingway makes little or no effort to identify the speakers. The first man has called the second Al (they are alike as two peas), and here in mid-passage we bump into the author calling one of them Al and must recall that "the second man" is to be Al hereafter. We go through the same difficulty upon learning later that the first man's name is Max. George's line "It isn't ready yet" might at first glance be said by anybody, and somebody's statement that it is five o'clock, coming as it does in a separate paragraph, also floats vaguely until the reader's wit has managed to salvage it. As a rule the speakers' names and the verbs of saying appear when they are not needed, are absent when they would greatly facilitate the swift reading that the author must have desired. And it is talk so bare that it could be wired for sound with almost no loss of sense, or said on the stage (with George's visible turning to look at his clock) with no loss at all. Story dialogue, potentially as vivid as that of radio, screen, and stage, may indeed add something that aural and visual mediums cannot use. For the written story must include, in fact, it consists of, a voice not in quotation marks: the author's. In the passage cited there are forty-one words of the voice, and for story purposes they are futile. That voice is an opportunity. The short-story writer who refuses to make use of it is merely limiting his range of material and his technique.

How effectively and unobtrusively this master voice can control dialogue, a passage from Henry James's "Paste" will illustrate. Charlotte, a young governess, has been summoned to the funeral services of her uncle, a country clergyman, and of his second wife. In the vicarage garden she is puzzled by the attitude of her cousin, Arthur Prime, toward his dead stepmother. He tells Charlotte as the story opens that he has found a number of personal effects which he wants her to look over, presumably with a view to disposal. Charlotte goes up to her aunt's bedroom and finds "a confused cluster of bright objects on a table in the darkened room . . . coronets and girdles, diamonds, rubies and sapphires. Flagrant tinsel and glass, they looked strangely vulgar" in the vicarage chamber; and the strange romance between their owner, an actress, and the "honest widowed cleric with a small son and a large sense of Shakespeare" begins to unfold.

"You see what it is—old stuff of the time she never liked to mention."

Our young woman gave a start; her companion had after all rejoined her and had apparently watched a moment her slightly scared recognition. "So I said to myself," she replied. Then to show intelligence, yet keep clear of twaddle: "How peculiar they look!"

"They look awful," said Arthur Prime. "Cheap gilt, diamonds as big as potatoes. These are trappings of a ruder age than ours. Actors do themselves better now."

"Oh now," said Charlotte, not to be less knowing, "actresses have real diamonds."

"Some of them." Arthur spoke dryly.

"I mean the bad ones—the nobodies too."

"Oh some of the nobodies have the biggest. But mamma wasn't of that sort."

"A nobody?" Charlotte risked.

"Not a nobody to whom somebody—well, not a nobody with diamonds. It isn't all worth, this trash, five pounds."

There was something in the old gewgaws that spoke to her, and she continued to turn them over. "They're relics. And I think they have their melancholy and even their dignity."

Arthur observed another pause. "Do you care for them?" he then asked. "I mean," he promptly added, "as a souvenir."

"Of you?" Charlotte threw off.

"Of me? What have I to do with it? Of your poor dead aunt who was so kind to you," he said with virtuous sternness.

"Well, I'd rather have them than nothing."

"Then please take them," he returned in a tone of relief which expressed somehow more of the eager than of the gracious.

"Thank you." [3]

Comparison with the three other passages shows a change here in telling medium, the means whereby the story is conveyed to the reader. The anonymous student, Owen Wister, and Ernest Hemingway observed their characters from outside all of them, reporting such of their words and behavior as, they hoped, would illuminate those characters' thoughts and motives, thus make them wholly clear. James selects Charlotte as the single carrier of the story; foregoing his evident omniscience as author, he imaginatively moves into her being to report the impact of the experience on her mind and senses. Thus channeled, the telling medium becomes at once more selective and more intensive, permitting closer proximity to the emotional values of the story, as Charlotte's own acts and words, as well as those of others, are filtered through her consciousness. (It would, you see, permit irony, too.) With the choice of a telling medium we shall have much to do later. For the present it is enough to note the gain here in clarity of dialogue. For we, the reader, follow the author into Charlotte's being and are permitted to use the comfortingly restricted range of her senses and the unilateral approach via her thoughts, instead of being swept past at high altitude and asked to take a hurried bird's-eye view of the whole scene. We are startled or puzzled only when Charlotte is. We live the story with her, forgetting that the author is anywhere around. He has used that master voice in a shrewd sort of ventriloquism.

This hidden-author vividness and close proximity to material has been aided by an astonishing variety of dialogue forms.

[3] From *The Author of Beltraffio and Other Tales*, by Henry James; The Macmillan Company. Reprinted by permission of the publishers.

Wister's monotonous inversion, Hemingway's casual reliance on *he said* can quickly become noticeable, distract the attention from the story, and finally set up a screen between the reader and that priceless illusion of life that the writer would maintain undimmed. Here an almost limitless abundance of methods for getting the idea of speaking across to the reader lets him all but forget that necessarily tiresome act itself, fixing his attention on what is said, what is not said (it may be more important), manner of speaking, and manner while speaking: all of them relevant means of portraying character. Common verbs of saying, uncommon ones, and verbs like *risked* and *threw off* that are verbs of saying only in this context; speech preceding the verb of saying as well as speech following it, speech preceded or followed by action, manner, or thought, connoting the speaker and permitting the omission of a verb of saying, speech that is clearly identifiable (since there are but two persons here) by implication of question and answer without the necessity of speaker's name, even; pauses, considered speech, impulsive additions and retractions—all of these small technical devices for limning the vagaries of human talk have been so ingeniously intermingled that the reader gets in short space a clear and solid representation of life without, unless he stop and investigate, becoming aware of any particular method used for producing it.

No dialogue is perfect, and this perhaps is too tightly and richly wrought to be so. Every story presents its special dialogue problems, dependent on the telling medium, the kind of people involved, and other considerations. Allowing for qualification by such special needs, the novice might strive for a method-of-all-work: dialogue attempting a mean between the intricate workmanship of James and the rough-shod reality of Hemingway, a technique in talk seeking the merits of both without going to the extremes of either.

To that end, now, we can formulate working principles. They will not be unexceptionable and should be taken not as

44

hard and fast rules but as groundwork on which the student's individual technique can be built.

Accurate reproduction of human speech is impossible: blurred sounds, peculiarities of intonation, and the unphonetic nature of dialect often defy spelling and syntax and the reader's powers of comprehension. Even if it were possible, such literal representation would be unwise, for most of us are forever repeating ourselves in talk, we get bogged down in incoherence, we throw out locutionary mannerisms and clichés, and take more time (which in story would be space) for the simplest statement than a short story could afford. But a convincing suggestion of reality can certainly be secured by selection of lifelike individual speaking traits, by thorough study and practice of technical devices for reproducing these, and by moderate exaggeration of some elements in actual human speech. As was pointed out in the discussion of Faulkner's "That Evening Sun," the storyteller must continually ignore large areas susceptible of record in order to focus the attention on, and maintain at a desired pace, that thin stream of graphic details which read like the continuum of existence. Selection in itself entails exaggeration, or at least distortion of some sort. But the end, significance as opposed to the unaccented jumble of complete reproduction, more than justifies this means.

Then our two main objectives are: first, that sense or suggestion of reality always to be gained through revealing character in action, by these or any other means; and, second, readability acquired by the most varied use of technical devices and dialogue forms consistent with the material.

For the first, reality, we must study and make use of many small mechanical aids, not the least of which is appropriate diction. This will include not only dictionary words, idioms, local colloquialisms, and slang, but contractions, omissions (How do? Seems if), and deliberate out-of-class or -character expression for irony (the rustic putting on airs, a spinster's baby-talk to her dearest friend). We must use the relative length, structure, and pace of sentences and whole speeches as indicative of character. Alfred Jingle in *Pickwick Papers* and almost anybody in Jane Austen will show nineteenth-century extremes of range. We must choose characteristic verbs of saying. I mean the use, for example, of *said* or no verb at all for a laconic or flat-voiced person. Or consider the overtones of *the minister inquired* as against *Mike wanted to know,* as verbs of saying coupled with speech. We must meditate and employ characteristic appearance, behavior, or action preceding, accompanying, or following speech—never interpreting by generality, always selecting and citing details. (A general interpretation: *He was at a loss.* Characteristic details: *He stopped suddenly, looked up, rubbed his chin.*) And whenever possible, for clarity's sake if for no other reason, we should avail ourselves of the advantages of a single point of view and hearing.

For the second objective, readability, we must assemble and use in variety all appropriate dialogue forms. Classified here are some of the possibilities in their simplest terms:

"I'll go." With but two people on scene, the speaker's name and a verb of saying can often be omitted without ambiguity, the reader catching the question-answer rhythm; but one should put in reminders now and then and prevent irritation at having to check back. With three or more present and speaking, great care to keep them identified must be taken, especially if their speech itself shows no sharp contrast.

"I'll go," Jim said. Here is the commonest form, to be kept in its relevant place.

"I'll go," said Jim. A slight but relieving variant, simple inversion. But we should avoid inversion of less common verbs (for instance, "I'll go," promised Jim), especially when the less common verb, as here, has a transitive as well as intransitive use and thus might offer the confusing suggestion that its subject is its object; especially also if a pronoun instead of a noun is its subject. Nobody today wants to read "I'll go," promised he. It is well to keep verbs of saying as simple as appropriate-

46

ness allows, reserving less common ones for characterizing purposes. Avoid the style-conscious bastard verbs of saying, such as *hissed* (there being no *s*-sound in the speech) and those denoting actions such as coughing, sniffing, cackling, during which understandable speech would be difficult or ludicrous; and mere glittery dialogue mannerisms such as *asseverated, opined, adumbrated,* except—and even here with caution—for humorous purposes.

Jim said, "I'll go." (Or conceivably, if rarely: *Said Jim, "I'll go."*) Another form of inversion.

"I'll go if you like," Jim said. With a small amount of material added, further variety becomes possible. Each succeeding example is of course susceptible to variants preceding.

"I'll go," Jim said, "if you like." With two or more clauses in the speech, new positions for the speaker's name and the verb of saying become available. The break may suggest that the speaker paused there, for some reason that the writer may wish to indicate.

"If you like," Jim said, "I'll go." More than one clause also permits inversion of clauses, giving further opportunities for character-drawing.

Jim said slowly, "I'll go." Several variations in order are now possible. But try to make the manner of speaking, if it is to be stated, precede the speech, so that the reader can get set for what is coming and will not imagine the words being said in some other way and have to correct his impression. Incidentally, adverbs can become a vice in dialogue, especially the large group ending *-ly*. They are weak words at best, and no other part of speech echoes so readily. There are better, if slightly longer, ways of describing manner. One of the best is to choose spoken words so carefully that they describe their own manner.

Jim flushed. "I'll go." Juxtaposition in the same paragraph of speech and action connotes the speaker clearly enough, allowing the omission of the usual identification for further variety.

"I'll—," Jim looked at her quickly, stood up. The context, part of a speech, plus an action do the job in still another way. We can use interruptions (in actual speech they are very numerous) by the speaker of his own speech, as well as by others. Some people, if interrupted, will simply raise the voice and plug on. Reading must be single-auditory; but by careful work we can approach the two- or multi-voiced harmony or cacophony of music. But never cut off speech or leave something unspoken unless you know, and are sure the reader will know, what would have been said.

Smiling, Jim flipped a thumb at himself and then toward the open door. Sometimes the most expressive dialogue can be carried on in silence.

As for general rules, a new paragraph is needed for each new speech. But this convention is often broken effectively when, for instance, the prime business of a paragraph involves the utterance, apposite or contrasting, of two or more persons; or when some special end is to be gained by massing, such as incoherent fragments of speech in a crowd, or several remarks by various persons having a single effect. These devices are space-savers for the short story. Rules for punctuation in dialogue are stricter. The novice should not be misled by stylistic idiosyncracies that have got into print despite editorial objections. Let him hew to the line in this matter, working for originality elsewhere.

Is all this too finicky? I do not think so. Talk in stories is worth time and will reward patient, painstaking labor with very small tools. Keep your ears cocked for idioms and even for small reproducible sounds in speech such as M-*hm,* H'm, Yeah, Yah, Hanh! Uh-uh (yes), Unh-unh (no). Use a dictionary, but discard it when you can tap a livelier source. Read the eighteenth- and nineteenth-century masters with skepticism in this respect: many of them held custom higher than reality, and speech changes faster than dictionaries can record.

Try four pages of dialogue for yourself. Say there are to be two speakers, of contrasted character (sex makes an easy contrast), one of whom wants something, the other being unable or unwilling to give it. Using all possible dialogue forms consistent with the material and your telling medium, make this situation clear merely by choosing and recording speech and action and, perhaps, thoughts of the medium—that is, entirely without explanation or comment by you as author. And never mind resolving the situation. One thing at a time. This isn't a story, it's just talk.

3

ACTION

I F WE EXAMINE any good short story with care, we shall find that its convincingness is to a large extent the result of the presence of two qualities. The first, spontaneity, is its ability to move by its own emotional momentum, without apparent propulsion by its author; the second, immediacy, equally valuable, its mysterious faculty of seeming to happen here and now, in the very presence of the reader as he reads. The presence of these two qualities is often attributed, mistakenly, to the genuine feeling of the author, his sincerity, his genius. The first two of these traits he must have, certainly, and with luck and toil he may gain the third; but they have nothing to do with the convincingness of his story. Spontaneity and immediacy are matters of technique. Technique is mental coordination: selected, planned, and practiced effort. From the opening lines to the final period, technique strives, deliberately and cunningly, to make the story run on its own power and to make it seem to happen here and now.

At first thought, the easiest and maybe the only way of making sure of these qualities would seem to be to tell all stories in the first person (not, of course, the author's person but that of a participant in or witness of the action) and in the present tense. Many long as well as short stories have been told by one or the other of these methods, and a few employ both. *Treasure Island* is related in the first person, successively, by several leading characters; *Henry Esmond* by the protagonist throughout. Eudora Welty's short story "Old Mr. Marblehall" uses the present tense (one must distinguish between the actual present tense, as found in Miss Welty's piece, and a colloquial use of the present for past, as seen in many stories of

Ring Lardner and Damon Runyon). And Faulkner's *As I Lay Dying* is written in the streams of consciousness (direct mental discourse, first person, present tense) in turn of all the characters in the novel.

But it would be absurd to limit storytelling to these devices. Technique should expand and discover, never restrict. First-person telling is disliked by some readers and may quickly become monotonous and distracting; also, as will be seen later, in certain conditions it can be either too close to or too remote from the material. The present tense has inescapably a theatrical air. The fact is, we are still too firmly rooted in the once-upon-a-time, it-happened-like-this tradition to welcome the present tense except in very rare moments of great excitement or as, naturally, a character thinks or speaks in what is *to him* the present. Prose-storytelling must come alive and be spontaneous, its past action must be made present and immediate to the reader, usually, by other means. The importance of such means becomes apparent as we acknowledge the fact that here again the stage, the screen, and radio have a technical advantage over printed prose. Their action is necessarily spontaneous, for the writer must remain unseen; is by nature present and immediate for it takes place even as we watch or listen.

I take up the second quality, immediacy, first: it seems more fundamental, it is relatively simple and compact in itself. Spontaneity will involve us in argument and the choice of a telling medium (for if the author is not to appear in person getting his story told, somebody or some vehicle must be found to do so), and thus can best be treated later.

A good thing about immediacy is that the reader helps create it—without knowing that he does so, of course. Even today, man still loves passionately to read. Somebody paid money for our story, somebody found time between pressing pleasures and business to sit down and tackle it; somebody came to the text not for the purpose of noting our name under the title (a hundred to one he won't even see that), not to be one of our reading fans or one of the magazine's cover-to-cover readers, not to improve himself, increase his knowledge of human nature, or acquire miscellaneous information; but for the sole purpose of living vicariously, imaginatively, for a little while in a land of daydreams. "The [reading] process," Stevenson says quaintly in his "Gossip of Romance," "should be absorbing and voluptuous." Readers can be "rapt clean out of" themselves. As readers "we plunge into the tale in our own person and bathe in fresh experience." Cynics may demur, and reservations for different kinds of readers are inevitable; but the enormous circulation of novels and magazines, despite competition of easier and cheaper story entertainment, proves the Teller of Tales to be right still.

Nevertheless, the author who relies wholly on this reader-imposed spell will soon come to grief. Many factors potentially within his control lie ready to break it. The spell once broken, even cracked, the editor has only to pick up another manuscript promising sounder workmanship, the reader to turn over a couple of pages into a daydream that doesn't wake him up on the floor. It is the part of wisdom to appraise this spell, this contribution by the reader to the writing craft; to be everlastingly grateful for it; but to exert every faculty toward preserving and stimulating it.

In order to find ways and means we must consider what different kinds of action are susceptible to narrative expression. If we take the amount of detail recounted as a *differentia,* there are three. Call a first kind synoptic, as in *John spent the winter at Palm Beach.* Imagine that sentence in a short story. It has a crisp sound and look, is objective and fairly specific, introduces a human being and a recognizable place: all to its credit. I would be the last to rule it out of narrative. But the question is, will it stand up as a manner of writing short story against other possible ways of acquainting the reader with approximately the same material?

Now the amount of detail in any human experience is obviously relative, depending on susceptibility to impressions, memory, physical and emotional condition, and so on. So too must be relative the amount of detail used in recording experience, depending on the psychic importance of impressions (as against the physical needs of the story), on the skill of the writer, and of course on the proposed or required length of the story. One writer, whose imaginary sentence I quoted above, deals with miles of travel and four months' time in seven words. Another, to suggest the extremes, might find a whole book in the first day, the first mile of the journey. The seven words are very much shorter, and the short story must be short. But ask yourself whether their brevity is a source of immediacy, which a moment's thought will show to be the result of singularity of detail; for as the present becomes past it becomes classifiable by association with other similar experiences; while it *is* present there is never anything just like it under the sun. Plainly the brevity, or the inclusiveness, of those seven words detracts from and even destroys possible immediacy in the action recounted. So John spent the winter at Palm Beach. Who cares? It's history now, dead and done with. In the group of three kinds of action capable of narrative expression the synoptic must, so far as the short story is concerned, take a low place. Don't rule it out, but have as little to do with it as possible. It is too rapid, superficial, and comprehensive to permit the presence of sensuous and emotional stimuli necessary to create and sustain immediacy.

Call a second kind of action customary or habitual. It can be identified by the presence of such expressions as *would, used to, was in the habit of,* or *sometimes* stated or merely implied with the past tense to indicate repetition by habit or practice. For example: *John used to spend his winters in Florida.* Analysis shows this kind of narrated action to have an even wider range than synoptic, for it not only skims over big units of time and space but does so for the purpose of grouping similar experiences. It is possible, of course, to narrate customary action in terms of much smaller time and space factors, and with carefully selected detail:

Johnny used to buy a green lollipop at the corner drugstore every Monday after school, to cheer him up.

Still the effect is that of letdown. Nothing doing right now. Repetition of experience detracts from immediacy, however necessary it may be for other reasons. We are well aware that hundreds of things happen twice or several times, in real life; indeed, our recognition of the boresome nature of repetition there may have something to do with our dislike of its representation in stories. Narrative that groups experiences has lost the bite, the air of unique venture—everything impending because nothing is the same—that a really convincing daydream must have. If it happened in headings and categories, who cares? It's biography if not exposition.

To the inexperienced the story opening offers the likeliest chance of disaster here, for the writer naturally feels that much must be explained and motivated before he can really get under way. The beginning of the student's story already cited for bad dialogue, "Jim Bent, Deserter," makes all possible mistakes in this respect with a gusto that is irresistible:

Jim Bent, Captain in the U. S. Army, found himself in a precarious position. In short it was this. His close friend and comrade at West Point had fallen violently in love with the Major's wife, and not only was it a very disgraceful proceeding, but his constant night visits, sometimes lasting most of the night, indicated that the matter must soon come to a head. Lieutenant Kane didn't mean to break up the Major's home, but he was passionately in love with the lady in question, and merely did not have the courage and the will power to control his passions.

Generalities and summary phrases, such as *precarious position,* are by nature synoptic; leading off here is the topic sentence of academic prose summing up the paragraph. *His close friend . . . at West Point* synopsizes experience twice time-removed, *had fallen violently in love with* synopsizes experience once time-removed from the immediate action, the present-past of this story. Clichés like *disgraceful proceeding, break up the Major's home, passionately in love with, lady in question* are bound to be synoptic, since they classify emotional experiences that are, and should be represented as, unique under broad typical heads. And those *constant night visits,* in spite of the amusingly solemn implications of *sometimes lasting most of the night,* cast a pall of habit over the whole passage.

Novelists, with plenty of space at their command and much more intricate problems of structure to solve, often use these less immediate kinds of narrated action for special reasons: transition, emotional relief, variety. They are willing to let you down a little, in order to set you up later. Even here, however, there is a growing tendency to do without synopsis and habit whenever possible. The pressing immediacy of much of the early part of *War and Peace* seems largely the result of Tolstoy's careful avoidance of them. James Boyd's *Long Hunt* abstains entirely, Hemingway's *The Sun Also Rises* almost entirely, from their use. The space limitations of the short story, its needed compression for intensity of emotion and singleness of impact, render them extremely undesirable for the beginner. A skilled craftsman can overcome the handicap: Stephen Vincent Benét, Sinclair Lewis, Scott Fitzgerald could and did, many times; the novice is wise in avoiding it until he acquires power.

As a last resort, however, if material essential to the story can only be stated by these weaker methods, let him consider the possibility of disguising their weakness. Synoptic or customary action screened through a character's thoughts—this of course must be done consistently with the general telling medium of the story—has not the same flaccid effect as that narrated directly to us by the author, because in the first instance our attention may be still held on the present-past time at which the character is thinking; whereas in the second instance everything stops while the author goes back and expatiates. For instance, *Johnny remembered how he used to buy,* etc. may be soundly integrated in the present-past of the story by that act of remembering; we are still living with Johnny at the time he did his musing, and see the time he mused about only as he saw it, in retrospect. (This consideration may have a bearing on the telling medium to be used for the whole story.) Again, fresh details and sense impressions may take the curse off the letdown. Maybe *Johnny remembered how he would lick off the hard green candy, one lick at a time, and taste the lime and sugar on his tongue even after supper.* And the use of language that the character might use if he were telling of the experience, possibly language characteristic of him at that earlier day, which has thus got naturally into his thoughts today, will focus the reader's attention on the present-past in which such telling (thinking, that is) occurs, not the past told about.

But in a sense these are technical subterfuges. Steady reliance on a third kind of narrated action is the best possible way of minimizing the other two, and it is the mainstay of the short-story writer. Call it continuously specific or dramatic action, or as Phyllis Bentley calls it, "immediate scene." It is created by forging a chain of, mostly, physical details portraying a particular time sequence—details selected, however, not alone for their ability to clarify this mobile scene, but for their powers of implying what preceded and what may follow it.

So once again John stepped off the Orange Blossom. Another winter, he thought. "Why, there's a palm!" he told the porter. "But where's the beach?"

This is pretty silly, for I have no story to write about John and Palm Beach. But something is happening before the reader's eyes, here and now. Things have happened before this, but they are subordinate, to be used only as a bearing on and revelation of what is happening now. Even if these words begin a story, the situation is clear enough, within its stated terms, to let the reader go on. I believe that readers care little about what is not told them, so long as what *is* told maintains this steady present-past sequence and is in itself clear. For here is that chain, that continuum of existence that means life in daydream. The details of the sequence, moreover, succeed in implying something about the past (other winters spent here) as well as something about the present (John's boredom, his wisecracking) which, if not thus integrated, would have to be told by synoptic and customary action, interrupting the sequence. To create this doubly functional narrative the author has omitted innumerable details generally applicable to the character, the scene, and the action, holding fast to his purpose to pack what little he tells with clarity and significance. From immediate scene, well done, no reader can escape. If he doesn't read every line, every word, he will lose the thread of the story. And if the author has supplied, besides clarity and significance, the interest that I, having no story to tell, had to leave out, not to lose the thread has become for that reader a matter of prime importance.

Accustom yourself to this kind of narrated action, the peculiar property of the short story and essential to its success. Wherever you go, get into the habit of recording sense impressions that imply action. Never mind smart expression, go for accuracy, the unique quality of the thing itself. Notice that not only the kind of sense impression experienced, but its aspect, will be dependent on your state of mind or emotion at the time; I mean, not only the sort of thing you observe or feel about a strange place, for instance, just after getting good news from home, but the quality or flavor of it, will be quite different from details observed and quality felt under opposite circumstances. These matters are far more important than smart expression; by studying and practicing them you will be a cut better than smart: you will avoid the ordinary and undramatic not by artificial stylistic means but by persistent search for and discovery of clarity, significance, interest—details having unique application to one person, one time, one place in a story. Successful here, whatever else your work lacks it will have immediacy.

In my files I find the first page of a story that never got written. Apparently I was keen about it, for the manuscript is clean enough to be fifth to tenth draft, but something happened; I got too keen and lost it, or something better turned up. The point is, this page seems to me, now after several years, to have the interest that John getting off the train lacked, as well as enough clarity and significance. Perhaps it won't seem so to you.

"Sure this is it?" he asked scowling, ducking to peer out the bus front window. There was no town there, just road.

"Take your next left," the driver said without turning, then added as if for the uniform: " 'Bout half a mile or so, you can't miss. We don't go in there any more, not enough call. Take it easy, Mac."

Take it easy. Outside he stood up straight, breathed deep, glanced round him, still puzzled. The bus swept on along the beautiful big wide dry highway. Cars snapped past both ways, hugging the oil smut on each lane. Nothing like what he remembered. He shook his head. There was water to his left, a narrow bay or river that made up past smooth ledges. Smelled good. There was an old wharf ran out, boats moored in its lee, and a few gulls sailing and circling over a seine on a big reel by some sheds. The shoal water was yellow-green in the sun, but it was darker offshore where the channel ran, and over across on the other bank the close-growing little pointed firs looked black. Looked good. His heart commenced to go it. The sort of thing you might see on a calendar in colors: "The Old Fish Pier," Vandah Grimes, Real Estate & Insurance, Try Us First.

The crackling began again in his head. Pay no attention, the doc said, whistle or something, take it easy. Take it easy for crisakes. He set off along the soft shoulder, digging in with his heels because no mines there, whistling between his teeth.

Perhaps I quit because I couldn't be sure I knew what a returned mental discharge from the South Pacific felt like. But here I tried to make clear through immediate scene that the boy had lived in this region and found something familiar mingled with his anxiety and its strangeness; and I tried to make you sympathize with him and so want to read on.

Try it. Do better than I did. Write a page of immediate scene that might begin a story. Work first for that chain of physical details that will make the present moment clear; but weave into it implications that will illuminate the past and if possible (in my piece Vandah Grimes was going to appear in person) unobtrusively point to and thus motivate the future; and try also to set up a character or a situation that will awaken the reader's desire to read on. You may actually get at a whole story while doing this. But don't write it yet.

4

YOUR MOVE

W E NOW REACH that matter of spontaneity, the argument that I referred to in the last chapter, and a critical point in the study of technique. The road forks here, and you have to decide which way to take. At the risk of being dull and dogmatic, I am going to try to influence your decision. But at the end of this chapter it will be up to you.

You have the general principles with which I began, the pros and cons of writing as a business, the functions and devices of dialogue, the fundamental value of immediate scene—in short, enough of technique to let you, if you really want to do this, write a story. The choice is, simply, between going ahead and writing it blind—that is, trusting method to instinct, letting fiction come out of you as it will—and investigating all possible ways of telling it and then trying to use the most suitable and effective. If you have a spark of genius, the first way may do no harm. And if you take the second, there will be a danger of technique-hyperconsciousness setting in, a sort of scrupulous mania which, by offering many possible methods but no imperatively best one, destroys the priceless certainty in you that there is, after all, a good story here to be written. Yet I strongly recommend the second.

What, precisely, is spontaneity? In a person we think of it as some outward manifestation of that happy and ebullient state of mind in which life is sweet and all achievement possible. This sparkling enthusiasm may conceivably be reflected— and often has been, see Dickens, Saroyan—in a writing person's story. Closely examined, however, it looks more like the first reckless flush of the amateur than the rational assurance of a professional craftsman. Already we have seen how quickly it may pass. It must usually be involuntary, depending on indirect and capricious factors like sound sleep, good appetite, health, peace of mind, successful adjustment to environment. But in a month of mornings any man with a living to make must work through many when perhaps he has not slept well, when all is far from right with the world and himself, and the only urge he feels is toward any vocation having nothing to do with blank paper and a typewriter. Shall he wait, then, for that sense of perfect attunement with life to come? Obviously not. If Stevenson, Clarence Day, Stephen Vincent Benét, Katherine Mansfield and other stout hearts in failing bodies had waited, they would have stopped writing and we should have lacked much good reading. Yet much of their work has the very quality we are seeking.

Spontaneity, then, can be an effect produced by the story, sometimes luckily supported by a feeling in the writer. Spontaneity is the quality of apparently independent emotional momentum. Having it, the story moves from first word to last without visible propulsion by its author. By writers of genius the quality may have been unpremeditated. By those less gifted or by the inexperienced it is created by technical means. The means are, first, by removing the author's presence, in fact and even wherever possible by implication, from the story; and, second, by substituting for him a telling medium or vehicle less distracting and more germane to the material.

For three reasons, one from each of the three angles of the essential writing compact between author, editor, and reader, I believe spontaneity should be, often must be, so created.

Consider the reader's angle first, his relations with reading matter in prose. Though unaware of technicalities, he recognizes broadly two kinds of reading: article and story. By the first, generally called expository, he expects to learn something; he expects diagrammatic inclusiveness of approach, directness of manner, thoroughness of method—his author telling all, writing all around and into and through the subject, in person

61

as author pontifically addressing himself, the reader. Through the second, narrative, he expects for the most part merely vicarious emotional experience; that is, selectiveness of approach (large areas susceptible of record ignored in favor of the thin stream or chain of details suggesting the continuum of existence he knows), and indirection of method, the author withholding much and allowing material to reach him, the reader, via some sort of dramatic representation or medium (character talking to character, overheard by reader; or character talking [thinking] to reader)—a method which by this very withholding, this restriction of material within relevant human channels, by preventing the author from telling all at any point, enhances the reader's suspense, the verisimilitude gained (for in real life who knows how an experience will come out?), his sense of illusion, and hence the convincingness of the experience vicariously received.

These expectations in the reader must have been preceded, among writers, by a rough division of motives. From the earliest human utterance on down, the expository motive has been that of making thought clear, of proceeding from the common ground of agreed hypothesis to previously unknown conclusions. Narrative must begin under a similar obligation: namely, to make clear the situation (characters and their motives on scene) from which it springs, as well as other resulting situations. But this is a pictorial clarity rather than a logical one. It has only the loosely shared area of human experience and the loosely acknowledged laws of probability, seldom any common ground in precisely defined fact, as basis; and its chief end being entertainment or enlightenment or both, instead of information, it must proceed at once from *any* mere clarifying to the inducing of an emotional reaction in the reader.

In the short story even the means for attaining clarity must be of a special kind, unknown to and unwanted by the expositor. They must be unobtrusive and implicit, if they are not to destroy the illusion of life building up—for life as lived provides no gloss, no footnotes; and the means must be swift if they are not to weaken the illusion by impeding the thin stream carrying it along. Above all the means must be autonomous. There is in every story reader a stubborn hostility to the intrusion of any distracting, external human agency in his daydream; he will "skip that part" and move on to a point where the fable lets him dream alone. The shorter the daydream, naturally, the stronger may be this prejudice. Even in a long story (Thornton Wilder's play *Our Town* is a case in point) illusion is difficult with a stage manager puttering about in full view. In long or short it is shattered beyond repair if the reader is allowed to "see the wheels go round." And in the case of the short story in inexperienced hands, if illusion is to be held intact, art-that-conceals-art entails concealment not only of narrative designs and measures for their accomplishment, but concealment of the presence of the would-be artist himself.

On behalf of the reader I am arguing not only for the exclusion of those personal appearances by the author manifest in asides, comments, apostrophic remarks (Dear Reader! . . . Our story opens on a bleak November morning . . . Blessed be all simple emotions!) those pontifical explanations and interpretations of behavior common in fiction of the nineteenth century and earlier, but since the beginning of the twentieth generally discarded. What I suggest is the adoption of some pervasive approach that will, besides making all such incongruous outbreaks unthinkable, reach down to the foundations of narrative statement and forestall even the implication of the author's presence on the scene.

Such a sentence as *Captain Jim Bent was angry and disgusted,* for instance, although taking the form of narrative by saying something at a moment of time about a fictitious person, is actually sheer exposition. By professing psychological authority, if not clairvoyance, in respect to his character's feelings the author has become visible by implication. Illusion cracks as the reader becomes aware of somebody explaining

63

something directly to him, over a character's head. At this particular juncture and at this particular moment, the author has told all.

Now the approach that we seek, although recognizing of course that the author does, in fact must, *know* all, *all* the time, requires a narrative withholding; its practitioner will tell only a little of what he knows, at any time, and that little only obliquely. Perhaps he will write:

> Captain Jim Bent looked across the sleeping town to the lighted windows of the Major's cottage. Frowning, he spat into the street.

This is not good story, but it is story, not exposition. Withholding his summary epithets, the writer has selected for statement a few details of behavior (looked, frowned, spat) which: 1. by indirection demonstrate Jim's feelings which the expository first writer affirmed as facts; and 2. by thus calling on the reader for a slight intellectual effort (the associative relationship between frowning and anger, spitting and disgust), divert his attention from the writer as external recording agent of the story. Most readers would not discern anybody setting down these apparently simple but significant details (for they are no more than what the character himself, if the story were coming to us through the medium of his consciousness, would be aware of), and would dream on, undisturbed.

This, then, is an approach to narrative which compels the dramatic or creative method. Dramatic because it allows character apparently to demonstrate itself by talk and action, to the reader's unfailing satisfaction. Creative because it produces an illusion of life, seeming to flow from no human force outside the story, through no outside agent; because it seems to move on its own emotional momentum, without propulsion by its author. In short, this is technical spontaneity in one of its many forms. It could hardly have dropped out of the sky upon writers' work tables; or been undertaken casually in a spirit of

64

whimsy: it is much the hardest sort of prose to write. Perhaps in part borrowed from the stage, certainly directed by the oral ancestor of story writing, which also required mental effort on the reader's part to catch the point, it must be the result of a long-standing demand by readers of short prose fiction for vicarious emotional experience unpresided over by the author's presence and undiluted by his comments.

Let us look at this matter, now, through the editor's eyes. Anything like a symposium of editorial opinion is naturally impossible, and I have no doubt that many editors, if questioned, would promptly reply that they don't particularly care how a story is written so long as it does something to them, or has snap or bite, or is sure-fire by some standard they intuitively know and use but have never taken the time to analyze. But here, at least, are the published opinions of three men who, during the last forty years or so, themselves wrote short stories and at one time or another directed the literary destinies of three different kinds of magazines: *The Atlantic Monthly, Adventure,* and *The Saturday Review of Literature.* The spread in time and kind is wide enough for their considered judgment to bear weight.

One would hardly expect at the turn of the century a specific contribution to the theory of short-story technique. Only a few writers here and abroad had given evidence up to that time of deliberate technical effort, and their achievements now appear isolated. In 1842 Poe had delivered his celebrated dictum about "unity of impression" and reading time; almost half a century later this had been followed by Brander Matthews's insistence on "a single character, a single event, a single emotion." So theory was as vague and scattered as production. Yet in 1902 Bliss Perry, editor of *The Atlantic,* assembling the fruit of his varied experience as teacher, short-story writer, and editor, must have been aware at least of the advisability of some such technical discipline as I have been discussing. In a chapter of *A Study of Prose Fiction* on "The Question of Form" he saw fit to quote Sir Walter Besant's precepts, three of which were: "Endeavor to be dramatic. A great element of dramatic skill is selection. Avoid the sin of writing *about* a character." In another part of the book Bliss Perry remarked:

[Short-story writing] calls for visual imagination of a high order: the power to see the object; to penetrate to its essential nature; to select the one characteristic trait by which it may be represented. A novelist informs you . . . what [his heroine] looks like. . . . If he does not succeed in making her real . . . he has a hundred other opportunities before the novel ends. . . . The short-story writer, on the other hand, has but the one chance.[1]

And among the exercises in his appendix Perry included: "Describe a room or a house so that each detail shall serve to indicate the character of the occupant," and "Write a conversation which indirectly reveals character." All these are but hints, perhaps; yet they all point in one direction—the elimination, by one means or another, of the author as visible telling medium.

Twenty years later, national circulation and advertising had made magazine writing a big and prolific business, and we find another editor much more specific about the troubles of the short story; Arthur Hoffman, long editor of *Adventure*— not to be considered a pulp magazine in those days. It ran Conrad's *The Rescue* serially—published *Fundamentals of Fiction Writing* as a protest against the academic emphasis on mere rhetoric and the commercial technique (formula) current at the time. In three chapters of this book, "Creating the Illusion," "Distractions," and "Adaptation of Style to Material," Hoffman proceeds logically from the need of eliminating the visible author to the need of substituting for him some telling medium integral to the story. He had found, he says, "unsoundness in both the editorial basis of criticism [of manuscripts submitted] and the writers' basis of creation." The latter

---

[1] From *A Study of Prose Fiction*, by Bliss Perry; Houghton Mifflin Company. Reprinted by permission of the publishers.

he laid to poor teaching, "In particular, lack of emphasis upon preserving the illusion." Over and over again he stresses the point: "This, it may be said, *is* fiction—the imposing and preserving of an illusion." The reader "must forget that there is such a thing as an author."

Fiction may of course include analysis, philosophy, technique, information and all the other things for which it is so often made the vehicle, but if it is to remain straight fiction, these must be really integral and necessary parts of it—analysis of or by the characters themselves, the information inherent in the material, the technique necessary for presentation, the philosophy of a character, locality or nation.[2]

Again:

The interrupters and destroyers of illusion are almost infinite in variety and number. The means of avoiding them, indeed, constitute a complete set of working rules for the writing of fiction.

Hoffman then lists small distractions: unusual words, foreign words, classical, historical and fictional references, unusual proper names. (Evidently many of *Adventure's* would-be contributors had not attended to their academic prose!) Then comes a more serious distraction:

Obtrusion of Author.—This is a crying evil, a serious damage to the illusion. The author has no more business to appear concretely in his story than a playwright has upon the stage . . . [The slightest personal appearance] compels a reader to realize that some one is talking to him. You can't be carried away in a dream when conscious that some one is telling it to you.

Another serious distraction, which I have called author's appearance by implication:

Not long ago there arose again the fad of beginning a story with a paragraph of philosophy. It has spread like a disease and, I think, is one.

[2] This extract and those immediately following are from *Fundamentals of Fiction Writing*, by Arthur S. Hoffman, Copyright 1922. Used by special permission of the publishers, The Bobbs-Merrill Company.

As constructive suggestions, first comes condensation. Hoffman puts it thus:

A story is at bottom a selection of certain bits of material from an almost infinite number of bits or, put the other way, the rejection of all material except the salient bits.

(In my terms, large areas susceptible of narration ignored for the thin stream of details suggesting a continuum.)

It is safe to say that many writers could make most of their stories not only more dramatic but more effective in general by greater condensation. . . . Instead of giving the reader setting and local color in discouragingly large pieces, weave them into the action.

(As could easily be done, for instance, by seeing the whole experience through some medium less inclusive and omniscient than your own view as author, some medium within the story.)

Instead of describing a vast plain, let a character ride over it.

Then he introduces methods covering the whole problem. In reading the passage, bear in mind that throughout his book Hoffman uses the word *technique* to mean fiction formularizing, which he hates; the word *style* he uses in the sense that I, and others generally nowadays, use *technique*.

All that an author has to convey to you comes to you through a single medium which we call his style and which in practice is singularly inelastic in relation to the great variety of things that must pass through it . . . [Style must be made more elastic, must be adapted to material.] That there are already in our fiction occasional and sporadic cases of this adaptation of style to material shows the soundness of the theory, for these examples are . . . instances in which the writer's art is sufficiently developed to break through his usual style and spontaneously adapt expression to the thing expressed.

Thereupon this editor discusses two of these spontaneous "styles," which he calls First-Person Narratives and Frames or

Brackets ("a story one of whose characters tells the main story"), finding merits and dangers in both. Warmer! as we used to say in the parlor game. But the short story was to find, soon after Hoffman wrote, more ways of substituting an integral telling medium for the unwanted visible appearance of the author.

Fifteen years later, in a series of editorials he called "English 37: the Novelist and the Reader," Bernard De Voto, then editor of *The Saturday Review of Literature,* went further, supplying needed psychological documentation for similar opinions that might otherwise have seemed arbitrary. "The most natural way to tell a story is usually the least effective way to write fiction," he there wrote as prelude to a thorough discussion of the dangers attending the visibly omniscient author.

[Fiction] demands of the writer a severe discipline and an expert skill. . . . Fiction today produces an engagement between [itself] and the reader which rests on an active coöperation not required in Dickens's time. . . . The immediate moment, the immediate scene, has a momentary illusion of being, if not more real, at least far more important—it has a higher potential.[3]

Again:

Little Red Riding Hood, Roland's horn, and the stories of the Rhine Maiden's gold . . . are immortal. They are impersonal, anonymous: the personality of the author has been completely absorbed in the self-sustaining life of the tales themselves.

It is this anonymity which short-story technique rediscovered as a third positive means (I call it the objective method) for eliminating the visible author. "Today," De Voto goes on,

any description which has not been converted to other uses of fiction is a stigma of amateurishness . . . Such passages . . . do

[3] This extract and those immediately following are from *The Saturday Review of Literature,* June 26–Sept. 4, 1937, vol. xvi, nos. 9–19. Reprinted by permission of the author and the publisher.

not move as fiction must if it is to be read with satisfaction. They are irrelevant to what happens, they are not part of the psychological process of the scene, and they are not engaged with the emotions of the characters. [Similarly] descriptions of persons are precarious. [And all data] are neutral until [details] acquire emotional import for one of the characters.

An explanation, no matter how completely it may be phrased in terms of the character, is expository, and in fact the more completely it is so phrased the more it is likely to reveal the author's hands on the puppet-strings. . . . It will bog the reader in a motionless mass of supplementary details from which . . . the reality of fiction is entirely absent.

At other points in the discussion De Voto applies the same reasoning to the intrusion of mere information supplied by the author or of the author's personal emotions. What happens, he says, upon the occurrence of any one of these things, is that

the flow has been interrupted, the illusion has been broken, the reader has slipped out of his engagement, what he feels is not produced of but occasioned by the [story] . . . A moment of hesitation that does not last long enough to produce resistance is also an impairment. . . . Such a hesitation or resistance means a failure or insufficiency in technique.

Technique is the application of methods designed to insure [stories] being read. . . . Fiction borrowed methods from other arts and worked out methods of its own. A purification, or at least a refinement, in their use has been one of the developments. . . . [For instance] Between Fielding's time and ours a sentiment, or a convention, has developed which holds: that an essay is one kind of thing and a [story] is another kind of thing, that a mixture of kinds is improper or ineffective, and especially that the interposition of the [storyteller] himself is discordant. . . . [This] is one of the determining principles of the modern art of fiction.

How can a [storyteller] relate his fiction without appearing in his own person? Much of the technique of fiction hinges on the question.

Whereupon De Voto, too, mentions over-all technical devices:

The event which is really seen at second hand will seem much more nearly to be seen at first hand if it is related not by the puppet-master but by someone whom it affects . . . the point of view held within the story itself.

Thus the elementary device of a narrator who speaks in his own person but is a character in the story.

Hoffman called this "First Person Narrative" and "Frame" or "Bracket" story. In my lingo, succeeding chapters will discuss "I" as Protagonist and "I" as Witness. Then De Voto adds a method developed since Hoffman's time:

One method of modern fiction avoids analysis altogether by transferring it . . . to the reader. In Hemingway, for instance, what the characters do and say is so rigorously selected and forms such a revealing system in itself that the reader is compelled to derive the motives behind it from the action itself.

This method is the third positive means I have already referred to and will discuss fully, as objective technique, in a later chapter. And a fourth, naturally unremarked by De Voto since he was chiefly treating the novel, will appear in due course.

Let us now consider the most important angle of the writing compact, in its bearing on spontaneity: that of the writer himself. Let us remember the paradox: for the most part a man can write convincingly only of what he knows at firsthand, although this area of first-hand experience is the very one in which personal prejudice and emotional distortion, capable of destroying conviction, are likely to be most prevalent. It is my belief that technically produced spontaneity will relieve this dangerous situation, simply by removing the author's ego (his prejudice and potentially distorting emotions about it) from the story and transferring his interest from this prejudice and his personal emotions to the organic life of what he has to tell.

"You write about your own experiences," says Mark Schorer,

but you must write yourself out of them. You are writing fiction, not autobiography. No one cares how you feel about your material; what is important is that the reader can feel something about it (besides distaste) and that the characters can feel something about

71

it. The most familiar characteristic of a beginner's story is that it tells more about the author than it does about his characters. Your prejudices, your moods, above all, your private motives for choosing this material in the first place, must be transcended by the material itself in its story form. You must, even after you have found your theme, achieve some kind of objective statement about it.[4]

All this at the cost, some students are apt to fear, of originality. But not if we understand what that quality is, and what it is not. Originality is not merely being different from other people: that is eccentricity. It would be truer to say that originality is being like other people in a different way. "True originality," Robert Hillyer has pointed out,

is a combination of three elements: a common speech, a common emotion, and an individual. Note that the individual has a right to but a third of the whole.[5]

Of course it must be doubted, anyway, whether originality is worth seeking, or worth being afraid of losing: that is, held as an end or good in itself. Certainly its presence will not of itself assure success in any human effort; certainly, lacking it one cannot create it by trying. Far too much has been made of it by careless readers and critics in the public press. It is a critic's word, a reader's word. As an entity, by the striving writer it had best be ignored.

But objectivity that often produces a highly original effect can be, and is in fact created every time a soundly-wrought story gets written. What happens in the creative process, I think, is this: the writer meditates upon some part of his experience, trying to see it clearly, to see it whole, and to grasp its possible significance as interpretation of human experience in general. To do this, usually, some modification and some exaggeration of the true facts of the original experience are neces-

[4] From "Clearing Some Hurdles," by Mark Schorer; *Pro Tem*, August, 1943. Reprinted by permission of the author.

[5] From *First Principles of Verse*, by Robert Hillyer; The Writer, Inc.

sary; and thus the writer's imagination transmutes, possibly by means of what T. S. Eliot calls an "objective correlative," what was a special and particular view of life into something that still closely resembles life but is both more generally acceptable (in the sense that other people than the author find kinship there with their own experience and emotions) and more significant than any small section of actual, individual living can be. If blind Milton had merely recorded at white heat his personal grievances at the hands of women, the account would have been read only by scholars and gossips; but *Samson Agonistes* is a fable for mankind. If Conrad had given us merely the log of his voyage up the Congo, it would have been a travelogue; but he saw that voyage as a quest, something universal—saw the heart of Africa as a workable symbol of savage malice and duplicity in the human heart and mind; and in "Heart of Darkness" his personal experience has been transmuted and forgotten.

This, I admit, is an ideal view of creative writing. But you might as well aim high. I do not mean, of course, that all short stories written today go through this process, or that all stories sold and published are the product of the technical discipline suggested here. It is only recently, and even so only incompletely, that some careful writers appear to have recognized the resultant gain in spontaneity; and hundreds of short stories are still written in any old fashion, sold, and read more or less approvingly by tolerant readers.

But the young writer needs a lodestar to keep him on the course of objectivity. Short-story technique supplies this one: spontaneity produced by the selection, adoption, and consistent maintenance of a single telling medium (not, of course, the author's) through which all of the story is transmitted to the reader. Such directing of his material, instead of restricting him, will free in him narrative forces that would otherwise lie powerless.

As much for encouragement as for persuasion, and at the risk of seeming presumptuous, I want here to analyze two early American short stories that lack spontaneity—lack it simply because at the time of writing the discipline that would create it was almost unknown. These writers were "young" as compared to the present 150-years maturity of conscious short-story technique. They were groping in darkness without guide or precept, often misled by false ideals; and by trial and error they and those who followed them slowly and painfully found the methods that we take more or less for granted today. Thus I mean no disrespect to Hawthorne and Irving, whose stories we shall examine as primitives; but I have chosen stories by these famous authors in the hope of establishing a clearer view of their work than is usually granted to students of the short story. We grow up with a sort of blind reverence for the "classics," a conviction that they must be great in all possible respects. And this attitude is confirmed in school and college by our teachers, scholars, and critics, continually finding new felicities in old work. But my point of view must be practical. I am trying to prepare you to meet present conditions of editorial requirements and readers' expectations. If I don't succeed, you will imitate blindly or triumphantly offer "big name" exceptions. Students of literature may kneel down to the "classics" for all I care. But as writers let us get up, then, and look them square in the eye. They won't fall off their historic pedestals necessarily, but we shall see them more clearly. I believe most editors would bear me out in the statement that, if by unknown hands, neither Hawthorne's "The Birthmark" nor Irving's "The Legend of Sleepy Hollow" would be publishable today. Both possess great stylistic skill, deep feeling, and a sense of narrative form; they both lack spontaneity for they lack its prerequisite: a single, consistent telling medium not the author's. Hawthorne's allegory is an example of inconsistency, Irving's study in local color one of consistency only to and with his own omniscience as author.

The theme of "The Birthmark," as jotted down in the author's notebook, was "A person in possession of something as perfect as mortal man has a right to demand tries to make it better, and ruins it." Bravely ignoring his lack of knowledge both of human nature and of science, Hawthorne attempted to illustrate this paradox by presenting a learned chemist who, married to a woman of surpassing beauty marred only by a birthmark on her face, tries to remove the blemish and does so, but in the doing kills her. Hawthorne's motive was obviously moralistic, as evidenced by the "signification" or "application" baldly stated in the final paragraph in the manner of the ancestors of all moral tales, Aesop and the *Gesta Romanorum*. His idea seems of dubious validity, at least unless a thoroughgoing psychopathic study of a warped mind is contemplated, for normal man deeply in love would more likely be blind to any single blemish. Hawthorne himself saw this weakness in conception as a natural result of his very cloistered life, when in the preface to *Twice Told Tales* he wrote of some of his short stories: "They have the pale tint of flowers that blossomed in too retired a shade." But it is his method of telling this story that concerns us.

In the latter part of the last century [it begins] there lived a man of science, an eminent proficient in every branch of natural philosophy, who not long before our story opens had made experience of a spiritual affinity more attractive than any chemical one. He had left his laboratory to the care of an assistant, cleared his fine countenance from the furnace smoke, washed the stain of acids from his fingers, and persuaded a beautiful woman to become his wife. In those days when the comparatively recent discovery of electricity and other kindred mysteries of Nature seemed to open paths into the region of miracle, it was not unusual for the love of science to rival the love of woman in its depth and absorbing energy. The higher intellect, the imagination, the spirit, and even the heart might all find their congenial aliment in pursuits which, as some of their ardent votaries believed, would ascend from one step of powerful intelligence to another, until the philosopher should lay his hand on the secret of creative force and perhaps make new worlds for himself. We do not know whether Aylmer possessed this degree of faith in man's ultimate control over Nature. He had devoted himself, however, too unreservedly to scientific studies ever to be weaned from them by any second passion. His love for his young wife might prove the stronger of the two; but it could only be by intertwining itself with his love of science, and uniting the strength of the latter to his own.

Such a union accordingly took place, and was attended with truly remarkable consequences and a deeply impressive moral.

This is not story but exposition in academic prose. The author is addressing the reader directly, over his characters' heads, in generalities that leave us doubtful of his assumed authority as a man who knows the history of science or the history of human passion. He mentions "our story" as something that will follow after the lecture on science versus love has ended, and rams home his moral at the start lest some dullard fail to catch it. This arbitrary, synoptic, and pompous opening sets up and flaunts in our faces the author's point of view, his assumed right to tell a story in person.

Immediate scene, always a help, is reached in the second paragraph as "one day, very soon after their marriage," Aylmer, apparently noticing the birthmark for the first time, "sat gazing at his wife with a trouble in his countenance"—notice this external view of Aylmer; we are still viewing the story with the author—"that grew stronger until he spoke."

"Georgiana," said he, "has it ever occurred to you that the mark on your cheek might be removed?"

"No indeed," said she, smiling; but perceiving the seriousness of his manner, she blushed deeply.

Now to state that a character perceives something is, patently, to report mental reactions or sense impressions; that is, to set up a point of view restricted by that character's consciousness— a shift from the medium first used. But this second narrative medium breaks down at once, in mid-sentence, as Hawthorne records the blush not as she feels it, in terms of warmth, but as an observer sees it—as he the author, or Aylmer the husband, saw it, in terms of color. And we are soon recalled to the author's medium as Hawthorne proceeds to describe and explain the birthmark as only he knows it.

The next excursion is into Aylmer's state of mind as he meditates on the birthmark. "Had she been less beautiful—" it is almost indirect mental discourse at this point—"he might have felt his affection heightened . . . but seeing her otherwise so perfect, he found this one defect grow more and more intolerable . . ." until "Aylmer's sombre imagination was not long in rendering the birthmark a frightful object, causing him more trouble and horror than ever Georgiana's beauty, whether of soul or sense, had given him delight." These of course are Aylmer's thoughts and sense impressions, though heavily presided over and analyzed by the obtrusive author. But in the very next paragraph we are snatched back into Georgiana's perceptions; she "soon learned to shudder at his gaze." The scene shifts to "late one night"—we have lost immediate scene in a welter of synopsis and custom—and we are held briefly in Georgiana's point of view when she "voluntarily" returns to the dreaded subject of her blemish, "with a feeble attempt at a smile" that is more an external impression than one that she herself would receive. " 'Have you any recollection of a dream last night about this odious hand?' " she asks. (The birthmark takes the shape of a small hand.)

"None! none whatever!" replied Aylmer, starting; (also usually external: a startled person would more likely be aware of his state of mind than its reflex in his body)

but then he added, in a cold, dry tone, affected for the sake of concealing the real depth of his emotion . . .

And there we are again, viewing the situation through Aylmer's perceptions.

"And did you dream of it?" continued Georgiana hastily; for she dreaded lest a gush of tears should interrupt what she had to say . . .

And back we rush, willy-nilly, into poor Georgiana. Now listen!

The mind is in a sad state when Sleep, the all-involving . . .

It is the foghorn voice of the author again, interpolating a short essay on sleep. Hawthorne's telling method has looped the loop.

It would be useless to multiply examples; the entire story is told in this peripatetic fashion as its author whisks us from his own findings to the thoughts and feelings of Aylmer, to those of his luckless lady, and thence to himself again. Even when the laboratory assistant, Aminadab, appears, Hawthorne cannot refrain from intruding into *his* thoughts for a brief soliloquy in something close to direct mental discourse, unheard by the others: "If she were my wife, I'd never part with that birthmark." The effect of this method, or lack of method, is confusion and emotional estrangement: Hawthorne never stays long enough anywhere to permit the reader sympathy or kinship with the experience represented; and conviction in the story is impossible when its events are recorded by means of the author's obtrusively superhuman powers instead of by any natural medium. In the hands of a less gifted writer, as almost any composition teacher can attest, the effect of this sort of catch-as-catch-can telling is sheer absurdity.

For a good allegory with consistent telling medium, read Franz Kafka's "In the Penal Colony" (*Partisan Review,* 1941, with explanation in *Southern Review,* VII, 2, pp. 363–5; the story is reprinted in Brooks and Warren, *Understanding Fiction,* p. 441). For Hawthorne's ability to set up and maintain a consistent point of view, himself, read "Mr. Higginbotham's Catastrophe" (*New England Magazine,* Dec. 1834, reprinted in *Twice Told Tales*). As an instance of modern storytelling marred by inconsistent telling medium, see Eleanor Green's "The Dear Little Doves" (*Harpers,* 1942, reprinted in the O. Henry Memorial Award volume of 1942).

But perhaps the effect will not be so bad, the lack of spontaneity and hence convincingness so striking, if the author merely remains within his own omniscient point of view. Let us see.

"The Legend of Sleepy Hollow" had been published twenty-four years when "The Birthmark" appeared. Hawthorne must have read it; he might well have noted the authentic atmosphere resulting from Irving's faithful portraiture of a specific and to him thoroughly familiar place. "The Legend" has other positive merits: it is just a tale, with no moralistic or allegorical trappings; and if the author is plainly visible from first word to last (notice, however, Irving's attempt in the "Postcript" to ascribe the telling to somebody else, a fashionable literary device of the time and a perhaps fortuitous step in the right direction)—if the author is plainly visible, at least he is a person well worth seeing and knowing. One hesitates, indeed, to criticize this venerable piece of American prose as a short story at all. Irving was an essayist and biographer, not primarily a storyteller. His motive here was the recording of local color and folklore. As he wrote to a friend: "I consider a story merely as a frame on which to stretch my materials." But so do students, unfortunately, and their not-so-good material gets stretched mighty thin.

Roughly 11,000 words in length, "The Legend" is half told before any immediate scene is reached with the words "On a fine autumnal afternoon"; and it contains but three words spoken by a character, the "Who are you?" gasped by Ichabod Crane at his ghostly pursuer, which elicit no reply. Yet it is all talk, really; it is a leisurely, genial, formally rhetorical monologue—by the author. Never was reader so utterly at a speaker's mercy. Beginning with the geographical location and historical associations of Tarry Town, digressing for reminiscences of squirrel shooting, remarks on witchcraft and superstitions in general, at its own good time it reaches a lengthy description of Ichabod, his school, the social position of the schoolmaster, and of Katrina Van Tassel and her father's farm, as well as of Brom Bones, with an interpolated essay on love ("I profess not to know how women's hearts are wooed and won," etc.)—all this entirely by means of exposition and synoptic and customary action, not once emerging into the present-past immediacy of any particular story. Once finally established on that "fine autumnal afternoon," in spite of very lengthy descriptions and one expository digression about the supernatural tales told of Sleepy Hollow, immediate scene is maintained until a page before the end. But here for once that quality is helpless. Irving's discursiveness, his omnipresence in the story, and his stubborn insistence on presiding in person over it have left him no chance, no space, no taste for an element far more necessary in fiction than descriptive detail: dramatic portrayal and motivation of character. For this is a love story with a comically unhappy ending; Ichabod presumes to the hand of the squire's daughter and is sent packing by a rival's ruse that plays upon his fear of ghosts. And we never know whether this gawky schoolmaster is to be taken for a villain, a fool, or a pathetic victim of class struggle. It is to be doubted whether the author himself knew. Yet this is a question of prime importance to the reader. If Crane is merely villain or merely fool, watching his defeat is unrewarding because the defeat was so easy. If he is to be taken as a victim, little or no pity is forthcoming in view of his meaner side and the clearly likable qualities of the people he tried to dupe. Katrina is equally vague. While dancing with Ichabod she smiles "graciously in reply to all his amorous oglings," as if favoring his suit. Then the schoolmaster leaves her and joins the storytellers to listen to the tale told by Brom Bones, who, "sorely smitten by love and jealousy, [had] sat by himself in one corner" while Crane and Katrina danced, but makes no move toward her when Crane leaves her free; and now Katrina is evidently ignoring both swains. As the dance breaks up there is mention of a tête-à-tête at which Katrina rejected

Crane, which incidentally makes all the rest of the story, the pursuit by the headless horseman and Crane's flight from the vicinity, superfluous. But at this crucial moment, when Katrina rejects the schoolmaster, Irving backs away with the confession, "What passed at this interview I will not pretend to say, for in fact I do not know." We can guess, of course; but guessing does not clarify Katrina as a person. How could she possibly endure, and even encourage, the advances of that human scarecrow? Was it conventional respect for his position? Feminine coquetry? Or did she plan to force Brom Bones's hand through jealousy? We can guess but we never know. These are some of the matters, vital to the craft of fiction, that Irving would have been able to present—and in far less than 11,000 words!—if technique, non-existent at the time, had taught him that the author as telling medium inevitably creates distractions that obscure and then vitiate the story.

Now it is your move. Write blind if you like. If you prefer a sight of technique contributed to us by the failures and slow success of many writers since Irving and Hawthorne, the next four chapters will, I hope, give it to you.

5

"I" AS PROTAGONIST

AN INTERESTING passage in "The Birthmark" recounts Georgiana's discovery of her husband's laboratory:

The first thing that struck her eye was the furnace, that hot and feverish worker, with the intense glow of its fire, which by the quantities of soot clustered above it seemed to have been burning for ages. There was a distilling apparatus in full operation. Around the room were retorts, tubes, cylinders, crucibles, and other apparatus of chemical research. An electrical machine stood ready for immediate use. The atmosphere felt oppressively close, and was tainted with gaseous odors which had been tormented forth by the processes of science. The severe and homely simplicity of the apartment, with its naked walls and brick pavement, looked strange, accustomed as Georgiana had become to the fantastic elegance of her boudoir . . .

This is pretty unscientific science, even for the date of the action in the late eighteenth century. The phrases "in full operation," "electrical machine," and "ready for immediate use" sound impressive without committing themselves to the vaguest picture; Hawthorne was faking it like a sophomore. But the important point, which he seems to have missed, is that there was no need to be scientifically specific and authentic, since the character through whose thoughts and senses the experience might have been filtered was herself undoubtedly ignorant in such matters. Georgiana would probably have identified the furnace (though she probably would not have personified it), she would have wrinkled her nose at the odor and soot, she would have noted the bare walls and brick floor, naturally; but the rest was merely clutter and disagreeable shapes of unimaginable things. In the first sentence "struck her eye," although a trite recording of the sense impression, does seem to be going to give us the experience through this channel. And Georgiana's reactions to the formidable equipment of which she is to be the victim would be dramatically relevant. But then the ubiquitous author takes over the job, and botches it with his pretentious faked inventory. The last two impressions—the close atmosphere "felt" by Georgiana and the severe simplicity that "looked" strange to her—come clear and convincing through the poor woman's senses. I like to believe that here, or in similar passages from other short stories, Hawthorne was experimenting and searching for a spontaneous telling method.

For the following year, 1844, with "Rappaccini's Daughter" he approached spontaneity by this means, improving his own stumbling efforts in "The Birthmark" and Irving's in "The Legend of Sleepy Hollow." Like the latter story, "Rappaccini's Daughter" is an example of the attribution to fictitious authorship fashionable at the time, as if the writer were *trying* to keep out of his story; "Rappaccini's Daughter" carries the rubric "From the Writings of Aubépine," and Hawthorne begins with a preface purporting to criticize the work of this imaginary Frenchman, whose name, however, is merely a translation of his own. This is perhaps a little better than Irving's "Postcript" coming so late that the disguise was futile, but still not very subtle or serviceable. The tale as a whole is no better than "The Birthmark." Its theme is over-moral and philosophical: a young man falls in love with a girl systematically nourished on poisons, discovers and administers an antidote, and of course does the poor thing in. The time span is loose and vague, allegory is laid on with a shovel, the point of view shifts to any character who happens to be on hand, and the story stops for author's comment and such apostrophic observations as "Blessed are all simple emotions, be they dark or bright!" There is a very large element of chance in the plot, the characters are shoved about by the author's will, and at the end several disturbing questions remain unanswered.

But the scene is Padua, a specific place instead of the vague Gothic limbo of "The Birthmark," and for the most part it is a garden between two houses in that city; this fact and the time of action, "very long ago," give us a satisfying contact with particularity, and hence reality. At least the author has pinned himself down. And as his young hero, a stranger in town, looks out of his window on the garden at the beginning of the story, for a thousand words Hawthorne all but disappears and the tale comes alive and runs on its own emotional momentum. The italics are mine:

Giovanni still found no better occupation than to look down into the garden beneath his window. From its appearance *he judged it to be* one of those botanic gardens which were of earlier date in Padua than elsewhere in Italy or in the world. Or, not improbably, it *might once have been* the pleasure-palace of an opulent family; for there was the ruin of a marble fountain in the center, sculptured with rare art, but so woefully shattered that it was impossible to trace the original design from the chaos of remaining fragments. The water, however, continued to sparkle and gush into the sunbeams as cheerfully as ever. A little gurgling sound ascended to the young man's window, and *made him feel* as if the fountain were an immortal spirit that sung its song unceasingly and without heeding the vicissitudes around it, while one century embodied it in marble and another scattered the imperishable garniture on the soil. All about the pool into which the water subsided grew various plants, that *seemed* to require a plentiful supply of moisture for the nourishment of gigantic leaves, and, in some instances, flowers gorgeously magnificent. There was one shrub in particular, set in a marble vase in the midst of the pool, that bore a profusion of purple blossoms, each of which had the luster and richness of a gem; and the whole together made a show so resplendent that it *seemed* enough to illuminate the garden, even had there been no sunshine. Every portion of the soil was peopled with plants and herbs, which, if less beautiful, still bore tokens of assiduous care, *as if all had* their individual virtues, known to the scientific mind that fostered them. . . .

While Giovanni stood at the window *he heard* a rustling behind a screen of leaves, and *became aware* that a person was at work in the garden. His figure soon emerged into view, and *showed itself* to be that of no common laborer, but a tall, emaciated, sallow, and sickly looking man, dressed in a scholar's garb of black. . . .

Nothing could exceed the intentness with which this scientific gardener examined every shrub that grew in his path: *it seemed as if he was looking into their inmost nature.* . . . Nevertheless, in spite of this deep intelligence on his part, there was no approach to intimacy between himself and these vegetable existences. On the contrary, he avoided their actual touch or the direct inhaling of their odors with a caution that *impressed Giovanni most disagreeably.* . . . *It was strangely frightful to the young man's imagination to see this air of insecurity.* . . . *Was this garden, then, the Eden of the present world? And this man, with such a perception of harm in what his own hands caused to grow,—was he the Adam?*

The scene continues, with Giovanni the ignorant but curious observer, through Beatrice's entrance and her talk with her father. Soon after its close Hawthorne breaks in with unwelcome comment ("But there is an influence in the light of morning that tends to rectify whatever errors of fancy," etc.); but for a little while we have been living the story in the being of that young Italian, through his senses, knowing only what he knew, lonely and eager and apprehensive as he was. The italics show how this was done, mostly by verbs that tell, not what the garden and flowers *were,* but how they *seemed to him.* Compare this passage with those in which Irving takes Ichabod through the forest or lets him read or listen to old wives' tales, noting how the genial essayist never lets the story out of his clutches. Compare it with Georgiana in the laboratory of "The Birthmark" and see the enormous gain in Hawthorne himself. No inventory of plants and herbs here; Giovanni was no botanist. No explaining, no telling-all such as we found in the opening paragraph of "The Birthmark" about Aylmer. The technique is not very subtle yet. Giovanni does a good deal of looking without much motive. The diction, phrasing, and sentence structure are no more appropriate to a young student than were Irving's to his simple rustics; the Aubépine ruse aside, they are obviously Nathaniel Hawthorne.

At the beginning of the passage the words "one of those botanic gardens which were of earlier date in Padua than elsewhere in Italy or in the world" are, unless one can improbably suppose that the boy knew this, a lapse into direct exposition. But this considerable sojourn within a character's sense impressions, with its marked gain in suspense and implicative force and its easy, natural culmination in indirect mental discourse, is a promise of complete and consistent spontaneity to come.

As I remarked in the preceding chapter, we shall see spontaneity developed by four principal methods, now become standard, but no one of which can be categorically called best. Each has merits and each, under certain conditions, has weaknesses and dangers; although I believe that the last to be treated will prove more generally serviceable than any of the others. But a telling medium should be carefully chosen, with reference to material and theme, for appropriateness and functional efficiency.

By many people Edgar Allan Poe is better remembered for his theory than for his practice of the short story. His theory, requiring that the story be short enough to be read in less than two hours and that it should possess "unity of impression," seems important only historically; in 1842 it was a good thing for the genre for somebody to have ideas about it. The requirements themselves are irritatingly vague. Some readers are twice as rapid as others. What is "unity of impression" and how, precisely, can a writer get it? Poe never said.

But in practice the man was vigorous, exact, illuminating, a pioneer in a wilderness, far ahead of his time. "The Cask of Amontillado," published only three years after "The Birthmark," is a triumphant demonstration of everything Hawthorne's pallid and gangling homily lacked. Let us take this story as an example of the first of four telling methods, which may be called "I" as participant or protagonist.

Using it, a writer gives us a record of the action through first-person telling by a participant, as if this character were actually talking to us or had written down the account for us to read. By this device the author, as author, is automatically barred from the entire story (except for the title and his by-line!). But certain difficulties beyond the mere imaginative agility involved in the act of seeing life convincingly through a fictitious person's senses are at once apparent. This telling, if it is to sound real, must be conditioned by three important factors:

1. The plausible articulateness of the character, his ability not only to think but to speak out on intimate matters; and, this determined, the quality of language natural to him as a coherent story vehicle. Imagine one of Hemingway's toughs trying to confide in us! Is a doubt cast upon some of Ring Lardner's low-brow monologues?

2. His plausible presence on the scene all the time, or at least his plausible contact with those who could keep him informed. If much dependence on the latter is necessary, will immediacy be lost? Or can dramatic profit be made of this very exigency, the teller receiving *but misunderstanding* reports and so becoming further embroiled?

3. His plausible dramatic sense. For good stories do not trickle naturally out of all people, and a man under emotional stress (as, if the story is moving, its protagonist must be) is not likely to exercise restraint to produce the suspense and surprise that readers demand and the author must somehow provide.

Poe met these problems with the patience and resourcefulness of genius:

The thousand injuries of Fortunato [he begins] I had borne as I best could; but when he ventured upon insult, I vowed revenge. You, who so well know the nature of my soul, will not suppose, however, that I gave utterance to a threat. *At length* I would be avenged; this was a point definitely settled—but the very definitiveness with which it was resolved precluded the idea of risk. I must not only punish, but punish with impunity. A wrong is unredressed when retribution overtakes its redresser. It is equally

87

unredressed when the avenger fails to make himself felt as such to him who has done the wrong.

It must be understood that neither by word nor deed had I given Fortunato cause to doubt my good will. I continued, as was my wont, to smile in his face, and he did not perceive that my smile *now* was at the thought of his immolation.

He had a weak point—this Fortunato—although in other regards he was a man to be respected and even feared. He prided himself on his connoisseurship in wine. Few Italians have the true virtuoso spirit. For the most part their enthusiasm is adopted to suit the time and opportunity, to practise imposture upon the British and Austrian *millionaires*. In painting and gemmary, Fortunato, like his countrymen, was a quack, but in the matter of old wines he was sincere. In this respect I did not differ from him materially;—I was skilful in the Italian vintages myself, and bought largely whenever I could.

So the theme of this story is revenge; specifically, an unfortunate and long-suffering citizen of medieval Rome lures his oppressor to the catacombs and walls him up alive. The story is told, as if to a friend, by the avenger, an educated and intelligent man whose family have suffered reverses. The action is wholly in immediate scene; even these opening three paragraphs, which explain the situation by recounting past events by means synoptic and customary, being covered by the implied immediate scene of the telling itself. Thus there are three levels of time: the past (with reference to the action of the story) treated in these opening paragraphs and once or twice, very briefly, later; the past-made-present by the immediate scene of the action; and the implied actual present of the telling. But the third requires no space, and the first can be dealt with, clearly and excitingly through the first person of the protagonist, in 250 words. Notice the gain in economy and swiftness: Irving needed 5,000 words to prepare us for Ichabod's flight from the headless horseman; Hawthorne took 300 merely to explain his underlying cause, Aylmer's marriage, and hundreds more to interpret motives at every dismal step of the way. But particularly notice the gain in spontaneity. Here is no presiding author, no external narrative agent whatever, but only the still-indignant yet icily calm voice of a man rubbed raw by slights and injuries, who fifty years ago planned and executed the perfect crime, and now feels the feat worth telling.

The first problem, the articulateness and coherence of the teller, was met by careful selection of character. Montresor, well-born and intellectually trained, sensitive and thoughtful, above all proud, brooded long over his crime before committing it and for fifty years before confessing it. If Poe had hit upon a different sort of man—impulsive or emotional, say— the telling medium he used would have been revealed to us as shabby artifice, the word-for-word recounting would have damned itself as implausible and false. But Montresor is recollecting in relative tranquility. The number of times he planned the murder, step by step, and the number of times, alone in his guilty knowledge, he has re-enacted it, word by word, have grooved the last detail in his obsessed memory. He is exactly the man for the job of doing and the job of telling. His detachment, almost his cool pride in the horrible deed, is maintained to the last: *in pace requiescat.*

The second problem, that of the necessary presence of the narrator on the scene all the time, was solved by rigid compression of characters to the two principals, and of the action to its actual climax, the murder itself. Although only the culmination of months, perhaps years, of provocation, and the basis of half a century of reflection, that act is made the whole story, thus reducing the time span of the action to a single evening, an hour or two—a fairly close analogy between reading time and the actual time represented. This done, the problem solved itself. Since complete conviction, however, is dependent upon whether we believe the facts of provocation Montresor has told us in those opening paragraphs and sympathize with his motive, a reservation as to whether Poe has not overcompressed his material must be left for further discussion.

The third need, that of the narrator's dramatic sense, was satisfied by two provisions. First was, again, Poe's carefully demonstrated conception of Montresor's temperament. Notice Montresor's choice of the carnival season for his act (at once a security measure and an ironical theatric touch), his proven ability to play a part as shown by the ambiguous smile in paragraph two, and his evident delight in the almost constant irony fully understood only by him and the reader: "I was so pleased to see him that I thought I should never have done wringing his hand." "How remarkably *well* you are looking today!" Then Luchesi used as bait. And after Fortunato's "I shall not die of a cough," "True—true." And "I [drink] to your long life." Then the reference to masonic orders. And "Let us be gone." The second provision was the author's skillful management of action and dialogue so rapid and full of implication that the reader has neither time nor inclination to be critical: far more necessary in prose fiction than on stage, screen, or radio, for with a book in his hand the audience may, if you let him, stop at any moment and check back.

We come, then, to the reservation. Without prejudice to the method generally, it must be said that in this story, since all those insults and injuries of Montresor are only referred to (and that only through the warped mind of the injured), instead of being dramatically and thus convincingly presented, as is the act of revenge; and since Fortunato drunk and half ill during that act seems more a pathetic victim than the vicious intriguer Montresor has made him out to be—reader sympathy has no outlet and poetic justice is baffled and thwarted. This dissatisfaction is increased by vague reference to Montresor's family and, particularly, his wife. Is all this merely a madman's whim, or *was* there real injury? Compare the definite and sustained pull on our sympathy of "The Pit and the Pendulum" for a mortal in agony and finally rescued. It is a weakness of content, rather than of technique, with which we shall have much to do later. It indicates the need of further caution, however, in choosing this method. Probably no able modern writer would use it for similar material without making the provocation as real to the reader (John Collier did precisely that, and with strikingly similar material, in "De Mortuis . . .") as Poe made the act of revenge.

The great merit of the method is intensity: it reaches the heart of the story and lays it bare. Its limitations arise from the normal, inevitable attitude of human readers toward a fellow human who tells his own story. If his acts were heroic, he is apt to seem a braggart; if they were villainous, even worse. And even in less extreme range of material, with any such failure to objectify experience as is the commonest failing of inexperienced writers, the "I" as protagonist is almost sure to sound either too conceited or too humble for his story to possess validity or move us deeply.

Yet the method represents a decisive step toward spontaneous technique; this telling medium is sound in principle and often effectively used today. For an example, read Sherwood Anderson's "I Want to Know Why," in which it was used for purposes of irony; that is, the theme of the story and its point are transmitted to the reader over the head of the puzzled narrator—not by the author expositorily—but between the lines of the narrator's own account.

It will help you to accustom yourself to this kind of telling medium if, without any particular story in mind, you will write, say, a thousand words of experience, in the third person but through the sense impressions (see Giovanni watching the garden) of a character, a particular sort of person who feels strongly about something that has happened or is about to happen to him. Make the experience, his individuality, and his emotion clear without explanation by you as author. Then rewrite the same material in the first person, as if he were telling or writing it to somebody, trying very hard to maintain the demonstration of *his* personality you got through third-person telling, not for a moment letting it merge with your own.

91

6

"I" AS WITNESS

W E THINK of the leading character in a story as its hero or protagonist. More precisely, a protagonist is the character without whom as motive agent the story could not occur, whose involvement in the action and whose success or failure at the end constitute its chief matter and interest. Such is Montresor, the narrator of "The Cask of Amontillado." In this position at the very heart of the story, the dangers of first-person telling referred to in the last chapter would seem greatest. If they can be avoided, however, emotional response should be strong. It is a case of risking much for a possibly great reward. But there is a widespread distaste for reading stories told by the protagonist, due perhaps—among readers subconsciously seeking emotional identification with him—to the intrusion of an alien ego on the scene. Curiously, this prejudice does not interfere with the enjoyment of "true" confession stories, which by this method trade on a pretense of actuality (thus possibly eliminating the desire for identification: "The poor thing is a real person, I tell you. She can't be *me*.") for cheap emotional response—pity, fear, envy, lust, and so on— from immature readers. In more honest fiction the prejudice is strong enough among the general reading public to suggest careful consideration of other possible telling mediums.

For there are, of course, degrees of possible proximity to, thus participation in, the action of a story; and each represents a position from which the story may be told, still in the first person. A character to be chosen as teller may have participated in the action without being its protagonist in the sense I have indicated; he may only have been present as an interested witness; or he may have been merely told about it, after it happened, by someone more closely concerned. This range is enormously increased by possible gradations in the personal identification of the teller, which run from a distinct individuality—a person known to us by name with a clear-cut character—to some anonymous, typical figure who happened to be on hand (a neighbor or bystander) and is identified as telling medium only by an infrequent first-person pronoun in his report. This latter extreme of anonymity, excellently illustrated by the method of William Faulkner's "A Rose for Emily," will eventually lead us to and merge with another method, to be called objective.

But for the time being let us consider an intermediate position and method that one might call "I" as interested witness. Remembering the potential strength and weakness inherent in letting the protagonist tell his own story, one can see at once that choice of a less deeply involved character as teller will radically alter the situation to be controlled by the unseen author. Similar conditions of plausibility (articulateness in the teller, his necessary presence on the scene, his dramatic sense) will still operate here. The danger of emotional distortion and consequent readers' dissatisfaction may be less. But there may be a loss of intensity as we deliberately leave the heart of the story and view it through any one of the great number of positions outside its heart—a loss that increases with distance. And there will be a new danger, of distraction. For unless the degree of personal identification of the teller chosen is precisely consistent with the amount of motive power he supplies—I mean, consistent with the relative importance of the part he plays in the action—his obtrusive presence on the scene, just like that of an unwanted author, will disperse and weaken the reader's emotional response. Inexperienced writers, using "I" as witness, sometimes believe they have shaded down their tellers' personalities to that of a neutral, detached observer whereas actually they are left looming all over the story, try-

93

ing in spite of themselves to steal it from the principals. Even skilled authors are occasionally guilty, as will be seen.

A short story whose narrator occupies a middle position between protagonist and anonymous bystander—who is known to the other characters, has an interest in them, and takes some small part in the action—will demonstrate the merits and possible defects of the telling medium. O. Henry's "A Municipal Report" is of this type. Widely circulated and often highly praised, like other stories previously examined here it is not wholly successful and has been chosen for that very reason. The general impression that well-known stories are invariably good stories should be corrected; and I believe that students are better off if not exposed exclusively (as too often they have been) to masterpieces that defy analysis and only engender a sense of inferiority. "A Municipal Report" was written in great haste, possibly while the New York *World* copy boy waited at the author's door, for the Sunday supplement of that newspaper; it is one of 130 stories produced in as many weeks, all of them under the space limitation of one newsprint page. Under these circumstances, to condemn O. Henry out of hand today is as foolish as it was early in the century to worship at his feet. His often keen eye, his whimsical wit, his warm heart, his unfailing gusto, and above all his whip-snap ingenuity helped to make the short story a known and needed commodity throughout the country.

"A Municipal Report" opens with a quotation from Frank Norris deriding Chicago, Buffalo, and Nashville as locales of novels. The slur at the first-named city Norris was later to retract by writing *The Pit;* the reference to Nashville merely gave the hard-pressed O. Henry another week's assignment. He begins expansively:

East is East, and West is San Francisco, according to Californians. Californians are a race of people; they are not merely inhabitants of a State. They are the Southerners of the West. Now, Chicagoans are no less loyal to their city; but when you ask them why, they stammer and speak of lake fish and the new Odd Fellows' Building. But Californians go into detail.

Of course they have, in the climate, an argument that is good for half an hour while you are thinking of your coal bills and heavy underwear. But as soon as they come to mistake your silence for conviction, madness comes upon them, and they picture the city of the Golden Gate as the Bagdad of the New World. So far, as a matter of opinion, no refutation is necessary. But, dear cousins all (from Adam and Eve descended), it is a rash one who will lay his finger on the map and say: "In this town there can be no romance—what could happen here?" Yes, it is a bold and rash deed to challenge in one sentence history, romance, and Rand and McNally.[1]

This engaging chatter is even further removed from the story that follows (editor's assistant finds starving lady poet and Negro cab driver supporting former's worthless husband, who finally dies and all is well) than was Hawthorne's sedate disquisition on love versus science at the opening of "The Birthmark"; for Hawthorne at least began writing about Aylmer ("In the latter part of the last century there lived a man of science," etc.) whereas these sentences are generalities bare of individuals, hinting only very vaguely at some story to be laid in Nashville, and even implying, falsely, that sectional loyalty will be its theme. It should be noted in O. Henry's defense that there was some precedent for the philosophically discursive opening (which Arthur Hoffman was to call a disease as late as 1922); readers were already used to it as practiced by Rudyard Kipling in some of the early tales he contributed to the Lahore *Civil and Military Gazette*—"Bitters Neat," for instance ("The oldest trouble in the world comes from want of understanding," etc.) or "In Error" ("There is hope for a man who gets publicly and riotously drunk more often than he ought to; but there is no hope for the man who drinks secretly," etc.). The precedent, indeed, might be traced far

[1] From *Strictly Business*, by O. Henry, copyright 1910 by Doubleday & Co., Inc.

back beyond O. Henry's knowledge to that literary ancestor of the short story which included, at the end instead of as here at the beginning, an instructive application or moral. But Kipling, at least, was seldom guilty of beginning a tale with such irrelevance and in this oracular mood, and then shifting to a character as narrator.

This O. Henry does without a blush. Immediately following the two paragraphs quoted comes an excerpt, plausible enough in wording, from some gazetteer or perhaps a chamber of commerce brochure on the city of Nashville, which provides the rather far-fetched title but also offers a neat contrast, by its stodgy prose, with the highly romantic aspects of a lost-cause South to come. Now these three short opening sections— the actual statement by Norris, the banter directed at Californians, and the sober prose of the "report"—are unmistakably O. Henry addressing the reader; nobody within the tale that follows would conceivably have begun his account of the episode in just that way. Yet the very next sentence is: "I stepped off the train at 8 P.M.," and thereafter the story maintains, if somewhat loosely, this immediate scene recalled through the point of view of the "I" here first mentioned. Who then is this "I"? If examined, his personality appears a baffling set of contradictions. He is a Southerner and a traveler, yet a stranger to Nashville. He has a mysterious business of his own, but has been given a sort of roving commission "from a Northern literary magazine," including control of its contracts with and payments to contributors; but he is scalped by a cab driver. His relations with one contributor, Azalea Adair, are far from businesslike, showing ignorance both of authors and of editors. He satirizes the city of Nashville while becoming fatuously sentimental over two of its inhabitants. He has command of a smart-aleck vocabulary calculated to drive most editors frantic, and uses it freely. Placed in this responsible position by the Northern "literary" journal (*The Atlantic,* perhaps!), he sees everybody he meets only as the broadest sort of type; he lies by telegraph to his boss; and is (with unconscious aptness) called a "duffer" by him. He emits solemn, stale generalities, obscure periphrases, mock-heroic euphemisms, and topical wisecracks with equal ease. At certain points in the story he exhibits almost miraculously acute powers of observation, yet fails to see what is happening under his eyes until long after the reader has done so. And throughout the story he sings of himself: his annoyance at Major Caswell, his delight in livers *en brochette,* his sophistication and cosmopolitanism, his grand manner toward human beings in general, and his unfailing generosity to the unfortunate and oppressed. Before the end is reached this "I" has become by all odds the most noticeable person in the story, although none of his fantastic qualities is in the slightest degree germane or even relevant to it. All that was needed was anybody who could pass money to Azalea Adair and notice, and finally pick up, a button.

This "I" is, of course, O. Henry simply being for the most part O. Henry, but trying very hard at times to be another person whom he didn't know well enough to make in the least convincing. My guess is that, so far as technique went, he wrote the story blind. Those opening paragraphs were a readable start—of something; they got him into the mood; and he patched up the telling medium as he went along, putting in desperate bits here and there as the intricate plot demanded. There was no time to revise. The outcome and the necessary properties (the torn dollar bill, the missing button) he had fixed in his head; the rest he squeezed and worried into last-minute conformity, trusting to his wit and the stock reaction to a pathetic female in distress to pull him through. In the case of thousands of readers insensitive to organic structure and easily doped beyond reality, this they have done and perhaps may continue to do.

But young writers need a clearer view; without it they will launch into worse mistakes. Underneath O. Henry's camouflage they will see here a workable plot idea: the slowly developing difference between appearance and actuality, through the senses of an interested and appropriate witness whose discovery is paced by the reader. If in "A Municipal Report" the difference proves not great enough to be worth all the fuss, if actuality seems hardly more real than appearance, that is no prejudice to the method. Except for the first page (a sound practice is to write a first page, or two first pages, or three, in the knowledge that that part is going to be thrown away when it has served its purpose of getting you into the real story)— except for that scrambled first page the story is consistently told by a witness. Stronger suppression of the witness's personality, unless it is relevant (in which case, more thorough understanding and more convincing elucidation of it), with consequent gain in space for the much more important character development of the chief actors, will result in that highest aim of technique: a natural, integrated medium for transmitting a moving story without benefit of author. Notice, for instance, how this end was achieved in Ring Lardner's "Haircut."

These two telling methods, "I" as protagonist and "I" as witness, are most useful where apparent compression and emotional unification are needed for material requiring a wide time span. The disparity between necessary lapses of actual time and their representation in narrative, always a problem in the short story, is far less noticeable to the reader, and thus less likely to shatter illusion, if covered by an immediate scene implied by the first-person telling of a character in the story. And this teller, if wisely chosen and objectively characterized, may supply naturally and convincingly the needed comment or interpretation that the author seeking spontaneity would rightly refuse to offer in his own person. In Faulkner's "A Rose for Emily" many years are covered convincingly and with small loss of intensity by allowing some person unnamed, a neighbor of the protagonist, to muse reminiscently (also, characteristically, and greatly to the author's purpose, *backward* in time) on the single day of the protagonist's funeral. Faulkner uses the method also, though differently, in "That Evening Sun"; and many other contemporary writers have welcomed the narrator-within-the-story, at one or another of his possible positions, as a means of reducing actual time or of pointing up for emphasis a needed emotional aspect or reaction that could not otherwise be provided without loss of spontaneity.

To sum up, then. Success with first-person telling mediums will depend largely on the following considerations:

1. The objectivity with which you portray the narrator. To lighten the problem, if possible devise a personality for the teller quite different from your own: not so like you as was the chatty, sentimental, casual show-off like O. Henry in "A Municipal Report," or as was the sensitive, introverted, proud, impoverished Montresor like Poe in "The Cask of Amontillado"; but, rather, as radically different as were Ring Lardner and the naive barber of "Haircut," or Sherwood Anderson and the passionate boy who loved horses of "I Want to Know Why." Perhaps then you won't be tempted to barge in.

2. The convincing detail by which you can present him. Stay within the range of your own observed experience; find a teller younger rather than older than yourself, for you will have lived through his years; a member of your sex not too far removed from your environment; particularly a person whom you know (in your mind, I mean—he may be a composite of several actual people) more closely than you know a broad type, such as millionaire, policeman, parson, hostess, etc.

3. The appropriateness of his degree of personal identification by the reader in the story. Minimize his personality to a point consistent with his function, without however leaving any doubt as to who is talking, where, and in what circumstances. The opening paragraph of "Haircut" is worth study:

66939

I got another barber that comes over from Carterville and helps me out Saturdays, but the rest of the time I can get along all right alone. You can see for yourself that this ain't no New York City and besides that, the most of the boys works all day and don't have no leisure to drop in here and get themselves all prettied up.[2]

Make sure the necessary facts are clear at the start. Then if in doubt of the amount of individual identification appropriate or necessary, play it down (as Lardner did here) rather than up—and this even if the narrator is the protagonist.

4. The plausibility of the narrator's function of teller of all the story. Would he naturally be there? If important matter has to be told him, is immediacy or intensity lost? Has he a reason for telling—if he is at or near the heart of the story, has he a strong reason? Would he naturally have the ideas and the language needed for the telling, the knowledge and understanding of other characters that the reader must receive for clarity, and the dramatic sense that you as author must make him convincingly use in the structure of the story?

Not all of these considerations, of course, will operate in every first-person told story. But all should be explored before the medium is adopted. If they seem too severe, you have the best reason in the world for seeking other, less artificial means for the creation of spontaneity.

But for practice, for there will come a time when only this medium will do, tell the same event (a fire, a dog fight, a holdup, an automobile accident) twice: first as if by a person actually involved, then as if by a disinterested witness. Adjust personal identification of the narrator to his relative importance, at both narrative positions making the needed amount of identification and characterization clear wholly through the medium himself.

[2] From *The Love Nest and Other Stories,* by Ring Lardner; Charles Scribner's Sons. Reprinted by permission of the publishers.

7

OBJECTIVE TELLING

EXCEPT at its best, the frame story told by one of its characters creates so much machinery for the concealment of the author that he may become noticeable by his very absence. Such a story seems to protest, like the chicken thief surprised in the hen coop, "Ain't nobody in here but us chickens." Its author seems to forget that the primary object of all stories is to represent fundamentally natural human experience, and experience manipulated for dramatic effect until it has the inevitable neat *un*naturalness of a dream defeats that primary purpose. Many such stories were written, as authors like Kipling and F. Hopkinson Smith carried the method to extremes, during the last years of the nineteenth and the early years of the twentieth century; and the type is still familiar. In the small hours of a bleak winter's night, five or six lean and hard-bitten cosmopolites who ought to have been in bed are gathered about a glowing hearth with their pipes, perfectos, and unlimited brandy. One of them, after much urging, and with every sign of unsuccessfully controlled emotion, tells a tale of, say, cowardice in the Punjab, which seems to have no particular point—until at its close one of the hearers gets up and staggers from the room, the self-confessed culprit. To the naked eye no author is present here; there is no comment, no analysis, no interpretation, no moral. Yet the thing smells of the lamp. Life, we feel, doesn't run that way. Truth may be stranger than fiction, but this wasn't offered us as truth, it was offered as fiction; and as fiction, *somebody,* we feel, must have planned all that artifice to make the tale come out so very clean. The only conceivable somebody is the name in the by-line, and there is the author after all. Contemporary writers have improved the method by removing the frame and making the storyteller explain himself and the immediate scene of the telling while the real story unfolds; but even in skilled hands the danger of distraction by over-manipulation may exist. In my opinion Henry James's "The Turn of the Screw," although far subtler and much more convincing than many frame stories of the period, suffers from this fault of over-concealment that really reveals. Indeed, as Edmund Wilson has pointed out, James here superimposed so much telling machinery that the probable full significance of the story is lost without a special interpretation of its narrator as a neurotic, the "ghosts" of the story merely as her hallucinations—all this information having been luckily supplied us, not by the story, but by appreciative commentators. Certainly a tale so wrapped in technique that full comprehension requires a gloss must be very good indeed on other counts to atone for its secrecy.

But is there no alternative? Are we not, perhaps, in danger of making spontaneity a fetish if we strive so hard for it that other, possibly more important, story elements are jeopardized by its achievement? If it is to be gained only by such negative means as "I" as protagonist, participant, or witness in person on the scene, how does it happen that fairy tales and folk tales by the score ("Little Red Riding Hood," for instance), apparently untouched by literary technique and not visibly told by anybody, exert such a powerful hold on imagination and sympathy that they outlive ten centuries? There must be some other way, perhaps some positive way as against the negative method of concealing the author behind a character's skirts, of attaining spontaneity.

There are at least two other ways at present generally accepted, and it is altogether probable that in the future more will be found. But don't imagine that these ways are going to be as easy as "Little Red Riding Hood" looks. They, too, may look easy as we see them in some author's able hands. Actually they will present even greater demands than do previously considered telling methods on your ability to create a fabric so light, so bright, so flexible and full of motion that its strength will never be seen. I would say "your ability to create art that conceals itself," except that people take fright at that phrase. But that is exactly what I mean. Would-be painters and composers acknowledge the necessity of learning to be artists, of undergoing discipline in their craft with the hope of rising above craft into art. Why should not would-be storytellers do so? I believe that they should, and make no bones about it. That many shrink from accepting or imposing discipline is perhaps due to two myths: that all you need to make a story is pencil and paper, and that writers are born and not made.

Deluded by these myths, many of us never guess that the discipline involved in the art of imaginative writing—a matter of verbal utterance—is essentially a discipline of the candidate's naturally articulate, if not outright voluble, character and personality: some sort of training that will do something about the unfortunate fact that he is by nature just an old windbag. But in the technical methods left for consideration it is precisely that; it exorcises the gassy devil born in him. I have suggested that these methods are positive, in contrast to the rather negative results obtained by planned concealment of the author through substitution for him of a telling medium within the story. Now I mean that, with this discipline of his garrulous nature effected, he may with impunity let the story come out practically as it will, with no fear at least that by so doing he will reveal something that should be concealed. But the discipline will be everything; it will be perhaps more than positive, it will be revolutionary; it may very likely make a new man of him. A man so intensely engrossed in his material that as author he has no self left: he is a lens, a window through which the light of human experience falls.

The first of the two technical methods resulting from this discipline I call objective. Let us determine its characteristics, consider how they are to be obtained, and try to discover for what sort or sorts of material this objective medium of story-telling is best suited.

I mentioned Faulkner's "A Rose for Emily" as a story whose narrator, some unidentified neighbor of the protagonist, stands at the furthest possible position from the heart of the story and still is within it; and I remarked that this narrative position closely approached the one here to be investigated, the objective. But there is, strictly speaking, one position still further removed from the heart of a story—that of its writer; and surely this position can still be called, without quibbling, within the story if the writer is willing and able to imagine himself precisely the sort of person, no more and no less, that the unidentified neighbor of Miss Emily Grierson shows himself or herself to be: that is, somebody who sees and hears what goes on without more than the average powers of interpretation or analysis, who is in touch with the surface facts only, and therefore whose discovery of what lies beneath the surface can pace the reader's discovery. A user of the objective method will have to do more than this, but this is his first step into objectivity and a large part of the discipline referred to— the renunciation of his omniscient author's self and the deliberate imaginative substitution for it of an observant but relatively ignorant self on the scene of the story. In that new self he will have no discernible feelings as author about the material, no pretensions to analytical powers of knowing what goes on under the surfaces of people and things, no opinions as author; he will be merely the possessor of co-ordinated senses and a willingness to record impressions as the experience impinges on them. Thus, to all appearance he will be a recording nonentity, as passive and mechanical as the needle on a cardiograph. He will be telling it in the first person, but with the first-person pronouns and the person that they denote, expunged.

Close reading of "A Rose for Emily" will show how near this

104

method that story is. The medium is established in the opening sentence ("When Miss Emily Grierson died, our whole town went to her funeral"), but in the first 1500 words of this four-thousand-word story there appear only two more first person plural (never singular) pronouns or pronominal adjectives keeping the telling agent lightly but plausibly in the back of the reader's mind. The authority of the teller, his plausible presence on the scene and knowledge of the facts recounted, is as delicately established by such phrases as "it got about," "the whispering began," and "some of the ladies began to say"; and the "we" and "our" are neatly varied by an indefinite "you" ("You heard a lot of laughing" when Homer and Miss Emily drove by) and a "they" ("They waited until Miss Emily was decently in the ground"). As the story moves on, these indices of the anonymous telling agent increase in frequency, however; for in the final scene there must be recognizable figures trooping upstairs to that tragic bridal chamber, and one of them ("one of us," the story has it) is to notice the impression left by Miss Emily's head in the second pillow and lift the "long strand of iron-gray hair" from it that at length reveals the horrible truth. In all there are forty-eight such indices. But there is nothing else. The masked narrator, just one of the group, shows not the slightest emotion of his own, although he or she records and is able to suggest emotion in others. We never know even whether it is man or woman who tells this story; the medium observes dispassionately and keenly, but always, from the author's point of view, superficially, both sexes in the town and the sex reflexes and complexes of Miss Emily, her father, and her lover. "Already we knew that there was one room in that region above stairs which no one had seen in forty years," the medium says. "They waited until Miss Emily was decently in the ground before they opened it . . ." Then the dust, the furnishings, the man's collar and tie on the dressing table, the suit neatly folded on the chair, and:

The man himself lay in the bed.
For a long while we just stood there. . . .[1]

That is all this narrator does—stands and looks and hears and smells and all but touches the people of this story. The author might *be* this narrator, if he were willing to pare down his personal prerogatives as author to the narrow limits of this narrator's sense impressions; so metamorphosed, he could do all this equally well, need do little or nothing more. Remove the forty-eight first-person-plural references to that narrator, substituting third-person references, and (though I don't say for a minute it should have been done) the author would have done just that, using objective telling.

Now it is true that, so written, the manner of telling—ingenuous, superficial as regards character analysis, steadily insistent only upon a surface record of sense impressions—would closely resemble the manner of those naively spontaneous folk tales that usually began, "Once upon a time." One can hear an opening cadence: "Once there was an old spinster of noble birth named Emily Grierson, and when she died the whole town (not "our" whole town, now) came to her funeral." This manner was, in fact, the original objective telling, and it was a lovely thing. We find it still in Tolstoy's *Twenty-Three Tales,* in some of Stevenson's fables, and of course, expressed orally, in the wondrous impromptu yarns that our parents told us and that we still manage, in spite of radio competition, to tell our children. But I think this primitive objectivity is no longer available to most of us in written prose; not so much because it has changed as because we have. The Reformation, the Renaissance and the Royal Society, Sentimentalism and Neo-Classicism changed us. The steam engine, the Bill of Rights, Darwin, Freud, the motorcar, the *Saturday Evening*

[1] This and the immediately preceding extracts are from *These 13,* by William Faulkner; Random House, Inc. Reprinted by permission of the publishers.

Post, the movies, the radio, and a far-reaching discovery neatly indicated by a line from *Porgy and Bess*—"It ain't necessarily so"—changed us too. The Romantic Movement exerted tremendous pressure toward *sub*jective, individualistic, and ultimately sophisticated expression. We could no longer be credulous children listening to a story beginning "Once upon a time," or taletellers uttering it. It took the positive counteracting pressure, first of the French Naturalists of the late nineteenth century, then of the disillusioned Lost Generation of the 1920's, to shape for us a new objective telling, having the manner of the old but having much beneath its manner that the old lacked. In that "much" lies the rest of the modern objective writer's discipline.

Guy de Maupassant's "The Piece of String" gives us an early glimpse of this method in the hands of an artist whose talents rise above technique, who would have been great regardless of manner. It is to be doubted whether Maupassant was aware of his objectivity. Under the tutelage of Flaubert he strove, simply, for the qualities that we now know inevitably produce it: acute observation, directness, simplicity, detachment, and economy of detail. In short, he surrendered himself as author to his material, becoming himself merely a lens through which it may be seen—but the lens of a microscope.

The theme of the story is a peasant's ruin effected by unfounded, but plausible, public opinion working against his own stubborn honesty. The time span covers several months; but of this period two thirds of the story is occupied with the first day, and by the time it is necessary to lapse from this immediate *physical* scene, there has been set up an immediate *psychological* scene in Hauchecorne's troubled mind of such momentum that time becomes trivial as the tale rushes to its pathetic end. Several time tags ("The next day," "On Tuesday of the next week," "About the end of December") are present but go virtually unnoticed, the usually destructive effect of synoptic action quite helpless and inoperative against the emotional pull established in the reader to "find how it comes out."

But the insight into Hauchecorne's mind and the sympathy for him which this insight creates in the reader are brought about by a curious detachment. We come to suspect that what objective telling might lose in intensity by its position far outside the heart of the story may be more than made up by the incalculable power of its restraint. Throughout the whole of that first day, the market day in Goderville, we are given very few direct glances via author into Hauchecorne. For the most part Maupassant has been content to remain an unseen, anonymous observer recording speech and behavior (just such a one as Faulkner's narrator of "A Rose for Emily" so closely approaches)—content to remain so because he well knew that the reader would have the intelligence to see for himself the jaws of the trap closing on the poor old peasant, and, reaching that knowledge by his own inference, would grow far more excited by it than if it had been pointed out to him expositorily. This excitement begins when Malandain, Hauchecorne's enemy, sees him pick up—something, which the reader knows is merely a piece of string. The drum of the crier, the announcement of the lost pocketbook, and Hauchecorne's summons before the mayor heighten the tension by cumulative stages, virtually without benefit of visible author. And by the time that first day is over, the way he tells the rest of the story hardly matters to the reader, so long as he does tell it—soon.

But to Maupassant the way he told the rest of the story had to be governed by what he had to tell. Consider the possible plot turns at the end of that first day. Hauchecorne jailed for theft on Malandain's testimony: that would be swift but it would mean only ruin by chance, something that might happen in real life, that often does; but something that would give us no outlet for sympathy, no perception of the inner workings of human nature. Or the whole matter dropped for want of evidence, Hauchecorne mistakenly congratulated by his neighbors, perhaps his head turned by praise until he finally comes

108

to believe that it *was* the pocketbook he picked up after all. A mere realist might have done it that way, willing to emphasize the frailty of man at the expense of truth to the stubborn peasant stock which Maupassant set out to depict. He was interested not in fate by chance, not in bitter, over-simplified thrusts at animalistic man, but in showing man's strength within his weakness and, thus, his ruin by unconscious human means. On the second day the pocketbook is found. The rest is a swift, inevitable obsessive neurosis, in which Hauchecorne's invulnerable honesty triumphs even as his mind wanders and his body dies.

To write this, the only method the author saw—and nobody can say that any other would have been better, or even as good —was a departure from the brilliantly suggestive and exciting objectivity of the first two thirds of the story, a telling method that lets us directly into Hauchecorne's mind and with frequent analysis, interpretation, direct as well as indirect mental discourse, with summary statements on his own authority as author, with synoptic and customary action, and with mere flashes of immediate scene like montage in the movies—in short, by every possible means that would promote swiftness— brings the story to its end.

Yet even with these irregularities from strict objectivity, in this tale of the French peasant ruined by himself and friendly gossip we have come a long way in power from the moralizing of "The Birthmark" and from its generalities and abstractions. The human area under Maupassant's inspection is minute in comparison, and every detail in it stands out with corresponding clarity. Not a word of comment on the story appears. It happened like this . . . That's enough.

By 1927 Ernest Hemingway had refined objective telling to an extent that, at least with reference to what he had to say, permitted full communication of material not only without comment, analysis or interpretation of motives, but virtually without summary or synoptic statement and entirely without recording, direct or indirect, of any character's thoughts. Except in technique "The Killers" is not to be compared with "The Piece of String" as a work of art. Its theme was peculiarly local and temporal, whereas Maupassant's is universal. The French realist's minor tragedy is inspiring; the American's, with all its ingeniously contrived sense of doom, leaves us deflated and cold. But the method of "The Killers," despite limitations of material and theme, seems as near perfection as human beings are likely to achieve. Certainly Maupassant would have admired it—if he could have understood the conditions behind the story it carries.

Even now, only twenty years after the appearance of "The Killers," comprehension is difficult for one who did not live through the terrors of gangsterism and racketeering of the 1920's. Yet its idea is so simple as to sound banal: two gunmen, paid murderers, are after a man they have never seen. In the story they don't even get him; but his refusal, when warned, to attempt escape, his sullen acceptance of coming death at the command, not of these men, but of some unnamed figure more powerful than justice or any protection his "civilized" nation can offer him, is more moving—or was at the time—than would have been the roar of the sawed-off shotgun and Andreson's last gasp. It is the triumph of strict objectivity that it can suggest so much of what preceded and what is to follow its recorded events.

Immediate scene is maintained throughout the time span of about two hours. The story is less than 3500 words. There are seven characters, the last two glimpsed but briefly, yet all of them stand clear. A very large proportion of the story is merely talk, but talk which complies with the requirements of character portrayal and gives information to the reader, yet remains natural—thus in large part performing the function that in other methods the author or his delegate might have to perform. The rest of the piece is bare but precise statement of action, brief details of description that anybody present would have noted, and three short, scattered, explanatory remarks ("Henry's had been made over from a saloon into a lunch-counter." "He [Nick] had never had a towel in his mouth before." And "He [Andreson] had been a heavyweight prize-fighter.") so unobtrusive that they could hardly distract by revealing a personal telling agent, but do serve valuably in scene-setting and motivation. The medium is still that of an anonymous, a selfless observer, offering no comment or interpretation, delving into nobody's thoughts, merely recording the surface aspects of what went on that night.

But then how does it happen that we understand the story at all?—that we catch motives, behavior, even thoughts *not* recorded?—that the place and the people seem real?—that, in the end, we know that Hemingway's purpose in writing was to show the effect of this brutal experience on young Nick Adams, who was not really involved?

The answer lies in the discipline which the writer was willing to undergo in order to achieve a second meaning, an overtone, for nearly everything he set down. This area of implication begins at the very start with Al's nervousness showing through his inability to decide on what he wants to eat. It hovers persistently over talk and action and mere hinted behavior, the most palpable element in the story. And it ends only when the story ends, with Nick's sudden resolve to get out of town and George's cynical implication that that won't help, he'd better just not think about it. Exactly as in the case of the first two thirds of "The Piece of String," these overtones are the more powerful because we come at them by inference instead of being told them outright by the author or any telling agent delegated by him.

From Hemingway's story it can be seen that objectivity is a natural medium for swift physical action. Before "The Killers" was written, readers of adventure stories in juvenile, pulp, and slick magazines had taken for granted various less subtle objective forms, relics of that older method which traces back through fireside and cracker-barrel yarn spinning to folklore. Since the 1920's we have seen Hemingway's archetype, requiring greater effort on the reader's part but offering correspondingly greater rewards, spread into stories of psychological action and thus into the so-called quality and experimental groups of periodicals. At the present time its demand for reader coöperation is familiar to and willingly accepted by all kinds of readers except, perhaps, those whose lips move as they read; and it appears to hold a very important place in storytelling. What will become of it, now following a Second World War, lies in the hands of thousands of young men and women who have returned from the world's far corners with the itch to write and more in their heads and hearts than has ever been told before.

Consideration of a recent story, chosen from many now using objective telling strictly and competently, will complete our study of the medium by suggesting a sort of trial balance up to date: its merits as vehicle for certain kinds of material as against its dangers and limitations.

DUMMY RUN [1]

by Jerome Weidman

"You hear what I hear, Clyde?" The fat man in the sheepskin coat shifted his heavy boots on the sill of the stove and looked up from his newspaper. "My ears maybe, or is that another batch?"

The young man at the desk raised his eyes from his book and listened attentively. From the street outside came the dry, crunching sound of heavy footsteps approaching on the snow.

"I'll tell them," Clyde said in a low voice as he stood up. "Too bad they have to come all this way for nothing on a night like this."

He glanced toward the door and then across the wooden railing

[1] Copyright 1943 by Jerome Weidman; originally published in *The New Yorker*, Dec. 18, 1943. Reprinted by permission of the author and the publisher.

that divided into two sections the single room of the small frame
building which served as immigration depot for the crews of ships
loading or unloading in this Canadian port or anchored in its
harbor while waiting orders to join convoys. The door from the
street opened into the office section of the room, which contained
the small stove and the desk, a couple of extra chairs, and, near
the door, a long, waist-high wooden counter. The other and larger
part of the room, dimly lit and very cold, was an improvised waiting room with wooden benches running along its bare walls.
About twenty seamen—American, British, Canadian—were asleep
or dozing on the benches; each of them wore a pink slip tucked in
the ribbon of his hat. They had come ashore that morning or the
day before on twelve- to twenty-four-hour passes and were now
waiting for the harbor launch to take them back to their ships.
Clyde saw that none of them had been roused by the approaching
footsteps. He walked to the counter. The door opened and he
dipped his head slightly to avoid the rush of wind and swirl of
snow that came hurtling into the room.

"Close it, Clyde," the fat man said irritably from the depths of
his sheepskin collar. "Tell them to close that damned thing."

The door slammed shut. Six men and a woman had come in.
They stamped the snow from their boots and stood in an awkward
group, blinking helplessly in the weak yellow light.

"Good evening," Clyde said pleasantly. "Terrible night, isn't it?"

The newcomers nodded very quickly, as though they had been
reprimanded for some unconscious act of impoliteness. Five of
the men were young—under thirty. They wore heavy blue mackinaws and blue pancake hats. A line of gold print, the characters
strange and foreign, ran around the bands of their hats. The sixth
man was older, perhaps forty or forty-five, with a strong, lean face
and very broad shoulders. He wore a thick brown overcoat and an
officer's cap without insignia. The woman was completely muffled
in an old raccoon coat with a huge collar that stood up around her
head and hid her face. They looked as though they had just come
from a shopping expedition. The five young sailors were carrying
clusters of small parcels, paper sacks with packages of toothpaste
and shaving cream sticking out of their tops, a string bag full of
oranges, and cartons of cigarettes. The woman had a large, un-
wrapped box of face tissues under one arm and, clutched tightly
in a mittened hand, a bouquet of gaudy artificial flowers whose
stems were wrapped in the glazed tan paper peculiar to five-and-
ten-cent stores. The older man carried no parcels. Clyde's greeting

seemed to puzzle and embarrass them. The five young sailors and the woman looked expectantly at the older man. He took off one glove, stepped up to the counter, and held out seven pink slips of paper. They had obviously been torn from the same pad as the slips that the sleeping men in the larger section of the room were wearing in their hats.

"Tell them to scram," the fat man in the sheepskin coat said behind Clyde. "There's no boats going out tonight."

"I know what to tell them, Coombes." Clyde spoke without turning, and his high voice shook with faint annoyance, but he smiled across the counter at the older man in the officer's cap. "I'm sorry about these," Clyde said, and tapped the pink slips in the man's hand. "We can't send you out to your ship tonight. A lot of ice has formed in the harbor and a lot more has drifted down from Bedford Basin. The launch can't get through it tonight in the dark. I suggest you try to find some accommodations here in town for the night, and tomorrow morning, at eight-thirty, we'll send you all out to your ships. We should be able to get through the ice or around it in daylight. We can't try it tonight."

The older man laid the pink slips on the counter and pointed to them with a large forefinger. It was plain that he hadn't understood Clyde's explanation.

"They're a bunch of Poles from that freighter came in last night," Coombes said from his place at the stove. "That's the captain or the first mate or something with his wife and those five young guys are his gun crew. They came through on the morning launch when Drew was on duty and he gave them twelve-hour passes. They don't talk English. Tell them to beat it till tomorrow morning eight-thirty."

"How can I tell them if they don't understand English?" Clyde said in an exasperated tone. "I wish you'd let me do this in my own—"

Coombes dropped his heavy boots from the ledge of the stove with a bang that rattled the kettle steaming on top. He stood up and walked over to the wooden railing that divided the room.

"Hey!" he called loudly. "Any of you men speak Polish?" The seamen asleep or dozing on the benches stirred. Several looked up and squinted at Coombes. "Polish," he said, his voice rising. "Any of you men speak Polish? Any of you understand it?" The men looked at one another and back at Coombes. Nobody answered. Coombes took the pipe from his mouth and spat across the rail in disgust. He walked back to his chair beside the stove and sat down. "No Polish. Nobody understands them and they don't understand us. Just tell them to beat it. Do it in sign language. Anything. Get them out of here."

"I'm afraid we cannot send you out tonight," Clyde said, spacing his words and enunciating with care, as though he were talking to a deaf man. "There is ice in the harbor. Do you understand? Ice? Ice in harbor? *No boats tonight.*"

The middle-aged Pole turned and spoke sharply to the group behind him. The five young sailors shifted their parcels and dug into their blue mackinaws. The woman put the bouquet of artificial flowers into her other hand and opened her fur coat to reach an inner pocket. The huge collar fell away from her face and the bulky coat dropped open, revealing an attractive, slender woman in her early thirties. She and the five young sailors handed small, square booklets to the older man. He bounced them on the wooden counter to make an even pile and pushed it across toward Clyde.

"No, no," Clyde said. "We don't want your passports. We saw your passports when you came through in the morning, when you went ashore, when our Mr. Drew gave you these twelve-hour passes." He smiled quickly, a friendly, strained grimace. "Nothing wrong with your passports." He waved his hand across the railing toward the men on the benches. "Nobody's going back tonight. These men are all staying over tonight, too." He pushed the passports back across the counter and then, remembering, began again to space his words, and raise his voice. "You find place sleep tonight. Hotel or rooming house. Come back in morning." He stopped. The older man was staring at him, the lean, strong face expressionless except for his eyebrows, which were rising slowly. "You can all stay here if you like. On benches like the other men. But I think—" Clyde stopped again and all of his thin face grew as red as the tip of his thin nose. "The lady with you. I think it's too cold for her to sit up all night in there. I don't think it would be—" His uneven voice petered out.

"Lay off the lady stuff," Coombes said drily. "That's his wife and these Poles get jealous easy. He'll take a sock at you."

Clyde looked with embarrassment at the Pole; apparently the older man had not understood. He put the passports in his pocket, his face still blank. With a deliberate, dignified gesture he pointed to a line of print on one of the pink slips: "Your launch will leave Bedford Wharf at ——." "10:30 P.M." was pencilled in the blank space. Then he pointed up at the old alarm clock hanging from a nail in the wall. The clock showed twenty-five minutes after ten.

"I know," Clyde said patiently, his high voice becoming more ragged. "Ordinarily we would have a launch going out at ten-thirty. But tonight we—" He stopped, struck by an idea. He took one of the pink slips, crossed out "10:30 P.M.," and wrote in "8:30 A.M." above it. "You see?" he said eagerly, tapping the slip with his pencil and leaning far forward across the counter as though he hoped to cross the barrier of language by bringing himself physically closer to the other man. "Not tonight. Not ten-thirty. To-morrow morning. Tomorrow morning eight-thirty. Time is changed. Because of ice. Ice in harbor. Too dangerous. No boat tonight. No—" He stopped again and pointed desperately to the figures "8:30 A.M." on the pink slip. There was no sign of under-standing from the impassive Pole. Clyde drew a deep breath and waved his hand toward the men in the other section of the room. "It's not only you. All these men—they're not going at ten-thirty tonight. All waiting for tomorrow. You better try to find a place to stay for the night. You can use the phone here to call a hotel. I'll help you if you want." Like a teacher explaining a problem with diagrams on a blackboard, he pointed to the box phone on the wall, flanked by a large Canadian Pacific calendar and a news-paper picture of Winston Churchill. "Find hotel," he said. "Or rooming house. And then tomorrow—"

The sound of laughter, low but derisive, came across the rail from the other section of the room. "How's about cutting out the jokes so we can sleep," one of the American sailors called. "If there was a room anywhere in this town, you think we'd be sitting up all night in this icebox?"

Clyde tugged helplessly at the folds of the woollen muffler around his neck. The middle-aged Pole looked without expression across the railing at the men sprawled on the benches, shifted his glance to Clyde, to Coombes beside the stove, and then back to Clyde. Slowly he pulled off his other glove, unbuttoned his thick brown overcoat, dipped into an inside pocket, and pulled out a fat wallet. He slid open the zipper fastener and, very deliberately, began to count out a pile of bank notes on the counter. Clyde stared blankly.

"Well, I'll be a son of a gun," Coombes said. Clyde turned, his face puzzled. "He didn't believe us," Coombes said slowly, getting up. "He thinks we're not sending them back because they're Poles or something." He pulled the pipe from his mouth and came up to the counter. "He wants to pay us for sending the launch out."

"We can't do that." Clyde swung back to face the Pole. "It's not a question of money. You're entitled to the launch trip free. It's the ice. Ice in harbor. No boat because of ice. *Ice. No boat. Dangerous.*"

The Pole drew several more bank notes from his wallet and added them to the pile. His face was still blank, but there was a suggestion of contempt in the movement of his wrist as he flicked the money over.

"Who says we can't?" Coombes' bilious face was creased with cold anger. He spoke to Clyde but he kept his glance on the Pole. "We can't send the launch because it might get banged around. Sure. But if this wise guy is willing to put up the dough for any damage, O.K." He grinned unpleasantly as he pulled the sheepskin collar up higher around his ears and buttoned it across his chin. "Stamp up those passes. I'll take them out."

"Listen, Coombes. That—"

"Stamp them up," Coombes said, his cold glance fixed on the Pole. "I'll take them out, the wise guy."

Clyde hesitated, then picked up the rubber stamp, punched it down on an ink pad, and began hitting the pink slips. He stamped six and stopped.

"I'm not going to stamp the woman's," he said. "The men, all right, if they insist. But I'm not going to stamp the woman's."

"Stop being a damn fool," Coombes snapped. "It's their funeral. They're asking for it."

"I don't care," Clyde said stubbornly. His voice quivered. "The men, all right, if they insist. But not the woman. It's too cold and it might be dangerous. I'm not going to—" Coombes snatched angrily at the rubber stamp. Clyde swung it out of reach. "No," the younger man said in a shaking voice. "If you stamp the woman's, if you take the woman, I'll report you, Coombes. The others, all right. They're insisting. But not the woman."

Coombes glared at him. "All right," he said finally. He came around from behind the counter and poked his finger at the five sailors and the middle-aged man. "You and you and you and you three. Not the woman. Come on." The middle-aged Pole said something sharply. Coombes shook his head. "I don't know what you're saying, brother, but if it's about the woman, no soap. Here." He thrust the pink slips at the six men. "You coming or not?"

The Pole turned to Clyde and spoke again, a stream of short, sharp words.

"No," Clyde said, his face white. "I'm sorry. It's too cold and it might be dangerous. I won't let the lady run the risk."

All the control seemed to go out of the Pole's face. He hit the counter with his big fist and spoke angrily, in a furious roar. The upper part of Clyde's body bent backward, away from the angry man, but the front button of his jacket still touched the edge of the wooden counter. He shoved the seventh pink slip behind his back and shook his head again.

"No," he said. "I'm sorry. She can't go. It's too dangerous."

The Pole drew a deep breath, turned to the five young men, and spoke in a low voice. The young men nodded. The middle-aged Pole placed his own pink slip on top of the bank notes, moving his wrist with the small, contemptuous gesture.

"O.K., he's staying behind, too," Coombes said brusquely. "Come on, you guys." He pushed through the swinging gate in the wooden railing. The five young Poles followed him across the room toward another door, which led to the dock. There was a flurry of movement among the men on the benches. "Don't get excited," Coombes said to them. "This is only a dummy run. There's no launch in the harbor can get through that ice tonight, but these birds are willing to pay for taking a chance. Relax, you guys. You got till eight-thirty tomorrow morning."

He pulled open the door, ducked his head into the wind and the snow, and the five young men followed him out onto the dock. The men on the benches sank back. In the other section of the room the young woman and the Pole remained erect, staring at the closed door. From the dock outside came the sputter of a motor. The sound became a roar, rose higher and higher, and began to fade. Soon it was gone and the only sound in the room was the gentle hissing of the kettle on the stove. Clyde's hand shook as he brought it out from behind his back to place the lady's pink slip next to the rubber stamp.

"Would you care to come in here?" he said awkwardly, with a gesture toward the stove. "The lady, she might be warmer near the stove? In here? Warmer for the lady?"

The middle-aged man gave him a long glance, full of hatred and contempt, stalked to the benches, and sat down on a vacant seat. The young woman followed timidly, clutching the box of face tissues and the bouquet of artificial flowers, and sat down next to the man. She placed the box on the seat beside her but still held the artificial flowers. The other men in the room stared at them curiously for a while, then relaxed into their former postures.

The Pole and the young woman sat erect and stared straight ahead, across the heads of the reclining men. Clyde sat down at the desk and picked up his book. During the hour that followed he did not turn a single page.

At last, muffled by the snow and the wind, came the purring roar of the motor. The men who were not asleep sat up straight. Clyde put down his book. The middle-aged Pole and the young woman turned their heads slightly. The purring roar grew louder and then it stopped. Clyde looked at the alarm clock. It showed twenty minutes to midnight. Feet tramped heavily across the snow-covered dock. The door opened and Coombes came in, followed by the five young sailors. Everybody watched as they crossed the room. Coombes walked with a firm, fast, purposeful stride, slapping fresh snow from his coat. The young Poles moved more slowly, uncertainly. They all looked tired and very cold. Coombes snatched the pile of bank notes from the counter, pushed through the wooden gate, and strode to the bench where the Polish officer and his wife were sitting.

"Here." Coombes dropped the money contemptuously into the man's lap. "We don't want your dough."

He shoved his way back through the gate, went behind the counter, and flung himself into the chair beside the stove.

"What happened?" Clyde said. "Did you—"

"What did you expect to happen?" Coombes barked the words as he filled his pipe, tamping the tobacco in with fierce thrusts of his thumb. "We couldn't get through. The ice is too damn thick and you can't see where the hell you're going in all that damn snow." He jerked his head toward the other section of the room, where the five young sailors were talking rapidly to the older man, explaining in Polish what had happened. "We used up a little gas, but at least we'll have some peace around here. Damn near froze their ears off, but now they can tell that wise guy when I say a launch can't get through, it can't get through." He lit his pipe, taking huge, angry sucks on the stem, and buried his head in the newspaper.

Almost immediately the door from the street opened and a man wearing a heavy coat sweater and a peaked cap came in. "Hello, Clyde," he said, brushing the snow from his sweater as he walked behind the counter. "Hello, Coombes."

Coombes grunted without raising his head from the newspaper.

"Hello, Drew," Clyde said. "You're early."

"The hell I am." The newcomer blocked out half of Winston

119

Churchill's face by hanging his peaked cap on one of the nails that held the picture to the wall. "That alarm clock is slow. It's after midnight. You been off duty five minutes already, Clyde, only you don't know it." He laughed, walked over to the counter, glanced idly at the papers there, and looked across to the benches. "This whole bunch waiting for the eight-thirty?"

"Yes," Clyde said. He stood up, took his neatly folded overcoat from the back of his chair, and slipped into it. "Their passes are all stamped. All except one." He finished buttoning his coat, picked up the unstamped pink slip from the counter, and marked it with the rubber stamp. "Those seven over there," he said in a low voice, keeping his glance on the man who was relieving him, "they're Poles. They don't understand English. You might make the lady a cup of tea if you get a chance." He nodded toward the kettle on the stove. "She'll be pretty cold by morning."

"Sure," Drew said cheerfully. "I remember them going through this morning." He looked across the railing at the woman and winked at Clyde. "Not bad, huh?"

"You, too?" Coombes said from behind the newspaper. "Why don't you two guys keep your mind on your work?"

"What's up?" Drew said with a sly grin. "Clyde been—"

"Quit it," Clyde said, his face bright red. "It's just she'll probably be cold and it's a long wait till eight-thirty." He walked out from behind the counter, pushed through the wooden gate, and stopped in front of the group of Poles. His hand shook as he put the pink slip on the middle-aged man's lap. "This is the pass for the lady." He spoke slowly and clearly, his voice quivering, like a convicted prisoner who knows the jury will not believe him but makes his final, hopeless protest of innocence for the record. He looked directly at the man and carefully avoided looking at the woman. "You'll all get through to your ship in the morning, when it's light. I hope the wait isn't too uncomfortable for you. Good night."

He swung around abruptly, pushed through the gate, and pulled his coat collar up around his narrow head as he walked stiffly toward the door, like a man who knows he may be shot in the back but is determined not to give way to his terror by turning or running.

"So long," Drew said. "See you tomorrow."

"So long," Clyde said, pulling the door open. "Good night, Coombes."

"Good night," Coombes grunted from behind the newspaper. "Close that damn door, will you? It's—"

He stopped and lowered the newspaper. Clyde was hesitating at the door. The middle-aged Pole had jumped up. Everybody watched as he took the young woman by the hand and helped her to her feet. He led her through the swinging gate, toward the door, his lean face expressionless. The young woman walked trustingly beside him. Clyde stood there, his hand on the knob of the open door, his head bent slightly against the wind and the snow that poured in and seemed to freeze him in his tracks. His frightened face grew white and he stepped back slightly when the Pole reached him, as though he expected to be struck. The Pole stopped and bowed stiffly. He took the bouquet of artificial flowers from the young woman and held it out. Clyde stared at the older man, at the flowers, at the young woman, and then back at the man. The Pole bowed again and held the flowers out further. The young woman curtseyed. Drew started to laugh. Clyde flushed scarlet.

"It's for you," Drew said. "He's making you a present."

Clyde reached out hesitantly, his hand shaking, and took the flowers. His fingers slipped on the glazed tan paper and he almost dropped them.

"Thank you," he mumbled. Then he cleared his throat and spoke louder. "Thank you very much."

The Pole bowed once more and said something in his own language. The young woman nodded gravely. Clyde stared at the flowers, which he held gingerly, as though he expected them to explode, and then his thin, scared face broke into a small smile of gratitude and understanding. He bowed stiffly, awkwardly, to the Pole. He whipped off his old felt hat and bowed to the young woman. Both of them bowed to him.

"Listen," Coombes called. "You going to close that damn door or you going to let the—" The door slammed shut and Clyde was gone. For a few moments the sound of his steps on the snow could be heard and then it faded out in the windy night. The Pole and the young woman walked back to their bench. The kettle hissed gently in the silent room. "What do you say, Drew?" Coombes said from behind his newspaper. "You going to make that lady that cup of tea now?"

This example of old-world courtesy in the new world, of a triumph of gallantry over shyness, non-communication, and misunderstanding, achieves much with a minimum of utterance. Told in another way it might be absurd or unbearably sentimental. The point of view is that of a fly on the wall, which only sees and hears. Yet the details have been so well chosen that overtones come through with startling vividness. This story proves that modern objective telling need not concern itself exclusively with frustration or bitterness; something like the inspiration of "The Piece of String" shines here through a medium far more rigidly limited than was Maupassant's.

Let us cast up that balance sheet.

It must be clear by now that readers will accept the recording of physical movements, sensory perception, the behavior and speech of characters as coming by means sufficiently impersonal as not to distract their attention from the matter of the story. It must follow that divergences from this narrow path of narrative are to be used only if some positive gain greater than the possible fracture of illusion can be foreseen. Such divergences, which are likely to weaken the reader's "willing suspension of disbelief" and may even invalidate the story, are arranged here in what seems to me an order showing progressively dangerous qualities:

1. Attribution to a character of awareness of a sense impression. (In "Dummy Run": "Clyde saw that none of them had been roused.") If such awareness had been (it is not) attributed to another character later, and perhaps another later still, injury to the method would be marked. Here it is slight and hardly noticeable, especially in view of the fact that Clyde is the figure of interest, as Nick Adams is in "The Killers." But Hemingway did not attribute awareness of sense impression to Nick or to anybody else.

2. Author's explanation of the situation. The three brief, scattered sentences in "The Killers" have been noted. In "Dummy Run," explanation nearly fills the long fourth paragraph; but note that it lies inconspicuously within statements of Clyde's sense impressions and actions: at the beginning "he glanced" and near the end of the passage "Clyde saw" and "he

walked" and "he dipped his head." No further explanation appears in the story. Weidman got these two dangerous elements out of the way early; he tied one to the other, implying that the view of the room and the circumstances involving the waiting sailors lay within Clyde's consciousness, and at the same time indicating that Clyde is the character of chief interest; and by doing this satisfied the reader's justifiable desire (something that Hemingway is seldom willing to do) to learn the facts as he starts reading.

3. Lapse from immediate scene.

4. Indirect discourse for important matter. The objective story must appear to give us every spoken word. Note Maupassant's care, even in the last third of "The Piece of String," to keep Hauchecorne and others actually talking. There is no indirect discourse in "The Killers," none in "Dummy Run."

5. Author's statement of motives or emotion, or his interpretation of behavior or speech.

6. Author's comment.

The method is obviously most appropriate as vehicle for the experiences of unthinking or inarticulate people. Its choice for this story built on a "barrier of language" was ideal. Its great ability to reveal the mental and emotional processes of such humans by an oblique view, to stimulate suspense by understatement and restraint, and to approach the immediacy of stage and screen reproduction seems equally clear. But that very nearness to drama is a warning of its limitations. The inevitable tendency of strict objectivity is to eliminate, rule out, pare down to something exactly like commonplace life, which seldom has much of any significance and is often simply not clear. And unless the storyteller is a genius who can make his local and temporal conditions symbols of universality, as Maupassant did, objective stories will need footnotes, as Hemingway's does now and as Weidman's will need them as soon as readers have forgotten the particular circumstances attending the desperate condition of Poland and the Battle of the

Atlantic in the Second World War. This kind of telling, in short, has the tough impact of timeliness, but also perhaps its short life.

To try your hand at it, you might write 1000 words motivating an event (that is, showing the human motives that brought it about) wholly by implication, through a record of chosen details of action, behavior, and speech—omitting explanation, analysis, interpretation, and characters' thoughts.

8

STREAM OF EXPERIENCE

W E HAVE SEEN the creation of various personal telling mediums within the story, and the elimination of any apparent telling agency—both accomplished for the purpose of presenting experience which, having spontaneity, moves on its own momentum without visible propulsion by the author. We have noted the merits of each method under certain conditions of character and situation, and the possible weaknesses in each. That they should have weaknesses, over and above the fallibility of any human effort, I mean, is only natural; since after all they represent the extremes of storytelling. "I" as protagonist stands at one extreme, too close for perspective in the very center of the story; while strict objectivity struggles for a clear view from its distant perimeter.

Theoretically, some sort of median approach not yet considered might seek the merits of both positions, intensity and objectivity, without encountering the difficulties of propinquity or remoteness. Such a method would naturally use a protagonist or important character as vehicle, for the sense of validity we get from his position, but perhaps without allowing him the freedom—for complete naturalness of character amounts to that: you can't find a born storyteller like Montresor every day —of telling it in person. Such a method, if plausible technical means could be found, would tell a story not *about* the protagonist, and not as if *by* him in the first person, but *through* him in the third. Conceivably a steady focus on a single personality could then combine with the dramatic force (suspense, restraint, overtones, etc.) inherent in objectivity. Telling it through him, you could still come as close or stay as far away as you found convenient.

Practically, however, the problem lies in the word *through*. It was not until James Joyce had made us familiar with the stream of consciousness and until objective telling had undergone its modern development that writers began to understand the possibilities of *through*. By what ways can narrative come convincingly through a character, without recourse to him as narrator?

Another glance at "The Killers" and at "Dummy Run" will give us a first condition. In both stories there is a character to whom the sympathy of the reader is directed and who is on scene the greater part of the time. Nick Adams sees everything that goes on in "The Killers" except a small amount of incidental action that takes place in the lunchroom proper after Nick and George have been taken by Al back into the kitchen and before Al has opened the connecting slide. If Al were to open the slide at once (plausibly he could have done this to maintain communication with Max and arrange the group immediately, in case Andreson came early), Nick would see everything in the story, for when he leaves to find Andreson of course the story goes with him, and by the time he comes back it has become really his story. As it is, Nick hears everything. For some reason, however—perhaps to avoid the slightest suggestion of sentimentality, which he hates and fears—Hemingway wrote the story without reference to Nick's sense impressions—unless the statement near the beginning, "Nick Adams watched them," can be attributed to Nick's conscious vision. The point is that Nick's senses of sight and hearing were physically available to the author without loss at least of clarity, if he wanted to use them.

Clyde's senses in "Dummy Run" were not available. The young man is on scene most of the time, he draws our sympathy strongly, but near the end he leaves the immigration depot and the story does not go with him; necessarily it stays inside the office while we hear the final words of Coombes to Drew, "You going to make that lady that cup of tea now?"

which reveal its main point. If from the start Weidman had availed himself steadily of Clyde's sense impressions (you remember he does that only once, for a special reason, with "He saw that none of them had been roused") and remained consistently within that locus through Clyde's departure into the storm and perhaps to his quarters, the story would lack this main point: the conversion, unknown to Clyde, of grouchy old Coombes. Or again, if Weidman had used Clyde's senses up to the time of his departure, and then let him go but held us in the office for the revelation told by other means (as Katherine Mansfield did at a precisely similar point in "Marriage à la Mode"), the credulity of a good many sensitive readers would have been strained by a demonstration of author's magic as dubious as Hawthorne's. Thus, close as his material brings him to the possibility of telling through the senses of Clyde, Weidman's choice of objective telling and adherence to that method are seen to be wise.

The first condition, then, to any method of telling a story *through* a character is that its main interest involve a person who draws the reader's attention throughout and whose sense impressions are continually available without loss of meaning.

Now let us consider specific means. Are sense impressions the only one? No, but before taking up others we should be sure of a full understanding of what is implied by this major one. Through his senses the character will be aware of his own behavior as well as of that of others, of his own actions as well as of theirs, of his manner of speaking and of his speech itself; all of these means of transmitting experience can be used by mere statement of the act or behavior (he walked, he looked up, etc.) if needed, without repeated direct reference to his senses as vehicle, secure in the reader's inference that his senses have made him aware of what is recorded. A wide area of description and narration is accessible by this simple and natural vehicle, which has the suggestiveness of objectivity plus the vividness of reaction to scene or situation by a character, which objectivity necessarily lacks. Without a mirror, you may fear that the area does not include himself as an object, perhaps an important part of the story. But for all practical purposes it does, it can be made to include himself. The mirror has already been overworked. In most cases the reader doesn't care. We have long passed the necessity of detailed description of features and figure, have come to regard such inventories as bad prose as well as bad story. Does it matter that you never know whether Nick's or Clyde's eyes are brown or blue? Of course the careful craftsman will seize upon some one detail, usually, that reveals character. And in the method under consideration, as in other methods, he will be able to transmit that detail—here by bringing it to his character's, and thus the reader's, attention. All we need to know about the appearance of Lonnie, in Erskine Caldwell's "Kneel to the Rising Sun," is the shape of his chin; and Lonnie, exactly in character, has the habit of bringing up his hand to hide that feature. We see it as he feels it. A tall man can stoop, or fail to and bump his head, when he enters a low doorway; a short one naturally looks up when he talks to others. Description by this indirect means may tax a writer's ingenuity a little, but more than repays his effort.

A further legitimate means of transmitting experience through a character is offered by his thoughts. How large and how useful this means is can be seen by comparing the amount of information imparted via thought processes of the anonymous narrator of "A Rose for Emily," for instance, with the lack of such matter in "The Killers" or "Dummy Run." The most brilliant objectivity can do little more than hint at what conditions created a situation, and in the passage of time hints soon lose their force; indeed, it may be that the apparent transience of the objective story is due to just this inability to sketch in causative background: Prohibition and gangsterism, the Battle of the Atlantic, or whatever facts of time and place the story rests upon. But this is exactly what the memory and reflections of the anonymous narrator of "A Rose for Emily" can do; we get from his thoughts a fifty-year sweep of the changing South, without which much of the drama would be lost. Besides this freedom in supplying background and placing the story in time, the thoughts of a character may offer a convincing medium for the thought of the author and for his estimate of other characters and events, either directly by agreement with him, or indirectly through irony when his estimate and the medium's thoughts are opposed. Expressed thought, though less subtle than thought implied by speech or action, thus can have the comforting functions of clarity and orientation.

But we must know how to use it, for thought processes as a vehicle for narrative can easily be misused, with disastrous effect.

The danger comes clear as soon as we realize that for the most part people do not think in words at all. There are exceptions, of course, in people and in situations: the precise thinker reviewing the content of his mind, or a person rehearsing mentally what he will say or do. But usually the mind has its own shorthand consisting of wordless images, instantly translatable to itself but incomprehensible to anyone else, and labored if not downright unnatural if rendered into prose. The pioneer efforts of Joyce and Virginia Woolf with interior monologue or stream of consciousness, useful as they are in the field of the novel, offer only suggestive help to the writer of short stories, which must be relatively short, swift, convincing, and therefore instantly clear. Seeing this danger of distortion, deceleration, and obscurity, the short-story teller will use expressed thought with caution, perhaps as a sort of last resort when other means of transmission are unsuitable; and the briefer each incursion, the less the likelihood of trouble.

If thoughts are to be expressed, most of the principles governing dialogue apply here. Certainly thoughts will be more credible if couched in the free utterance of characteristic speech.

Verbs of thinking substitute for verbs of saying. Methods parallel those used for conversation; namely, direct mental discourse and indirect mental discourse:

He thought, *I'll go*.

He thought he would go.

—direct thought being phrased in the first person and present tense, indirect in the third and the past.

Both these methods of expressing thought are useful, but in their use careful writers will exercise discrimination over and above the caution recommended before employing quoted thought at all. In talk, direct discourse is almost always preferable to indirect, because of the vividness (at some cost of space) secured. In quoted thought, the opposite is the case. Direct mental discourse, the interior monologue or stream of consciousness, is fatally easy to write and soon runs into space out of all proportion with its worth in vividness or as story vehicle. At its first appearance, possibly because of the fallacy upon which it is based, readers will feel unease and embarrassment, and the margin of their credulity on which the story is being kept alive will run thin; if the mental monologue is long continued, the margin may be lost and illusion may break under a pressure of unreality similar to that of some of Iago's plotty soliloquies. The growing custom among writers and publishers of setting such passages in italic type only increases the strain. Italics have been used so long in narrative for emphasis or excitement induced by the author (He crept to the rail. The boat *was gone!*), that is, as a sort of super-exclamation point, that it is almost impossible to read words so set without getting with them this artificial air of tension. They look as if they must have been shouted, instead of being merely thought. And if their intent was to convey some such commonplace reflection as *Let's see, where's my other shoe?* the incongruity produced may be greater than any possible good effect planned. Certainly in the short story, direct mental discourse should be used only very rarely, for moments of emotional intensity natural to the situation and the thinker, and then only very briefly.

Indirect mental discourse, on the other hand, or something closely resembling it, can extend unchallenging and unchallenged throughout the story. Well-done, instead of endangering illusion, it steadily supports and enhances it.

Assuming always the continual presence of a character through whom the writer can transmit the experience, and assuming the writer's imaginative ability to shed all of himself but his ability to record and get into that character and feel the experience through that character's senses, a kind of expanded indirect mental discourse now takes shape as the fourth, and a very powerful, telling medium for the short story. I call it stream of experience. It may be introduced, and occasionally emphasized, by the appearance of a verb or verbs of thinking; but readers have already become so accustomed to this technique that such verbs are unnecessary; and, strictly speaking, unless one goes so far as to maintain that a person is usually aware of the act of thinking in addition to his awareness of the matter thought, they are inconsistent with the method. Some people perhaps would be, others not. The important point is that by this stream of experience the writer is afforded complete flexibility of expression within the character used as medium. He can, if he likes, write the entire story in language which that character would use if he were thinking, without committing himself to the limiting and dangerous channels of literally quoted thought. He can be unilateral for the purposes of plot, if he likes. He can be apparently direct and simple and graphic, while actually retaining complete control and opening realms of subtlety, understatement, and irony. Only when the language appropriate to his medium forces him beyond accepted usage in grammar, diction, or idiom must he pause and consider whether he can afford to risk illusion by putting the passage in first person, present tense, and quotes or italics to represent direct mental discourse, or whether he can tone it down to consistency with accepted usage, or had better simply cut it out. And since Joyce and Gertrude Stein such an occasion will be very rare. Accepted usage referred to is of course colloquial usage, including words and phrases added to our speech long before being pinned into dictionaries. The area of acceptance is so broad, it is safe to say that editors and readers will take anything intelligible, provided it is in character and not so conspicuous as to be distracting. Generally, indeed, language close to the character is preferred; but it must be really close to him, the product of thorough knowledge and close application by the author, not merely typical dialect of the Shure, Begorry, or Whah you all gwine? schools. Perhaps it would be truest to say that such language must be grounded in self-respecting prose, prose of which any person thoughtful enough to be plausible medium for stream of experience would be capable if he applied himself to the job of thinking it out— yet prose spiced with the characteristics of impromptu speech. The first thousand words of "Rappaccini's Daughter" illustrates all the devices of stream of experience except this final convincing touch of language. It is narrative transmitted through the sense impressions and indirect mental discourse of a character who draws our interest; but the words of the passage are not those natural to a young student, they are plainly the bookish, brooding Hawthorne's.

It was Mark Twain and Bret Harte who prepared the way for this final touch by getting close to spoken language. Hampered by Victorian rhetoric and typographical traditions, of which this rough young country was inordinately conscious, their efforts had always to be priggishly surrounded by quotation marks (for slang), as evidence to the cultured reader that the author knew better. As late as 1887 Hamlin Garland wrote in "Mrs. Ripley's Trip":

. . . his tireless old wife, who, having "finished the supper dishes," sat knitting a stocking.
. . . they couldn't afford "none o' them new-fangled lamps."

132

carefully including both suspect phrases in quotation marks, as if in apology. A modern writer would seize them eagerly as characteristic matter but let them ride without interfering, by formal punctuation, with the flow of Uncle Ethan Ripley's stream of experience. Whether a verb of thinking introduced the passage and thus put it literally into indirect mental discourse, or was merely implied by the use of the language itself, would matter not at all.

Examples of the method as used in several stories published in divergent markets during the last thirty years, and complete reprinting of one will show the range as well as the convincing spontaneity of stream of experience.

Susan Glaspell began (1917) "A Jury of Her Peers" as follows:

When Martha Hale opened the storm-door and got a cut of the north wind, she ran back for her big woolen scarf. As she hurriedly wound that round her head her eye made a scandalized sweep of her kitchen. It was no ordinary thing that called her away—it was probably further from ordinary than anything that had ever happened in Dickson County. But what her eye took in was that her kitchen was in no shape for leaving: her bread all ready for mixing, half the flour sifted and half unsifted.

She hated to see things half done; but she had been at that when the team from town stopped to get Mr. Hale, and then the sheriff came running in to say his wife wished Mrs. Hale would come too —adding, with a grin, that he guessed she was getting scary and wanted another woman along. So she had dropped everything right where it was.

"Martha!" now came her husband's impatient voice. "Don't keep folks waiting out here in the cold."

She again opened the storm-door, and this time joined the three men and the one woman waiting for her in the big two-seated buggy.[1]

This stream of experience is not wholly consistent or convincing, but in 1917 it was a stout try. The author ran afoul of the

[1] First published in *Every Week*, 1917. Reprinted by permission of the author.

perennial conflict between the medium's familiarity with environment making detailed elucidation of it seem unnatural as against the reader's total ignorance of it and need to be informed. She chose to be clear rather than strictly characteristic: "Mr. Hale" (that is, Martha's husband), "the sheriff," and "three men and one woman" are not quite the terms Martha would have used for those people; the terms she would have used (first names or nicknames for everybody) would at that stage simply not have been clear. But strict consistency might have defeated itself here; few readers would notice a breach so early in the story, even fewer would be bothered if they did; and without clarity nobody would go on reading. There are a few slight inconsistencies later. But as an early attempt at stream of experience, these paragraphs and indeed the entire story are notable. There is no direct mental discourse, but the quoted passage is alive with the cadence and phrasing Martha Hale would have used in thought or in speech. In the moment before she joins the others outside we have been admitted into this woman's personality so that we can thereafter feel the experience as she feels it. Even when the narrative merely follows her movements, its language implies her consciousness of them ("scandalized" sweep of the kitchen; and "she had dropped everything right where it was"). The sense impressions, too, are hers (her husband's voice "came" to her) and are phrased as she would record them (she "got a cut of the north wind"). And although no verb of thinking or remembering appears, what had happened up to that moment is told us in language close to her habits of thought ("It was no ordinary thing that called her away—it was further from ordinary," . . . "Her kitchen was in no shape for leaving," . . . "She hated to see things half done." And "She had been at that"). One can all but hear Martha Hale thinking, recalling swiftly, or telling a friend later about this great adventure. In two hundred words the author has told us enough of a dramatic situation for us to want to go on reading about it—and told us this via the stream of experience of a character who demonstrates her personality (her haste, her dislike of disorder, her willingness to stand by the sheriff's wife in a pinch) in the course of having the experience. This kind-hearted, simple-minded, hard-pressed Iowa farm wife proves an ideal medium for the story. She is going to be taken to the scene of a crime. She will there discover, in a way characteristic of her, the clue to the murder—but carefully suppress it, through sympathy with the murderer, another farm wife. And the strong hold she has gained on our sympathy will make that act of complicity understandable. In her place we would have done the same thing, because we *were* in her place right through the story.

Toward the end of Erskine Caldwell's "Kneel to the Rising Sun" (1935) occurs this passage:

The creeping forward began to work into the movements of Lonnie's body. He found himself springing forward on his toes, and his body was leaning in that direction. It was like creeping up on a rabbit. He forgot for a while what he was doing there. The springing motion in his legs seemed to be growing stronger with each step. He bent forward so far that he could almost touch the ground with his fingers. He could not stop now.

The fifteen men were drawing closer and closer. The dawn had broken enough to show the time on the face of a watch. The sun was beginning to color the sky above.

Lonnie was far in advance of anyone else. He could not hold himself back. The strength in his legs was more than he could hold in check.

He had so long been unable to buy shells for his gun that he had forgotten how much he liked to hunt.[2]

This is stream of experience as genuine as that of "A Jury of Her Peers," and more subtle and far-reaching. Caldwell had a tougher problem. Martha Hale in Miss Glaspell's story was a thoughtful and mentally alert person; everything needed for

[2] From "Kneel to the Rising Sun," reprinted from *Jackpot* by Erskine Caldwell, by permission of the publishers, Duell, Sloan & Pearce, Inc.

the story could be carried on the stream of what she did, felt, and might have thought. Here is a totally different case. Lonnie, a poor-white share cropper, becomes the unwilling and imperceptive instrument of the lynching of his negro friend Clem. The purpose of Caldwell's story was to show the racial struggle, the brutal fact of his being torn two ways, working in Lonnie, a mentally unalert coward: a struggle of whose significance and implications he was quite unaware. This matter had to be got across to the reader through Lonnie and yet, literally, over his ignorant head; via his mental reactions and sense impressions and yet outside of them. In short, it must be made apparent to the reader by its very absence from Lonnie's consciousness. This passage just before the lynching shows how intelligently the problem was solved. The two verbs of *forgetting* are the key to Caldwell's method. They keep us within Lonnie's consciousness, at the same time calling attention to what lay beyond it. After all, this pursuit (of Clem) was only a kind of hunting; he had always loved to hunt. Merely by following his sense impressions through characteristic action long fixed in him by heritage and environment, Caldwell is able to indicate the full extent of Lonnie's tragedy: that in this case he had betrayed and was hunting a man, his friend. And note the care with which Caldwell has refrained from attempting to draw our sympathies toward this character undeserving of them. None of the picturesque idiom of Southern speech has been used; the language throughout the story is not *un*-characteristic of Lonnie, but it does not admit us into his personality as did Martha Hale's. It is simple, neutral, flat, almost objective. Again stream of experience proves an appropriate medium. Lonnie had senses, feelings, which are used. But he had a personality not worth sharing, and no mind worth mention. Thus in form as well as content is the medium able to suggest a tragic condition by the very absence of an element of which its human vehicle is unaware.

The ease and naturalness with which stream of experience

can set the emotional key of a story, at the same time supplying background, situation, and characterization—not before but actually *as* the story begins—are well shown by the opening lines of Leane Zugsmith's "Back to Work":

Breakfast was special with two eggs for him and Mildred barely able to nibble her toast for watching him. Each time she cleared her throat, he knew it was not because of what she found hard to say but because of what she wanted to avoid saying. With a bread-crust he mopped his plate clean of egg, at the same time keeping a sharp watch on the alarm clock beside him. Then he held out his cup for more coffee and, as she poured from the dented pot, he noticed once more how thin her arms were and how the bones at the base of her neck stood out like a little boy's bones. But she wasn't a little boy—she was a young woman, his wife, who had been faring on anxiety for more than three years. Only it was all over now. There would be no more relief jobs. He had handed in his resignation. This morning he would begin— his eyes reverted hastily to the clock—back with a private firm for the first time in over three years. The solemnity of the occasion suddenly caused his hand to shake; some coffee slopped onto the saucer.

Instantly Mildred spoke. "It's so perfectly marvelous, Seth," she said, her voice high and rattling. "I keep thinking, it's like a painter getting his brushes back and his easel and, oh, you know, everything. Isn't it? Don't you think so?"

"Hey, how do you get that way?" His voice was teasing. "I'm no artist. Nixon, maybe he calls himself an artist; but I'm just an operator, don't you forget it." He grinned. "And a damned good one, don't you forget that, either."[3]

No footnotes will ever be needed to explain this story of the depression of the early 1930's; what Hemingway and Weidman were unable to communicate and remain consistent, what Miss Glaspell got in by main force at some cost in verisimilitude, is here blended with the action so firmly and smoothly that the reader is informed without his realizing it. Both characters are clearly seen in their environment, through the senses and

[3] Reprinted by permission of Random House, Inc.

137

thoughts of one of them, and, consistently within that medium, by implication as neatly economical as that of objectivity. (The dented coffee pot and the alarm clock on, obviously, a kitchen or dinette table. And "Instantly Mildred spoke." And "His voice was teasing.") Emotional tone is ingeniously set by the hurried opening sentence, by Mildred's nervousness, the short sentences of indirect mental discourse, his own hand shaking, Mildred's overstatement of the occasion. Notice that we are deep within Seth at once, so deep that only a pronoun can convincingly designate him until his wife has called him by name; and that a family idiom ("Breakfast was special"—one can almost hear him use the phrase) confirms this deep narrative position by stream of experience (a single "he knew" followed by indirect mental discourse) without the jolt that interior monologue might probably have given us. Notice also the author's planned pull on our sympathy, not only by the situation itself (man long out of work about to be reinstated), by this intimate association with Seth, and by his pity and love for his wife, her loyalty to him, but by his kidding her and bolstering up her courage and his own. But I think the best thing in this opening of a story about the young photographer who finally gets a job but loses it through ineptitude, the result of his long idleness, is the premonition of disaster it manages through this medium to convey. Just how this was done defies exact analysis, but choice of the method was surely a large factor. Only by stream of experience, I believe, could we be made to feel that these nice kids are too high, that their elation is a hostage to fortune and their luck won't last—precisely the hint, the shadow that Miss Zugsmith wanted to hover over that breakfast table.

Now, finally, let us examine a complete story in stream of experience, Sally Benson's "The Overcoat."

THE OVERCOAT [4]

By Sally Benson

IT had been noisy and crowded at the Milligan's and Mrs. Bishop had eaten too many little sandwiches and too many iced cakes so that now, out in the street, the air felt good to her, even if it was damp and cold. At the entrance of the apartment house, she took out her change purse and looked through it and found that by counting the pennies, too, she had just eighty-seven cents, which wasn't enough for a taxi from Tenth Street to Seventy-third. It was horrid never having enough money in your purse, she thought. Playing bridge, when she lost, she often had to give I.O.U.'s and it was faintly embarrassing, although she always managed to make them good. She resented Lila Hardy who could say, "Can anyone change a ten?" and who could take ten dollars from her small, smart bag while the other women scurried about for change.

She decided that it was too late to take a bus and she might as well walk over to the subway, although the air down there would probably make her head ache. It was drizzling a little and the side-walks were wet. And as she stood on the corner waiting for the traffic lights to change, she felt horribly sorry for herself. She remembered as a young girl, she had always assumed she would have lots of money when she was older. She had planned what to do with it—what clothes to buy and what upholstery she would have in her car.

Of course, everybody nowadays talked poor and that was some comfort. But it was one thing to have lost your money and quite another never to have had any. It was absurd, though, to go around with less than a dollar in your purse. Suppose something happened? She was a little vague as to what might happen, but the idea fed her resentment.

Everything for the house, like food and things, she charged. Years ago, Robert had worked out some sort of budget for her but it had been impossible to keep their expenses under the right headings, so they had long ago abandoned it. And yet Robert always seemed to have money. That is, when she came to him for five or ten dollars, he managed to give it to her. Men were like

[4] First published in *The American Mercury*. Reprinted by permission of the author.

139

that, she thought. They managed to keep money in their pockets but they had no idea you ever needed any. Well, one thing was sure, she would insist on having an allowance. Then she would at least know where she stood. When she decided this, she began to walk more briskly and everything seemed simpler.

The air in the subway was worse than usual and she stood on the local side waiting for a train. People who took the expresses seemed to push so and she felt tired and wanted to sit down. When the train came, she took a seat near the door and, although inwardly she was seething with rebellion, her face took on the vacuous look of other faces in the subway. At Eighteenth Street, a great many people got on and she found her vision blocked by a man who had come in and was hanging to the strap in front of her. He was tall and thin and his overcoat which hung loosely on him and swayed with the motion of the train smelled unpleasantly of damp wool. The buttons of the overcoat were of imitation leather and the button directly in front of Mrs. Bishop's eyes evidently had come off and been sewed back on again with black thread, which didn't match the coat at all.

It was what is known as a swagger coat but there was nothing very swagger about it now. The sleeve that she could see was almost threadbare around the cuff and a small shred from the lining hung down over the man's hand. She found herself looking intently at his hand. It was long and pallid and not too clean. The nails were very short as though they had been bitten and there was a discolored callus on his second finger where he probably held his pencil. Mrs. Bishop, who prided herself on her powers of observation, put him in the white-collar class. He most likely, she thought, was the father of a large family and had a hard time sending them all through school. He undoubtedly never spent money on himself. That would account for the shabbiness of his overcoat. And he was probably horribly afraid of losing his job. His house was always noisy and smelled of cooking. Mrs. Bishop couldn't decide whether to make his wife a fat slattern or to have her an invalid. Either would be quite consistent.

She grew warm with sympathy for the man. Every now and then he gave a slight cough, and that increased her interest and her sadness. It was a soft, pleasant sadness and made her feel resigned to life. She decided that she would smile at him when she got off. It would be the sort of smile that couldn't help but make him feel better, as it would be very obvious that she understood and was sorry.

But by the time the train reached Seventy-second Street, the smell of wet wool, the closeness of the air and the confusion of her own worries had made her feelings less poignant, so that her smile, when she gave it, lacked something. The man looked away embarrassed.

II

Her apartment was too hot and the smell of broiling chops sickened her after the enormous tea she had eaten. She could see Maude, her maid, setting the table in the dining-room for dinner. Mrs. Bishop had bought smart little uniforms for her, but there was nothing smart about Maude and the uniforms never looked right.

Robert was lying on the living-room couch, the evening newspaper over his face to shield his eyes. He had changed his shoes, and the gray felt slippers he wore were too short for him and showed the imprint of his toes, and looked depressing. Years ago, when they were first married, he used to dress for dinner sometimes. He would shake up a cocktail for her and things were quite gay and almost the way she had imagined they would be. Mrs. Bishop didn't believe in letting yourself go and it seemed to her that Robert let himself go out of sheer perversity. She hated him as he lay there, resignation in every line of his body. She envied Lila Hardy her husband who drank but who, at least, was somebody. And she felt like tearing the newspaper from his face because her anger and disgust were more than she could bear.

For a minute she stood in the doorway trying to control herself and then she walked over to a window and opened it roughly. "Goodness," she said. "Can't we ever have any air in here?"

Robert gave a slight start and sat up. "Hello, Mollie," he said. "You home?"

"Yes, I'm home. I came home in the subway."

Her voice was reproachful. She sat down in the chair facing him and spoke more quietly so that Maude couldn't hear what she was saying. "Really, Robert," she said, "it was dreadful. I came out from the tea in all that drizzle and couldn't even take a taxi home. I had just exactly eighty-seven cents. Just eighty-seven cents!"

"Say," he said. "That's a shame. Here." He reached in his pocket and took out a small roll of crumpled bills. "Here," he repeated. And handed her one. She saw that it was five dollars.

Mrs. Bishop shook her head. "No, Robert," she told him. "That

141

isn't the point. The point is that I've really got to have some sort of allowance. It isn't fair to me. I never have any money! Never! It's got so it's positively embarrassing!"

Mr. Bishop fingered the five-dollar bill thoughtfully. "I see," he said. "You want an allowance. What's the matter? Don't I give you money every time you ask for it?"

"Well, yes," Mrs. Bishop admitted. "But it isn't like my own. An allowance would be more like my own."

"Now, Mollie," he reasoned. "If you had an allowance, it would probably be gone by the tenth of the month."

"Don't treat me like a child," she said. "I just won't be humiliated any more."

Mr. Bishop sat turning the five-dollar bill over and over in his hand. "About how much do you think you should have?" he asked.

"Fifty dollars a month," she told him. And her voice was harsh and strained. "That's the very least I can get along on. Why, Lila Hardy would laugh at fifty dollars a month."

"Fifty dollars a month," Mr. Bishop repeated. He coughed a little, nervously, and ran his fingers through his hair. "I've had a lot of things to attend to this month. But, well, maybe if you would be willing to wait until the first of next month, I might manage."

"Oh, next month will be perfectly all right," she said, feeling it wiser not to press her victory. "But don't forget all about it. Because I shan't."

As she walked toward the closet to put away her wraps, she caught sight of Robert's overcoat on the chair near the door. He had tossed it carelessly across the back of the chair as he came in. One sleeve was hanging down and the vibration of her feet on the floor had made it swing gently back and forth. She saw that the cuff was badly worn and a bit of the lining showed. It looked dreadfully like the sleeve of the overcoat she had seen in the subway. And, suddenly, looking at it, she had a horrible sinking feeling, like falling in a dream.

Like "The Birthmark," with which I began a study of spontaneity, this story, which ends the study and our investigation of technique, has a moral. A comparison of the two would provide a full inventory of technical developments over the hundred years between them. Not, of course, that "The Overcoat" is a masterpiece; not even that, technically speaking, it is consistently expert. But it was written with a full understanding of organic unity producing illusion and the means of achieving this, which Hawthorne lacked; and it has aspects bearing on the range of possibilities in stream of experience worth noting.

Its telling position is within the protagonist, as shown by the verbs of thinking establishing the medium, the close following of the protagonist's movements, and the carefully adapted language. But like Caldwell in "Kneel to the Rising Sun," Miss Benson has assumed a relatively detached position within her protagonist, as if to say "No sympathy, please. She isn't worth it." This aloofness is first indicated by reference to the woman as "Mrs. Bishop"—perhaps her vanity would make her capable of this reference to herself, especially since her given name happens to be the extremely low-brow "Mollie"—a formal reference the exact opposite of Miss Zugsmith's indication of a very close narrative position by Seth's reference to himself as "he," inviting sympathy. Further signs of this standoffishness are Miss Benson's restraint in the use of language characteristic of Mrs. Bishop ("She felt horribly sorry for herself" is an instance), like Caldwell's restraint in the case of Lonnie and in contrast with Miss Zugsmith's and Miss Glaspell's free abandonment of language to their protagonists' idiom. And Miss Benson's relative aloofness is implicit in repeated verbs of thinking (seven in the first 500 words), with no direct mental discourse, which in their frame allow something approximating author's analysis by such statements as "inwardly she was seething with rebellion" without impairing the illusion. In fact, so detached is the narrative position that at one point—"Her face took on the vacuous look of other faces in the subway," of which Mrs. Bishop was certainly *not* conscious—Miss Benson slipped over into the external view of objectivity. But all this

143

was done, I believe, to the good purpose of rejecting intimacy with the character, warning the reader against identification with her or granting her sympathy.

At two points stream of experience proves an excellent vehicle. The first of these is the fourth paragraph, in which Mrs. Bishop's stupidity and extravagance reach the reader by irony via her own self-pitying protestations of innocence, with great economy (to show these qualities by her actions would have taken much more space and might have been misleading) and without a suggestion of didacticism. The second passage, where she arrives home and finds her husband lying on the couch, is even better. Her view of Robert with the newspaper over his face, in his old felt slippers, recalling by contrast their younger married days, must have been written with the utmost care. Everything she sees about him is true from her point of view, yet every detail could, and does, support the author's more favorable view of him which we, the reader, have been invited to share by a thorough understanding of the pampered wife's self-revelations. That is, he could be as she thinks a heedless, unromantic husband without ambition or pride; but he could also be merely dead tired and worried and hungry. Very briefly, and almost wholly by technique—for there is nothing deeply moving here—Miss Benson here touches the short story at its best.

Early in this chapter I mentioned the flexibility of stream of experience. These four stories illustrate that quality. As medium they have used a farmer's wife, a share cropper, a young photographer, and Mrs. Bishop. The telling position, within the medium, has varied from the close association suggested in "A Jury of Her Peers" and "Back to Work" to the aloofness near objectivity of "Kneel to the Rising Sun" and "The Overcoat"; and in each case the language used to represent stream of experience was adjusted to the position. The four stories were accepted by a popular weekly, a literary monthly of the old type, an experimental, and a liberal magazine. It is doubtful whether four so different stories, all using any one of the other three techniques here discussed, could be found in such widely different markets over a similar period of time.

Stream of experience, a steady view of experience through a character's senses and thoughts, voiced in appropriate language, is perhaps the best telling medium the short story has so far discovered. For the most part it has been formulated and perfected by American writers. It makes the greatest demand on the author's knowledge (requiring first-hand details), his imagination (demanding renunciation of his own personality or merging of himself with the self of the medium), and his self-control; but is the most conducive to immediacy and spontaneity, and *seems* to the reader the most natural way to tell a story. Here again, as in objective telling, the author has relinquished his birthright as author completely to his material, in this case submerging himself in the person of his protagonist. Here, more than in any other method, technical discipline and his imagination may allow him to transmute his own experience into something detached and objective, yet potentially intense—something universal.

Now choose a telling medium and write that story. It probably won't sell, but never mind, try again.

PART II

CONTENT

9

READER'S NEEDS

M RS. BISHOP saw her husband's overcoat on the chair near the door. "One sleeve was hanging down and the vibration of her feet on the floor had made it swing gently back and forth." But how much did Mollie Bishop weigh, two hundred? And was this home of theirs some tree hut, lean-to, or otherwise ramshackle edifice put up by Robert in his spare time? No. It is only reasonable to suppose that Mollie had kept her weight near a hundred and fifty. The living-room floor she crossed was solid oak or parquet tiling supported by the steel and concrete of a modern apartment house. Try it yourself: hang a coat on a chair and walk, trot, stamp, gallop past it. See if the vibration of your feet on the floor can get a quiver out of the garment. Perhaps, though, Mollie Bishop merely made a mistake; this is in her stream of experience; women aren't too sure about such matters; maybe she *thought* it was the vibration of her feet that made the coat sleeve move, but it wasn't. No. This is Miss Benson's mistake. There would be no point in allowing Mollie to misinterpret the cause of the swinging sleeve; to let her do so leaves the reader with a distracting wonder as to just what was the cause. I believe Miss Benson wanted to bring the coat sleeve to Mollie's attention; the desire was right and proper for her telling method; but she hit on the wrong way to do it. The minor slip gives us a text for the study of short-story content.

As a beginning it may be well to give some thought to the question: what, chiefly, is fiction about? Some tired editor once said there are only three subjects, love and war and love. Erd Brandt, once one of the best agents alive, then one of the best editors, put it better: "You've got to treat the fundamentals."

These could easily be listed—ambition, jealousy, motherhood, violence, sacrifice, what-have-you—and the hopeful writer could plod down the list. Edward Weeks, in a discussion of past best sellers, once remarked jokingly that the most promising topic for a story should be Lincoln's doctor's dog, combining the three most popular subjects in his editorial experience. As a doctoral dissertation at the Sorbonne Georges Polti once wrote *The Thirty-Six Dramatic Situations:* a book now translated into English and not long ago given wide publicity so that young writers might struggle confidently with such themes as "Self-Sacrifice for an Ideal" and "Conflict with a God." Robert H. Davis had a favorite story opening: he wanted a man to arrive at the middle of a great bridge, take out his watch and note the time as 2 A.M., replace the watch and produce a revolver, climb on the parapet and shoot himself "through the temple." I once became fascinated by the prospect of a story beginning as follows:

On Wednesday they found the wallet. They had looked for it Tuesday, but something went wrong—Vincent said the signs weren't right, and he wasn't sure they hadn't better pick up and move on anyway, the girl didn't appeal to him, the whole thing looked bad. Then on Wednesday they found it.

Of course it was empty. . . .

And I tacked a story onto that and sent it in; a magazine bought it, but the editor said if it was all the same to me he would just delete the first two paragraphs, it seemed to go better without them.

I don't believe fiction is about anything like this. I doubt whether any such prescriptive business will do us any good. Everybody is different. Content can't be forced, by the writer or by anyone else. A man has got to come at what he wants to write by himself, without artificial aid. He has got to feel that this particular theme is the only thing that matters right now, and even if nobody wants it some good will have been done by getting it out of his system. Readers are different, too, from one year to the next and from one century to the next. Many good stories have been written that have nothing to do with love or war, or anything from classical mythology, or even anything fundamental.

This is what makes content much more difficult to discuss than technique. Dogma and formula and prescription must be avoided, it seems to me, and the result will be necessarily abstract and general. Of a given story one can say, "That ought to be told objectively, for these reasons," etc.—being specific and fairly concrete. But it will do nobody any good to say of a given story, or of the short story in general: it must begin with a marriage, or a murder, or a girl in a shower bath. A short story *could* begin that way, but not this story that you want to write—that would make it another story, my story, not yours; and not any story that anybody wants to write. We must deal with abstract generalities, largely with the management of material in the round, through its effect on reader and editor, leaving concrete details of execution to your experience and ingenuity. If these fail, I can't interpose some remedy and expect you to apply it. I can only say, No story, try again.

And the danger that I mentioned in an early chapter, of hyper-consciousness of technique (which I hope you have met and survived), in spite of all I can do will now be replaced by a danger of cynicism about content—content, at least, regarded as pure emotional precipitate. Nobody can come through a serious study of short-story idea and substance still believing the genre a lyric cry. Analysis of material may result in a conviction that there are no such things as pure story values—as there should be no such thing as writing blind to method—but that, instead, we have at our disposal an enormous supply of reader impulses and reactions (like red and green lights that will go on for us when the circuit of his intelligence is closed), from which we must choose the best available under certain circumstances governing the demonstration of a particular story idea. In short, the danger is that most story reading will cease to be fun. You will see not only the wheels going round, the technique that you see now; but the gasoline flowing from tank to carburetor, mixing with a little hot air (no pun), meeting spark at the right moment, and exploding, driving pistons. This is too bad, perhaps, but one cannot really study anything and remain a fan, an outsider. And at least you will write better stories. Perhaps you will not always get worked up over the tale itself, but you will get worked up over getting a reader worked up over it, and this in the end may prove even more satisfying.

What basic things, what general elements are needed by the reader of a short story? Get at them by listing what you, as a reader, hope to find when you pay money, open a magazine, and begin reading one; what satisfies you and justifies your expenditure and your mental effort?

I put this question to a picked class of college students, all of them hoping to be writers. Only five of the forty members offered answers. A girl who really preferred poetry to prose said she wanted mood; pinned down, she wasn't sure what she meant by mood (is anybody?) but decided she meant atmosphere. A V–12 naval cadet taking six courses, an attentive listener and note taker, said he read stories for vicarious existence. A 4–F graduate student said he regarded story-reading as an intellectual exercise. A pre-draft scholarship holder said he looked for but one thing: purpose. There was discussion of these four answers, agreement and disagreement, but the majority were ready to admit them and any number of others as legitimate reader needs. We were getting nowhere rapidly when a hand went up in the back of the room. It was another V–12, a boy who seldom talked, who couldn't write well but read everything he could find. He said he had decided what he read stories for. Contact, he said.

I believe it is as simple as that. Even the aesthete and the graduate student had to agree, everybody agreed that contact was basic and universal.

Contact could be elaborated a little without running into the confusing end products of the first four answers. Contact with life, certainly. Much of this must be human, personal; not with living people but with a human concentrate: characters that resemble living humans. But a great deal, too, resides in place: sea stories, business stories, stories of foreign lands, of slums and pine barrens—the locale almost as strong as a personal appeal. And of course much in action, physical or merely psychological, or in idea; or, best of all, in both action and idea. The proportions of these three reader's needs will vary widely with individuals, running off into the sophisticated or self-conscious ultimates referred to. We might hazard a norm and give one-third value to each; remembering, however, that the first is indispensable: contact with human beings.

Definitions of the short story have always attempted to express these needs, but with success that varied in accordance with the definer's ability to divorce form from content without losing sight of either, to be specific and concrete without becoming prey to the temptation of critical jargon. It is useless to say, with some anonymous analyst, that "A short story is a story which is short." The gentleman has repeated a term (story) which itself needs definition; his receipt is nonexclusive, for neither the anecdote nor the parable is a short story, necessarily, though both are short. Poe did a little better without doing really well:

Unity of effect or impression is a point of the greatest importance. [It] cannot be thoroughly observed in productions whose perusal cannot be completed at one sitting . . . requiring from a half-hour to one or two hours. . . . Having conceived, with deliberate care, a certain unique or single effect to be wrought out, [the writer] then invents such incidents—he then combines such effects as may best aid him in establishing this preconceived effect. If his very initial sentence tend not to the outbringing of this effect, then he has failed in his first step. In the whole composition there should be no word written, of which the tendency, direct or indirect, is not to the one pre-established design.

The merits of this pronouncement seem to be its demand for economy (still echoed until recently by *Liberty's* announced reading times) and for unity. But unity of what? Kipling's "Without Benefit of Clergy" has a beautifully significant opening sentence ("But if it be a girl?") which, however, is not borne out by the story that follows, since mother and child both die, leaving the protagonist just where he started instead of struggling with a suggested problem of miscegenation. I doubt if unity of effect is so necessary a factor today as it seemed to Edgar Allan Poe in 1842 as he considered loose-jointed European narratives and set about, for contrast, "The Fall of the House of Usher." Unity of effect can become a dangerous idol. The opening paragraphs of *Bleak House* (fog here, fog there, fog darn near everywhere) possess unassailable unity of effect of the sort that an inexperienced writer might easily get bogged in without ever remotely approaching a short story. This plea for single effect, in fact, good as it may be when combined with pleas for other needs, if voiced to the exclusion of others soon gives rise to the specious sanctity of mood (the mood of the author, as a rule), that impressionistic bane of the short story's existence, inducing in the reader a strong moodiness to be relieved only by throwing the story out the window. Unity of idea, not merely of effect, is I think what is needed.

Twenty-seven years later, in 1869, some anonymous editor of *Appleton's Journal* did much better than Poe:

No doubt one of the most agreeable things in literature is a thoroughly good short story. At the same time it is one of the most difficult to obtain. We have few or no trained workers in this branch of composition. Our professional novelists rarely attempt the short story, and, when they do, are far from increasing their reputation thereby. Since the time of Poe there has been no one eminently successful in this branch—no one whose invention or art has been sufficient for success. A good short story should have one fresh central incident, two or three well conceived and sharply drawn characters, a certain symmetrical unity in construction, a deep significance in the catastrophe or climax—not necessarily a moral, as ordinarily understood, but as nothing should be purposeless, the short story should illustrate some defect or virtue in human character, or portray some special experience whereby the imagination of the reader may be gratified, his sympathies awakened, or his knowledge of the world increased. It is not easy to fix the limitations to the short story. Its construction is an art, far more so than is generally believed; it has its laws, and bears very nearly the same relation to the novel that the song does to poetry, which always properly possesses one definite idea thrown into a compact, symmetrical form. Writers of short stories cannot hope to attain success unless they make this form of composition a profound study; they must have brevity of expression, conception of character, keen feeling for unity and symmetry in art, and very dramatic perceptions. All these qualifications are necessary, but many of them can be acquired by study.

Taking its date into account—that is, after Irving, Hawthorne, Poe, but before Mark Twain (except for "The Celebrated Jumping Frog of Calaveras County"), Bret Harte, Stephen Crane, O. Henry, Garland—this statement seems highly remarkable. It is description rather than definition, perhaps; but a definition not only of the good short story but of the good short-story writer is there. It ignores Poe's nonsense about one sitting, corrects his preoccupation with mere effect, and actually predicts future requisites—just about the requisites of today, too—instead of merely collating the past. One could wish definers of the short story had stopped right there, letting writers go to work on this sound basis.

Perhaps for the most part they did, and perhaps the great upsurge in the craft at the turn of the century was a result. But meanwhile Brander Matthews had put in a word so widely quoted and so generally reverenced that it should be mentioned. In an article in *Lippincott's* (October, 1885) called "The Philosophy of the Short-Story," later published in book form, we find:

A Short-story deals with a single character, a single event, a single emotion, or the series of emotions called forth by a single situation . . . [and is thus distinguished from] the story which is merely short.[1]

One can see what he meant. But is this not an overstatement, an arbitrary recall to the unity of effect required by Poe? Certainly a character, an emotion, an event will often be ascendant; but can a convincing illusion of life be produced if one of these single elements is dealt with to the exclusion of all others? In the hands of an artist—Joyce, for instance—perhaps illusion can be held intact. But must all craftsmen move toward that formula? Certainly Matthews's is too narrow a conception of the short story, barring adventure and romance, calling in a loud voice for Art and thus inviting the merely arty.

Perhaps no definition will help us actually to write short stories. The best ones help us to see what should be there, in us and in our product: in us, the ability to express briefly, an understanding of people, a sense of unity and a sense of the dramatic; in the product, a fresh, central incident, a few sharply drawn characters, unity of conception and construction (including technique, I hope), and some meaning behind the words. But these are all critics', not writers', terms and tools. Who, sitting down to his typewriter and a cold blank sheet of paper, will do himself any good by muttering, "Now for a fresh, central incident," etc.? No, a writer will be simply obscuring the search for what he wants by giving it a categorical name. What is needed, what will begin to satisfy a reader, is either something more or something less than a definition. For something more, let the man looking for a story close all the books and his mind to their terminology, and turn straight to the people and events in his own experience that have moved him, that seemed to him striking, worth record. Then, thinking of the short story merely as a catalyst, a quickening agent on the chemicals of life, let him try to invest some such felt

[1] From *The Philosophy of the Short Story,* by Brander Matthews; Longmans, Green & Co., Inc. Reprinted by permission of the publishers.

156

experience with a meaning that will move others as the experience itself moved him. If this fails, for something less than a definition of the whole short story let him consider this suggestion about how to begin one:

Anybody, clearly seen by the author and interesting to the reader, plus something or somebody he wants and apparently can't get, or something or somebody he doesn't want that seems likely to get him—will always start a story.

Let him, drawing in so far as possible from people and things he knows, start thus—not yet writing, perhaps, but thinking. If he can be a writer, he will be able to go on from there. The result may not make him famous, may not even sell; but it will have some of the attributes for which we have been looking, the presence of which in good stories the definitions point out without telling how they may be created. It will be, not history, essay, autobiography—but short story.

A Nieman Fellow in Journalism at Harvard handed me a clipping from the *Rutherford* (Tenn.) *Courier* saying it was written as news, but didn't it not only fill the requirements of the short story but do this by meeting the reader's needs that we had been discussing. The piece was written by Ed Bell, and it appeared in the issue of March 7, 1944, in a column called "Tales of the Town."

An old negro woman told us about Little Pheedie, the crippled child of a couple starving slowly on a rocky farm back in the hills. He had one foot shaped like a brick and his shoulders were crooked.

A wild-looking child, she said, with a big wobbly head covered with hair that was like a nest of blacksnakes, and she swore he had a film that would shut over his eyes like a frog's.

He played alone because there were no close neighbors. If any other children caught him out on the road they rocked him home.

She told about one hot summer morning when he came to the house to get a jar of water. He said he wanted to get Baldhead a drink.

She asked him who was Baldhead.

"I play with him," Little Pheedie said, "up yonder in the stump pasture. He's a big water drinker."

The woman smiled at him and fixed the water. He didn't smile back. Little Pheedie never did smile much, but sometimes you could see it in his eyes when the frog lids were not down.

"Baldhead's not like them others," he said. "He's good."

Little Pheedie limped away with the jar of water back past the barn and up the pasture slope. The pasture had been cleared a long time. All the stumps but one had been blasted out and burned. The old stump stood at the upper edge in the shade of the woods. They called the field the stump pasture.

With the mother and father slaving all the time he was free to prowl where he pleased, and most of the summer he spent up there in the stump pasture somewhere and seemed happier. The old negro woman said Pheedie didn't eat much except sometimes a little bread and slices of meat.

One day his mother heard him laugh out in the yard. He never laughed much anytime. It scared her.

"What you laughing at, Honey?" she asked.

"Something Baldhead said."

"What'd he say?"

Little Pheedie looked at her solemnly. "He told me not to tell anybody," he said.

Again she asked him why he didn't bring Baldhead down to the house sometime, but Little Pheedie said his playmate didn't like big people.

The mother got worried and named it about his make-believe friend to the father. The father laughed and said that all little children played with ghosts.

Pheedie took something to eat up there another hot afternoon, but returned soon with the empty fruit jar and stayed in the yard. He sat out in the sun staring away at the rocky hills. His mother asked him what was the matter.

"Baldhead swallowed his boiled egg and mine too," he said. "I slapped him in the face and he run off. I guess I ain't got nobody to play with now."

She asked didn't he want to come in and sleep a while? She would make him a nice cool pallet on the floor. He shook his head, but later he did come in and slept on through the afternoon.

The father came across the fields at dusk carrying something. He had cut across the woods and hill. When he saw his wife standing on the porch, he laughed and held up what he carried.

"Old grandaddy," he said. "Twenty-one rattles and a button. He was laying up there by that old stump where he lived, I reckon, and I just whacked him with the hoe."

Little Pheedie, waking up, had come to the doorway, and when he saw what it was cried out, "You oughtn't to done that."

Then he ran out into the dark past his father, dragging his bad foot and crying.[2]

Certainly it is short story, not reporting—although we have no reason to doubt the reporter's word that it happened; it is short story because the reporter shaped and arranged for fictional requirements the facts he learned. If he had followed news writing requirements, his leading sentence would have stated the key fact of the incident: child playing with rattlesnake. But he held that back, letting the reader pace the parents' discovery of it. Further management is indicated by "hair that was like a nest of blacksnakes," the appropriate restraint of language, the attribution of the tale to the old negress, for veracity (an interesting variant of "I" as witness), the free use of direct discourse, the playmate strain (other kids rocking Pheedie home, and "Baldhead's not like them others. He's good."); and above all, the created unity of theme and structure, the significance, strongly implied but never stated, that the whole piece reveals: namely, like to like, the little human monster, cast off by his own kind, so lonely he makes friends with another hated being, the animal monster. In short, though basically true, its historical authenticity is overshadowed by the truth to nature read into it and evoked from it by the author. Incidentally, here is a person clearly seen and worth attention wanting something (my suggestion for starting a story); the rest of the story simply telling how he got what he wanted for a time, then lost it. But notice that, through the author's careful management, the reader does not know exactly what it was that Pheedie wanted, and for a time got, until he learns that Pheedie has lost it.

[2] Reprinted by permission of the author.

With equal certainty, it seems to me, the author has filled the requirements of definition by meeting the reader's needs. The human concentrate—hard-working, starving parents, the sympathetic neighbor, the crippled child himself—is poignant from the end of the third paragraph on. Place lives here too: the stump pasture clearly seen, the hot sun in the yard, the rocky hills, the cool pallet on the floor—these few details bodying forth the scene and atmosphere. Action runs throughout, the long time span well condensed by the telling medium so that it all seems to be immediate scene and everything moves toward the final afternoon; and best of all, every bit of action integrated in the demonstration of the chosen theme.

Poe would have liked this story; the anonymous editor and Brander Matthews would have approved it. But more to the point, few readers could fail to respond to its appeal.

10

EDITOR'S NEEDS

THERE must be several thousand managing editors, many thousands of associates and assistants and editorial readers controlling the selection of contributions to American periodicals. It cannot but be foolhardy for anyone to invade this huge, many-cubicled sanctum, try to analyze its operation, and set down anything specific enough to be applicable to various would-be contributors and at the same time in any sense generally true. A thorough survey is impossible. Much of what follows, therefore, may sound arbitrary; exceptions to particular statements may pile up; and even the general principles evolved may appear partial, lacking much, offering little. I hope, nevertheless, that an individual view—formed by the experiences of one writer and those of his writing friends over the past twenty-five years—will at least be better than none, and better than the misconceptions born of rumors that can come between author and editor, author and reader.

To get at the editor's needs we must first get at the editor and try to understand him, then at the kinds of manuscripts, publishable as well as unpublishable (for merely good stories cannot always be his only desideratum), among which he has perforce to choose.

I used to picture the editor as a dreadfully austere personage seated at a big desk with a checkbook at his left elbow, a mail chute at his right, and piles of shopworn manuscripts before him; if he reached for the checkbook it was with a grudging frown, but when he used the chute he moved with a flourish and chuckled happily.

As soon as one begins to meet editors, the picture grows more real if not at once more human. Most writers must serve an apprenticeship in understanding these men and women. It seemed to me that they habitually said, wrote, and did inexplicable things. I remember one day one remarked, "You know, if Robert Louis Stevenson walked in here with the script of *Treasure Island* under his arm, I don't believe I'd buy it." Editors would buy perhaps six or ten stories in a row, and then suddenly reject as many. They would ask me into their offices, into their homes; one would come a thousand miles, preceded only by a wire, "just for a talk"; another would pay my expenses to meet him somewhere on a hurried trip. Not me alone, of course. Usually I found a stream of writers and illustrators filing through the editorial field headquarters in some hotel bedroom. The chief was always rushed to death, but he would have time to outline his confidential plans, big and far-reaching. He would tell me where I fitted into the scheme. Naturally I would leave such a conference with my head in the clouds and begin to think of buying a new car. Then my next story would be turned down cold, or be tentatively accepted subject to extensive revision in accordance with a long, hurried, and incomprehensible outline in accordance with some new confidential plans, big and far-reaching. Once such a story was painfully revised, paid for, and published. The only words from my manuscript to appear on the first page were my name.

It is easy to suppose that there was a time when writers could climb into towers of ivory, open their precious hearts, and just write. But I doubt if this was ever really true. Certainly it has not been true since middle and lower classes became literate in this country and magazines were born. The story of fiction writing has been a story of compromise between personal taste and pocketbook, between what lay in the writer's heart and what readers hoped to find on the printed page. Most good writers have always written, I believe, not primarily to please themselves but to please others. Beginners must start with and never lose sight of the fact that writing for pay is, no less than playing the saxophone or walking the tightrope, a public performance; and it lives or dies by public approval.

But here is that nuisance, the editor, standing between us and the people whose needs we know and whose approval we want to receive. If he seems capricious, illogical, or plain stupid, running off in a huff may soothe our vanity but won't help us write. Trying to understand him might. I have no sympathy with the sort of pride that makes an unpublished writer feel that his creative soul will be smirched by trying to understand people.

Many editors were once, or wanted to be, writers. With this fact in mind their inveterate fondness for fiddling with manuscripts becomes understandable. Most national magazines now send author's proofs of material to be published, and if this practice does not quite give the writer the last word, it is more tolerable than the high-handed methods of the past. A hundred and one editorial considerations of which no writer can be fully cognizant govern proofreading revisions. Writers' objections to such changes are often out of proportion with their importance.

Many editors are former newspaper and advertising men. Weeklies, even monthlies of the better grade have to a large extent become journalistic. I don't mean that they publish news exclusively, although a tabulation of their pages will reveal a high proportion of factual material. I do mean that even in many short stories to be found in magazines of large circulation there is apparent the hustle and bustle of superficiality, the sensational or sentimental glitter—sometimes miscalled realistic—that we have come to associate with newspapers; and that timeliness of material has risen to a place of prime importance. American haste, American devotion to fads, American interest in striking personalities, American insistence on keeping up with the Joneses are some of the roots of timeliness. Perhaps its taproot is the dependence of magazines on advertising, and resultant competition. Editors must be waging a pitched battle all the time. Publicity plus popular stories equals bigger circulation, which means higher advertising rates and more advertisers, which permit bigger publicity and more popular stories—and so on and, we hope, up. A writer may secretly deplore this capitalization of literature, this absorption of what might be art into the hard struggles of the market place; but unless he can afford to found and maintain a private periodical for publishing his own work, he must try to effect a compromise. Let him, for instance, determine to give only the very best of which he is capable, on suggested editorial specifications, and there will be small danger to the integrity of his aesthetic soul.

Editors are habitually overworked. Running a magazine is peculiarly a one-man job if the magazine is to have, as the good ones do, personality, and if business and editorial staffs are to be reconciled and integrated; yet so greatly and intricately has the job expanded that a superman is called for. The least of the editor's tasks is that of being head reader: that is, he must read every word that finally goes into each issue and many thousands that, in this last test, are left out. He does it in his spare time, usually when you and I are asleep. For all day he is "seeing people," settling disputes, solving problems, pacifying his business manager and publisher, thinking up new schemes to scoop his competitors, presiding at conferences and previews, attending luncheons and cocktail parties and meetings of his tribe. If authors and bank directors and agents and promoters live all the way from New York to Hollywood, as they do, much of his work must be done on the move. If his printing plant and business management are separated from his office, as often these days they are, his decisions must be quick for his moves will be by air, and it's devil take the hindmost.

And we crouch in our little ivory towers and wonder why the man had to pick on us!

The editor who turned down an unpublished *Treasure*

Island, by the way, explained his decision. "I have found costume stuff expensive and risky lately," he said. "And it happens that I just bought a long sea story. Readers' letters show they are thinking more about the future than the past. And I know where I could get the same sort of thing—pirates, treasure, all that— for less than I'd have to pay R.L.S. In short," he summed it up, "availability is everything. Few stories get turned down here just because they are badly written. Practically none are bought just because they are well written. It's rough on writers, but perhaps in the long run it works out. I have to be a jump ahead of those people across the street. And I believe good writers get to be better writers by being turned down now and then."

Editors usually don't have time to stop and try to understand writers; as a rule they must take what comes, make what they can of it. We are the sellers, the burden of proof rests with us; it is we who should go more than halfway. Better understanding makes for a greater tolerance, a less impersonal and more human relationship. When the fear of an editor leaves a writer, he is free to do his best. I believe that it is unwise to play favorites with editors or magazines; that the best policy is, once you get started, to have enough manuscripts out at various places so that one rejection won't seem a catastrophe. I believe in living, as Cosmo Hamilton once phrased it, "with an ear to the ground"; and I also believe in forgetting one's writing problems, once in a while, and letting an editor talk about his. For these people are just as much up against it as we are; their hard bright manner is only camouflage; we can sit inside, independent, quiet, everything under control; they must be up and out, taking orders, giving them and seeing that they are carried out, with a hundred details on their minds each day, many days getting nowhere; they are struggling as we are, losing here, winning there.

"A good friend," Kenneth Roberts once wrote, "is a highly desirable part of every author's equipment." Roberts was referring to a writing friend, Booth Tarkington. I have had two good friends. Since they were both editors, it is only natural for me to think that an attempt to understand the man sitting between the mail chute and the checkbook may be more than worth the effort.

But consider him again, not as a person but as a reader; consider the editor in relation to what he wants for his magazine as compared with what he gets to fill it. I rule out the material he conceives and plans with an author, although much of that is published. I also rule out amateurish efforts that he never sees if his assistants do their work properly. Consider the unsolicited good stories he gets and, not because of space limitations or lack of money, but because of editorial policy, he cannot publish.

A glance at any newsstand suggests the vast assortment of periodicals, similar and divergent, that the American magazine —which started simply as fashion book, almanac, and Sunday school guide—has now become. Chaos it is, and chaos is unclassifiable; even any rough grouping by types will prove faulty. We can see juveniles, pulps of many kinds, weeklies and monthlies on slick paper, and a quality or literary group (including experimental or "little" magazines)—all publishing fiction, each with its specifications and its taboos. Over-simplification might discover but two kinds: those for readers who like life represented about as they know it, and those for a much larger class who want to daydream of life better, or, comfortingly, worse than that they know; that is, the reading realists and the reading romanticists or escapists. Some schools of journalism recommend close study and detailed tabulation of stories in selected markets—the highest paying, perhaps, or those nearest the writer's taste or abilities—with a view to reproduction of the type. Such statistical exercise will do those who will never make much of their writing no harm, but it may confuse, distract, and balk the young writer with something to say.

I am still thinking of the editor who finds a pile of manuscripts on his desk, all well written, of which he can, if he likes, buy a few. I am trying to look at writing and at writers as he sees those phenomena, whatever the editorial purpose and policy of his magazine may be. I believe he would find three approaches to story material engendering the somewhere-purchasable manuscripts before him, and that he would pay great attention to this classification of his and follow it pretty closely.

No matter what we may do to prevent it, our manuscripts tell the practiced editorial eye a great deal about us. The ideas we dramatize, the kinds of people we choose for actors, the sort of place we like to write about, the way we shape our material, even the words, phrases, and sentence patterns that constitute our language give him strong evidence of our literary creeds. Thus we expose ourselves and confess without meaning to, often meaning not to. Almost as plainly as if the writers of them sat across his desk and spoke their hearts out, one group in that pile of manuscripts will say to the editor between the lines of story:

Literature is bankrupt. Convention, commercialism, and repetition of the contents of the conscious mind have stripped writing of its freshness, vigor, and originality. But I am new, I am different; nobody on earth has ever been quite like me before. Let me therefore express myself, my subconscious and my unconscious. Let me find novelty of substance and expression, beauty in the strange and exotic and esoteric—let me find beauty in ugliness so-called, revitalizing the dead things of the soul. Communication and the reader be damned! A story, as MacLeish said of a poem, should not mean but be. There are still a few of us who can understand me, or who don't need to understand so long as, reading my work, they can feel that I am there. The rest don't count.

This is the creed and approach to material of the *avant garde,* of the "little" magazines of the twenties, of *Broom, transition, This Quarter;* of Gertrude Stein, Paul Valéry, Julian Green, Joyce, early Kay Boyle, Kafka, and a persistent small band of imitators today. It is a belief that recurs periodically in literary history, that of the rebel. When genuine and backed by skill, it has value: it reaches for new fields of endeavor, keeps us on our toes, stimulates the intellectual side of literature. At its worst it is an ostrich, head buried in sand; or a form of narcissism; or a kind of creative writing tending toward the ultimate of a blank page, the reader invited to guess what the author's thoughts were, or think his own. It has, always will have, but few readers—most of them either in college or the sort that, spiritually, never got out. If the editor's magazine is experimental, or perhaps of the liberal or quality group, he will read such manuscripts attentively; something there may be just what he wants. If he heads the staff of any other variety of magazine, some subordinate will suffer for having wasted the editor's time.

Another group of manuscripts in the pile will say to him:

To hell with art! Writing is a business if not a racket. I have to make a living, and I want to make it that way. Of course everything has been said, but that's because the public likes the same old stuff over and over. All I have to do is find out what this old stuff is—I'll call it the eternal verities or something highbrow like that—and then say it, with new trimmings of course, over and over. To hell with posterity! I won't be here then.

Our editor finds this group large. It bespeaks the attitude and approach of the pulp and slick fiction writers. Like the creed of the first group, when honest and efficiently implemented, it has value. It has produced thousands of well-plotted, readable, convincing stories, which have brought entertainment to millions of readers and millions of dollars to authors; the alertness and adaptability it requires in the writer is probably good for him; and I believe that many stories of this type—Clarence Budington Kelland's, James Hilton's, or Mary Roberts Rinehart's, for example—are often wrongly scorned by those whose hypercritical pose suggests sour grapes: mass appreciation alone may give them a relative permanence that such judgments cannot foresee. At its less than best, too, this attitude can produce horrors of fiction: prose that has luster and little else, shopworn situations, two-dimensional characters, pornography disguised as romance, a distorted view of life. Still, good or bad, such stories (glamorously illustrated, of course) attract readers by the million. If the editor runs a magazine of wide circulation, he will look carefully here and select the best of the assortment his assistants have sent up to him.

The third group will be small. But I believe that every manuscript there, if it must be rejected for reasons of policy or schedule, will be rejected with regret; and that, whatever the magazine, its editor will watch the writers' future work and hope to get it. Between their lines these manuscripts will say:

It's true that everything has been said, but the fact has no bearing on my work except to warn me against conscious imitation or mere novelty. It's a negative matter. My positive effort is to write what I know about so faithfully to readers' legitimate needs that it will seem to them both familiar and new.

And it is that sort of creed that makes editors forget policy and pocketbook, buy the piece because they like it and to see how it goes. Often it goes well in the unlikeliest places.

This third creed aims high. So far as I can discover it has been the creed of the great storytellers. Usually it receives enough monetary reward to satisfy those who are willing to profess it. And it seems to me the only approach that offers a workable and healthy compromise between writer's ego and reader's ego as construed by the editor. It can be practical without commercialism, preserve aesthetic integrity without holing up in ivory towers and starving.

Those who subscribe to it will find management of material more important than material itself; not simply manner of telling, which we have studied as technique, but selection, order, proportion, and presentation of story material. Neither the manner of telling nor the kind of material or theme will matter so much as this adjustment of material to a reader's needs as visualized by the editor, which covers the whole of content.

It is the amount of emotion you can draw out of a story that rules content. The factors governing that evocative quality of short fiction will hereafter be our chief concern. By amount of emotion I mean of course reader's emotion. Not author's emotion *per se,* although that may have been the now remote first cause and may still be present, properly disciplined, channeled, and objectified.

But how is a reader to be stirred emotionally? Certainly not, today, by fireworks—profanity, obscenity, or physical violence. Our reader has seen everything. Of the short stories already discussed, "The Piece of String" is the least violent yet perhaps the most moving. Certainly not—at least in the way desired— by author's judgment or feelings visibly at variance with the reader's. How then?

If you could get him to speak, and supply words representing his usually wordless instincts and intuitions, the editor would, I believe, answer the question somewhat as follows:

To be evocative, fiction must first be clear and credible. It must somehow contrive to start and keep a reader reading. It must show people enough like himself to give him sympathy with them, yet people in some particulars unlike anybody he ever heard of before. It must make him feel that on finishing the story he has been somewhere. It must relate its action to some idea having significance beyond the bare facts. And it must present this idea and its supporting action dramatically, allowing the reader to discover the meaning of the story for himself.

Then the factors in management of material which govern the evocative power of short stories are: plausibility, to be clear and credible; suspense and surprise, to start and keep the reader reading; characterization, to give him people familiar for sympathy, strange for interest; place and atmosphere, to make him feel he has been somewhere; theme and plot, to relate the action to an idea; and indirection and restraint, to let the reader discover the meaning for himself.

These factors we shall take up and discuss in detail. They

are as old as the hills. They have concerned better writers than we are, and, well handled, have stirred countless readers. It would be stupid to ignore them as outworn; there are no others. Blind worship of them might be equally futile. Rather, let us bring them to bear on our individual, our unique experience, and see if by so doing we cannot make them new.

11

PLAUSIBILITY

Fact and fancy in print, competing for public approval, are confused in the public mind. Hungry for excitement, escape, emotional identification with big deeds and famous people, the public lights on both fact and fancy with relish, often mistaking one for the other without caring, so long as its appetite is appeased. Hardly a story, it seems, gets written but some friend of the author, or some enemy, calls it autobiography or near-libel. The rise of realism and naturalism in the last century, and two world wars in this one, may have raised fact to new prominence, somewhat overshadowing the emotional appeal of fancy. The editors of the *Saturday Evening Post* admit their strongest competitor is *Life*. Possibly without connection, a recent serial in the *Post,* Leslie Ford's *The Philadelphia Murder Story,* included the editors themselves, real-named and accurately illustrated, as characters in its fictitious murder mystery. In much propaganda, in confession magazines, and in advertising, fiction masquerades successfully as fact. In many historical novels and biographies, in autobiographical novels and *romans à clef,* fact passes for fiction. Sensationalism and hero worship, in newsprint, over the air, and on the screen seem ever reaching for new levels. It is doubtful whether the general public goes to the movies to see a story or a Hollywood celebrity: it appears to derive the same satisfaction from either.

But short-story writers must cleave through this muddle and preserve a sharp distinction. For they must use both fact and fancy, knowing at all times which is which; must start with fact as an area of agreement shared with the reader, and on the facts build fiction with which, if they are not careful, the reader may flatly disagree. Their great concern will be to pass from one area to the other so credibly that the reader, detecting no change, will feel at the end as he did at the start, "That's true!"—whereas most of the story isn't, in the sense he applied at its start, true at all.

Yet in view of his confusion of fact with fancy, his gullibility, really, how can a reader disagree with a story; why won't anything go? In a few scattered exceptions—tales of the future, tall tales, ghost and fairy stories—perhaps almost anything will; though I think each of these has its special standard of credibility too. In a vast majority of short stories generally considered, anything certainly will not go; for no matter how muddled, the reading public will never forget that "Fact is stranger than fiction," with the converse inference that fiction should be not strange but somehow natural; and even a hurried reader has the time, lacked in mid-story by movie-goer and radio-listener, to remember and apply this proverbial saying. And besides this vague but stubborn conviction and the chance to reflect as he reads, every reader has his own knowledge of life—the life that fiction contracts to mirror—to use as standard of comparison with the life the story represents; he has not only that but a very human eagerness to find something wrong in what he reads—and write the editor about it, too. No matter how well as author you know your subject, some reader will have made it a veritable hobby and know much more. All of us, as readers, have felt and have heard others say disparagingly of stories, "Oh, fair enough; but of course highly improbable."

The "of course" is what hurts. A short story permitting that thought has failed of complete credibility. The study of plausibility seeks means of obviating such comment, not only by allaying doubts of authenticity before they occur, but by building up some positive reaction in the reader that absorbs all his attention and makes doubt impossible.

Storytellers use facts in fiction almost constantly. I mean not

173

only historical dates, deaths of prominent persons, precise words of a popular song, characteristic town names in Minnesota, and the flavor of turnips. I mean how to tie a bowline and when, an electric drill, the Atlantic Charter, the cost and material and suitability of a dress, Rosicrucianism, Boyle's Law, plastics; I mean what happens when you chuckle, why people flush, how a compound fracture or a piece of metal in you feels, and innumerable other matters, great and small, subjects of more or less common knowledge—facts about the existence, composition, appearance, and behavior of people and things. The pattern of fiction has been borrowed from the pattern of history, recorded fact. But the storyteller, lacking the historian's authority and the history-reader's relative credulousness, must know: first, how to make the facts he uses quickly convincing to readers of varying intelligence and stocks of information; and second, how and when to build upon his basis of fact some larger conception, unhistorical, merely conjectural and hypothetical, but sound by the reader's standards and therefore acceptable and convincing to him as truth, not so much to fact as to life.

No reader supposes that the events of a short story actually happened, and no author expects him to. The reader is there to daydream. The past tense generally used, another borrowing from the form of history, is merely a symbol of make-believe. The extent of the reader's credulity is that these events might happen, and the temporary make-belief that they did will be enjoyable or enlightening to him, or both. Strictly speaking, of course, the events—much of the material, in fact—of a story, conceived by the author extra-factually but presented as if literally true (that is, in the past tense, with specific details and every effort for authenticity and verisimilitude), are false. But this historical falsehood the storyteller himself has a right to believe more devoutly, consider more important, than many recorded actual facts; for it is one that can reach its own level of truth based on but transcending facts, and thus in the end can justify its literally untruthful aspects and repay the reader's loan of credulity, principal and interest.

The level of truth it is after is abstract as opposed to the concrete, and general as opposed to the particular facts on which it is based. It is truth to nature (boy gets girl, boy loses girl, or any other plausible story outcome) experienced, synthesized, and dramatically demonstrated by the human author, and recognized by the also-human reader on the strength of *his* experience, *his* understanding of and sympathy with other humans, as the right and fitting theme and outcome. That reader felt it all along but longed to have it said; as Pope wrote with other reference, this higher truth is "What oft was thought, but ne'er so well express'd." It has never been coded, never will be. It is subject only to the author's and reader's shared concept of the capricious operation of probability, and to the reader's anticipation, desire, and sympathy, which the author tries to discover, then direct and stimulate.

Now of course no writer is steadily conscious of the facts he uses as literally true, of his theme or outcome (the fiction) as true to nature or significant. He is far too deeply engrossed in the only thing that seems to him important: getting people down on paper in some way that will keep a reader reading about them and make him feel at the end that reading has been worth the effort. But he does, if he is an honest craftsman, what is better than being aware of any aesthetic distinctions. First he makes dead sure that he has what he calls "something to write about" and what I have called a demonstrable theme or outcome true to nature and neither too obvious nor too obscure. He checks this with what he takes to be his reader's anticipation, desire, and sympathy throughout the course of the story. And he scrutinizes for probability every least detail on which his theme or outcome is based. Even these three acts he may do instinctively, calling the three steps merely "catching a story." In later chapters we shall watch him take the first two. It is the last, the act of scrutiny, that we are to investigate here. The experienced author performs it by writing only of people, places, and things of which he has or can get first-hand information; and by avoiding the marvelous, fortuitous, or coincidental, however literally true. Beginners will be satisfied to restrict their material to their own fields of experience, knowing that these fields widen with every lived day. They need some clarification of miracles.

"But it's true!" a young writer says of his manuscript that a reader has found implausible. "My brother was there and he told me." Disregard the possible area of error caused by the brother's telling, and assume that the facts told and retold did actually happen, fact by fact. Perhaps because of the confusion between fact and fancy, there is a widespread delusion that literal truth makes convincing story, and this easily spreads to the belief that the more startling or extraordinary the literal truth, the better the story. The opposite is the case.

The startling fact is that children sometimes fall from considerable heights to hard surfaces without serious injury. It is the sort of occurrence that newspapers like to record, boxed, in bold-faced type. In less than three years, a single metropolitan daily published the following items:

Poised on the ledge of the third-floor window of his home in Brooklyn, N. Y., Raymond Bjornland, 3½, blond and blue-eyed, shouted to his mother on the sidewalk below, "Here I come, mamma." His mother screamed and bystanders ran to catch the child. Raymond, rolled up in a ball, landed on the sidewalk. The child was taken to a hospital, where it was discovered that he had suffered virtually no injury. He promised not to jump again.

MATTAPAN GIRL FALLS 30 FEET, SCRATCHED

Three-year-old Barbara Brabazon, daughter of Mr. and Mrs. Edward Brabazon of 562 Rover St., Mattapan, fell more than 30 feet from the second-floor window of her home yesterday. Taken to City Hospital, Barbara was found to have suffered only a scratch of the face. She was held overnight, however, for observation.

BABY FALLS 5 STORIES, RUNS TO MEET PARENTS

Michael Babyak, Jr., 14 months old, leaped on a bed at his home today, bounced out the window and fell five stories into a rear yard. When his parents dashed into the yard, Michael jumped up and ran to them. His only injuries were abrasions of the scalp and wrist. Clothes lines broke his fall.

SOMERVILLE CHILD PLUNGES 40 FEET

Suffered Only Abrasions on Leg, Doctors at Hospital Find

Gertrude Kehoe, 3, balanced herself on a windowsill on the third floor of her home, 58 Oliver St., Somerville, her back against a screen. Unthinking, she pressed too hard. In a second, the child and the screen plummeted 40 feet to the ground.

Horrified neighbors ran and picked up the girl from the gravel road where she lay. Edward Metcalf, worker on a WPA project on the block, rushed her to Somerville Hospital. Doctors said Gertrude suffered only abrasions on her left leg and unless internal injuries were revealed, she could go home today.

The names and addresses are provided as evidence and a challenge to the skeptical. Barring the possibility of internal injuries revealed later and not reported, this miraculous fall-without-injury actually took place at least twice in three years in Boston, twice in New York. To support its occurrence we have the general belief that a child or a drunk falls relaxed because ignorant of what is coming. Yet every reader knows that in a great majority of such falls, the head being as likely to hit the ground first as any other part of the body, death or severe injury is the result. No statistics are necessary or even relevant; the reader knows, you cannot budge him. Probability operates uncontestably. Suppose you wrote a story about marital troubles, and let a child's fall and escape from injury be the cause of its parents' reconciliation—as it well might be in story, as it may have been in fact. No matter how carefully worked out, how well done in other respects, the story depending for its outcome on that startling fact would not be convincing to readers.

To be suspect, an event need not be so rare as this. Coincidences happen to all of us, almost every day. We meet people we want or don't want to meet, by sheer chance. Something that we have not even thought about for years comes up at just the moment when it seems to have some bearing on our present lives. Lichen pictures appear on headstones peculiarly appropriate to the characters of the people buried below. We escape cloudbursts in the nick of time, lightning strikes the next house, a land mine killed Jim but left John next him whole. And so on. In fiction, the less of even these minor miracles the better. Readers will see the long arm of chance as it begins to reach, and credulity will weaken accordingly. But to rule the fortuitous completely out of fiction would be to distort our representation of life by eliminating a commonly accepted element. (Poe based "The Mystery of Marie Rogêt" on "a series of scarcely intelligible coincidences." Joseph Conrad wrote a novel called *Chance;* and his works are scattered with references to luck, a large factor in seafaring psychology.) There is a good way and a bad way of handling the problem. Occurrences beyond human control such as a chance meeting, a hurricane, the long lost's appropriate return, if they come early in the story and are apparently of no great consequence to the plot, have no effect on plausibility. The later they appear and, particularly, the more importance as motive power they assume, the more dangerous as story material they may prove.

A literary agent once put the situation thus:

Many short stories lack plausibility because the authors don't understand what makes a story and what does not. *Man bites dog* does not; it is news, maybe, but not fiction. A newsreader can marvel and enjoy the sensation without loss of faith: the paper says it's so. The state of mind you want in a story-reader is not one of wonderment but one of tense anxiety and sympathy. Both these must be based on the small, undoubted facts about life in general, not the sensational, unique, or spectacular occurrence—even though it may actually have happened.

Perhaps G. K. Chesterton came as close when he said, characteristically, "I find you can write successfully of ordinary people doing extraordinary things, or of extraordinary people doing ordinary things; but not of ordinary people doing ordinary things, for you will not be read; and not of extraordinary people doing extraordinary things, for you will not be believed."

The short-story writer deliberately attempts less than the spectacular in an effort to achieve something more—something that goes deeper and stays longer in a reader than passing wonder. His air is as calm as an antiquary's; he ballyhoos nobody; it is commonplace life, or one cut above it, he seeks an audience for, not Siamese Twins. About all he seems to say is: "Given people of this sort, environment of this sort, physical laws such and such, and psychological phenomena such and such (with all of which you are familiar or are in the course of the story made familiar)—given all that, this is bound to happen."

But actually he is far from calm. Execution of the simple proposition is a painstaking, often a heart-rending affair. He must be sure of his facts and of his reader's comprehension of them; knowledge varies enormously, and he must be clear to the dullards without being obvious to the quick-witted. He must, with the literal facts clear, begin to prepare the reader for agreement with his fiction by preliminary, unobtrusive reference: to traits in people, details of place, foreshadowings of action—all of which will later, being recalled, invite agreement with the story.

Different short-story ideas, with proposed means for their demonstration, present widely varying degrees of difficulty here. A tale mostly of physical action enacted by relatively simple characters in a generally known, typical milieu—city slums, deep woods, the sea—proves plain sailing so long as the writer knows what he is writing about. Difficulties with clarity of fact and credibility of fiction increase as we pass from the

179

familiar to a less known setting, from physical to psychological action and, thus, from simple to complex people. Hardest of all, probably, is the idea or the means for its demonstration either based on the supernatural or admitting a supernatural interpretation. Let us look at two such stories, the first wholly successful in this respect, the other only partly so.

In Stevenson's "Markheim" a young man enters an antique jewelry shop on a dark Christmas afternoon ostensibly to buy a gift for his fiancée. Talking with the "little pale, round-shouldered dealer," Markheim remarks that he has "done well on the Stock Exchange" and is, happily, about to marry wealth. But his manner belies his words. He seems ill at ease, rejects a hand glass almost with horror; and then, while the old man is fumbling under the counter for another offering, Markheim suddenly stabs and kills him. Taking the dealer's keys despite the terror and guilt that now nearly paralyze him, Markheim shuts the shop door and goes upstairs to find the old man's money. He closes the drawing-room door and feels safe. Whereupon, although alone in the house except for the corpse, Markheim hears a step on the stairs. The knob turns, the lock clicks, and the door opens.

Fear held Markheim in a vice. What to expect he knew not, whether the dead man walking, or the official ministers of human justice, or some chance witness blindly stumbling in to consign him to the gallows. But when a face was thrust into the aperture, glanced round the room, looked at him, nodded and smiled as if in friendly recognition, and then withdrew again, and the door closed behind it, his fear broke loose from his control in a hoarse cry. At the sound of this the visitant returned.

"Did you call me?" he asked, pleasantly, and with that he entered the room and closed the door behind him.

The theme is very simple: conquest of man by his conscience. The outcome is ironic: Markheim, who had planned his crime with care and intelligence and executed it with skill to escape detection, is betrayed by himself—first by his fear, then by his awakened sense of sin. The telling method is for the most part objective; perhaps a thousand words only, between the murder of the dealer and the arrival of the "visitant," with Markheim alone on scene, necessarily being analysis of sense impressions, thoughts and emotions; and a single sentence at the end, when he is again alone, interpreting thoughts and action. Published in 1885, the story antedated stream of experience, which might seem its natural medium, by at least thirty years.

But one can't be sure that Stevenson would have used stream of experience even if the medium had been known to him. If so written, from the death of the dealer on—more than four fifths of its length—the story would have represented Markheim alone and talking to himself. The "visitant," who knows him well and likes him and has often tried to "help" Markheim, whom Markheim takes to be the devil and whom a piously minded reader might take to be his guardian angel, is really only himself, one side—the better side—of himself. In stream of experience much of the story might have been dull. But as Robert Louis Stevenson wrote it, must it face a more serious charge? Is it plausible at all? Can it be fair for a writer to say that somebody enters a room, talks with his protagonist and persuades him to a course of action, when he means that no second person is there?

Turn back to the beginning of the story and note the literal facts Stevenson used and the preparation for agreement with his astounding fiction he undertook through preliminary, unobtrusive reference to traits in people, details of place, and coming action. To gain agreement, preparation had to surmount three hurdles: motivation of the murder, appearance of the "visitant," and Markheim's surrender.

"Some [customers] are dishonest," the dealer says at the start, holding up a candle to scrutinize Markheim (the shop is shuttered), "and in that case I profit by my virtue." Markheim blinks and cannot meet the dealer's gaze. No matter how reasonable the young man's story, from here on his motive is suspect; but the touch is very deft, Markheim has just come in off the street, the blinking might be normal reflex; this is the first unobtrusive reference, slipped in for post-operative recall. Others follow. We learn that Markheim had prepared what he would tell the dealer, and once he is launched on this line he seems more at ease. When the dealer stoops to draw an object from the showcase, leaving himself unprotected, Markheim's emotional reaction is suggestive; it is when the old man repeats the movement to withdraw another object that the knife is to fall. Markheim snatches the hand mirror and confronts the dealer with it; the dealer starts back at this threatening gesture, but "perceiving there was nothing worse [than a mirror] on hand," chuckles and goes on. So much as preparation for murder, a mere physical act resulting from motives preceding the story, and, itself, coming early; thus the easiest of Stevenson's three problems in plausibility.

The second, the appearance of the "visitant," was difficult enough in 1885, though "Saki," Lord Dunsany, Walter de la Mare, and others were soon to make mysticism and fantasy welcome in England; it might well have proved insuperably hard in our hard-boiled American twenties; since Kafka, Katherine Anne Porter, John Collier, and Ben Hecht, however, such material has become only moderately difficult again. Stevenson's efforts to prepare for this apparently supernatural event can be traced through his portrayal and step-by-step embodiment of young Markheim's fear. They begin with the story: Markheim's blinking in the candlelight, his failure to meet the dealer's gaze, his unease—all bits of behavior suggesting fear. They soon become more explicit as Markheim stalls for time, describes the hand glass as a conscience, and after the murder sees himself reflected in many mirrors, thinks his own steps are those of pursuers, takes the sound of rain to be footsteps or whispers—his terrors becoming more and more incarnate, hallucinations merging with reality so that he (and we, equally important) can hardly tell which is which, and "one portion of his mind was alert and cunning, another trembled on the brink of lunacy." The final preparations are the jovial gentleman beating on the outside door and calling the dead man by name, Markheim's palpably false sense of security upstairs, and the comfort wrought in him by the sound of innocent children outside singing a carol. Then comes the "visitant," cool and friendly. To Markheim he was an utterly real person. Though sharing his hysteria, one side of the reader's mind, too, has been carefully kept "alert and cunning," and he knows that Markheim has been hearing and seeing things that weren't there. And the reader knows now what Markheim does not know: that the "visitant" also is not there, except in Markheim's frantic imagination. The success of the author's handiwork is attested by the fact that nobody will question or worry about what becomes of the "visitant" at the end of the story. He never visibly or audibly leaves as he came in; Markheim is simply alone again; neither he nor the reader notices or misses the departure of the "visitant," because there is no departure. In fact Markheim has been alone (with his conscience) from the murder to the entrance of the servant at the close of the story. The apparently supernatural is thus solidly grounded on reality.

The third problem, repentance and its active result, surrender, was the most difficult of all. Strong passions, deep emotion, and, especially, deep emotional change—these things in real life take time, and the short story has no representative space to spare. Will a man who could cold-bloodedly murder with intent to rob repent the act, give himself to the gallows, and find peace, in an hour or so? Offhand, hardly; yet by the time he opens the door to the servant Markheim's change seems natural enough, the only thing to do. To discover Stevenson's ways and means of motivation, we must go back once again to the beginning of the story and pick up the clues he laid down to work upon us unawares. At the start Markheim's manner is engaging, though we know there is something fishy about it; the dealer's ironical reference to the uncle's cabinet (as the source of objects Markheim has previously come to sell) and Markheim's straightforward denial call for sympathy; we feel that the dealer is the stronger of the two men. This is important, for a logical outcome depends on sympathy for Markheim; the reader must not be led to think that Markheim is a hardened criminal or a capricious fool. In a pause, the ticking of many clocks in the shop may be a symbol of the passage of needed (for plausibility) time that the storyteller is not going to be able to recount literally. Markheim's interpretation of the mirror as a conscience before the murder is, after the act, emphasized by his seeing his reflection in dozens of mirrors— "his face repeated and repeated, as it were an army of spies; his own eyes met and detected him." (A lead.) The voices begin: the clocks ticking, a boy's feet running outside, all the town clocks striking three. And the moving candle flame makes the shop a jungle of swaying shadows, into which the slit of daylight from the shop door ajar peers and points "like a pointing finger." The act accomplished, time again looms over Markheim; time stopped for the dead man, time (to escape?) beginning for him. He sees flaws in what he has planned so carefully; he feels the constable's hand on his shoulder, sees "the dock, the prison, the gallows, and the black coffin." Turning over the body of his victim, he remembers his horror as a child at finding famous crimes pictured at a fair. "The thumping of the drums" and "a bar of that day's music" bring "a qualm . . . a breath of nausea, a sudden weakness of the joints, which he must instantly resist and conquer." He forces himself to look at the dead face, remain unmoved. Penitence? "Not a tremor." (This is a strong lead.) But the rain brings voices again. He has a growing feeling that he is not alone in the house, and upstairs at last, goes to pieces again. Weird tricks of nature revealing his crime occur to him: "the hands of God reached forth against sin. But about God himself he was at ease; his act was doubtless exceptional, but so were his excuses, which God knew; it was there, and not among men, that he felt sure of justice." (A remarkable lead.) Then the sense of security with the drawing-room door closed, and the children's singing voices reminding him again of his childhood, now happily—"back again to church, and the somnolence of summer Sundays, and the high genteel voice of the parson . . . and the painted Jacobean tombs, and the dim lettering of the Ten Commandments in the chancel." (Gently reared, after all. An echo of the appealing personality suggested at the start.) All this time we have suffered with Markheim; from the entrance of the "visitant'" to the act of repentance an even stronger pull on our sympathy is exerted. For the "visitant" argues contrariwise, his proffered "help" is to get the money, murder the servant, and slip away. Markheim stoutly refuses, disavows baseness, insists his first crime is to be his last.

"And are my vices only to direct my life [he cries], and my virtues to lie without effect, like some passive lumber of the mind? Not so; good, also, is a spring of acts."

The "visitant" remarks coldly that Markheim's past life promises no great change. Then the doorbell rings, the maid returning. The "visitant" makes a last quick plea, showing the way to escape. But the young man, awakened, desperate, resolved at last, is ready.

Markheim steadily regarded his counsellor. "If I be condemned to evil acts," he said, "there is still one door of freedom open—I can cease from action. If my life be an ill thing, I can lay it down . . ."

And we, too, are completely ready for his simple, courageous words to the servant: "You had better go for the police. I have killed your master."

Beside this strong texture and beautiful workmanship St. John G. Ervine's "The Conjuror" looks shoddy. General comparison of the two stories would be unfair, since Stevenson's aim was enlightenment whereas the Irish playwright wished only to be amusing; but our point of contrast is simply plausibility of material and management, with special reference to a common element in the two stories, the supernatural. "The Conjuror" appeared in 1928; its method is stream of experience, evidently chosen for the irony to be obtained by letting the reader know in advance a story solution which the dull-witted protagonist must think out for himself. One George Butt Bellis, a professional conjuror on vacation in a provincial town, witnesses several remarkable performances by a newcomer to the profession, a magician who calls himself "Diabolo." At first scoffing, Bellis is forced to admire the man's skill; Diabolo does trick after trick for which Bellis can think of no explanation. Finally he offers to assist the performer on stage, with the idea of discovering his technique and showing him up; but in a spectacular manner Diabolo fools Bellis again. Full of naive admiration (and a "strange smell" that he had noticed ever since his first attendance at Diabolo's show), Bellis goes backstage and offers the brilliant magician a partnership in his own act. Diabolo smilingly puts him off. Bellis bubbles over with admiration: "I don't mind telling you you gave me a turn. . . . It didn't seem humanly possible to do that trick." "No," says Diabolo. "It *isn't* humanly possible." And Bellis, seeing at last who his rival is, mutters, and makes for the door.

One can't help feeling that Ervine's chief trouble was attempting too much, for no discoverable reason but whimsey. It is as if the author suddenly said to himself, "Just for ducks I'll put the Devil himself on a stage and let him make a fool of one of these small-time magicians." But he made his task too easy. Ervine's devil doesn't make a fool out of Bellis; the man was a fool before Diabolo went to work on him. How Bellis could ever have performed the most elementary bit of sleight of hand before a group of tolerant friends without mishap is a mystery. So the contest is grotesquely unequal. Bellis's incredible failure to recognize Diabolo, and the author's patronizing air in setting down the poor fool's stream of experience take all the bite out of the story. Having seen who Diabolo is very early, we have to wait interminably for Bellis to find out. When he does find out (by suddenly granted inferential powers quite foreign to him before), the story ends. There is, in fact, no contest. To bring the devil to life and let him be seen in the flesh by many people is a task to tax a Goethe or Marlowe; get him alive for the purpose only of making sport of a nitwit, and all you do really is make a fool out of His Satanic Majesty himself. This may be a delicate British sort of humor that goes over our heads.

The specific means of accomplishment, the facts which should work for agreement, prove no better than the fictional theme. Perhaps you noticed something a trifle, not obscure, but hazy about Stevenson's date and scene in "Markheim": the dialogue, the interior of the shop, and particularly the "skewer-like dagger" seem European and medieval, whereas mention of a Stock Exchange, a constable, the dealer's reference to the hand glass as guaranteed fifteenth-century, and the description of the church recalled by Markheim indicate a later period, This I believe was deliberate and is useful in suggesting fantasy and the universality of the story. In contrast Ervine's date is the present, the setting is "Westsea" (Swansea, Brighton, or another coastal resort), and place names such as Liverpool pin the reader, and the author too, unfortunately, down to a contemporary, strictly English world of reality. But the worst trouble is that infernal smell. It occurs four times in the story, like a character-tag whenever Diabolo appears. Ervine wanted the reader to understand it was the smell of brimstone, but without letting Bellis identify it. The reader got it the first time, Bellis never gets it. But Bellis's far-fetched conjectures about this smell, and its strength and persistence coupled with the failure of anybody else in the crowded theater to notice it or, noticing, do anything about it, simply mislead and befuddle and irritate the reader out of all proportion with the bit of preparation this odor of brimstone could, even if convincingly brought in, have effected. For the reader, first suspecting the identity of Diabolo when the name is used very early in the story, is going to have his suspicions confirmed long before Bellis tumbles, anyway. This is hurried, gawky, journeyman's work, lacking the firm and fine touch that plausibility must have.

No inexperienced writer should attempt even the semblance of the supernatural. Far more necessary, because more generally needed, will be skill in preparation for agreement with natural outcomes by reference to commonplace, unremarkable things. In the following chapter—for suspense and surprise depend on plausibility as counterweights depend on their fulcrum—we shall see how O. Henry performs a minor but veracious, inevitable miracle in "The Gift of the Magi."

12

SUSPENSE AND SURPRISE

Now we have to consider," I said to a class in short-story writing, one day several years ago, "the element of surprise." The words were no sooner spoken than a long thin hiss in some part of the room rose to a piercing whistle, which ended in a tremendous bang. Smoke spread slowly. In the stunned silence, one student in a far corner began to laugh.

That was pretty good timing. In fact, they all thought I had planned it; I thought they had. The truth was, it simply happened. A big towhead Swede had planned something, but not that. During lunch hour, at a joke shop in town he had bought one of those spark-plug bombs with the idea of hitching it to a friend's jalopy. Delayed, he had ducked into the classroom with the bomb still in his overcoat pocket. His seat was down front by a window, under which stood a radiator. Harvard doesn't always recognize mundane things like coat hooks, and the room was filled; naturally the boy draped his coat over the bubbling heater. Some law of physics operated promptly. The lone laugher was the intended victim, who had guessed what had happened. The overcoat was ruined, and it was said that two philosophers upstairs refused to come out from under their desks for an hour.

Anyway, we had an example of surprise. It was worth discussing whether that episode could be properly motivated in character, or whether it would have to be faced as chance. However, anything I could say about surprise afterward was anticlimax.

Suspense and surprise make, together, a major factor of interest in fiction generally, but in the short story particularly, because if properly managed they comprise its main design:

hiss, whistle, bang! There is no letdown, the sequence runs to a single climax. Not, of course, that suspense and surprise are the only elements that awaken and hold interest; we shall find others more permanent if not more pervasive, others much deeper and truer to life. But none more exciting. It is my belief that suspense and surprise create the strongest temporal (that is, while-reading) interest in probably the greatest variety of readers—no mere mild approval or "willing suspension of disbelief," but a spell, an intoxication that will keep a reader's eyes on the story despite opposition by *his* other interests. The two should be studied together, for they are complements; suspense preparing for surprise, surprise relieving suspense that has become intolerable.

Suspense is the reader's emotional reaction to information withheld by the author. Wilkie Collins placed its importance in storytelling high: "Make them laugh, make them cry, make them wait." That is, give them a person they want to read about and a motive (in my terms, somebody or something he wants and can't get, or somebody or something he doesn't want that seems likely to get him)—and then keep them on tenterhooks to see how it comes out. George Pierce Baker, teaching the drama, had his own recipe: "Just get a good character up a tree, and then stand off and throw rocks at him." Serials, comic strips, and soap operas were devised to assist by external means whatever internal suspense the author can manage.

In the structurally simplest narrative, picaresque or episodic, a mere series of adventures in which the hero always wins (but in each of which he might lose), the very length of time and printed space it takes to tell the shortest episode builds up an impatience in the reader, his thoughts outrunning the recorded action, to see how it comes out. The tingling feeling that anything may happen—the sensation described by Stevenson in Shakespeare's coined words, *miching mallecho*—is alone a valuable part of suspense; it resides often in place or atmosphere, a certain kind of light or black darkness, small movements closely visualized, silence, rapid action, or merely a sixth sense of things impending. In these simple forms, pace becomes of importance. To tell all in a sentence, particularly if precursive or summary, denies and aborts suspense; while to prolong the situation beyond the value of the initial interest in the character involved thins down your reader's reaction to apathy. The stronger the appeal exerted by the character in the toils, and the more natural the situation in which he finds himself entangled, and the less disparity between the actual time the action would take and the time you take to tell it— the longer is suspense possible without impairment.

This slowing-down or withholding of information is subject to two provisions. First, it must be legitimate: if you merely suppress information which your telling medium would at that stage of the story logically know or be likely to remark, you risk collapse of illusion and everything that implies. "It happened like this—" has been your unspoken, but heard and agreed-upon, promise to the reader, and it must at all costs be kept. Even if not until the end of the story the reader finds that it might have happened some other way, or, worse yet, might not have happened at all, you will have only yourself to blame. Poorly written mystery stories keep John J. Whodunnit until the proper (for the author) moment simply by suppressing all reference to him. Often they apparently get away with it. Honest craftsmen have better ways of preparing for surprise. Remember your contract with the reader, for by neglect of the second provision governing suspense you will lose him as easily as you can by this trick. The second provision: suspense may not encroach on clarity. Mere confusion or mystification of the reader is not real suspense. It can be readily induced, and one suspects has been, deliberately, by Hemingway among other writers, as a substitute for telling a story. At its best it is bad story, at its worst just bad prose. One can easily see the dishonesty inherent in a muddling of words by comparing the same effect produced by arbitrary restriction of the range of vision, or arbitrary speeding-up of the camera in the movies. In the first Falcon film, for example, we were allowed to see the murder on which the whole tale hung, but the incident was seen only in a blurred flash of light and shadow and showed merely two pairs of legs, one pair buckling, the other running away. The film or story which tries to create suspense by making *all* characters suspects in one way or another is perhaps doing a shade better than muddling, but no more than that; such treatment certainly impairs plausibility, which is built on clarity. Our reader, with time to reflect and his knowledge of life to use as comparison, must be in possession of all facts available to the telling medium, and he should be in possession of suggested lines of conjecture so that he has at all times a (to him) clear and plausible, interesting supposition on which to continue reading; although these lines and this theory may, and usually do, prove to have been wrong.

True suspense is of three kinds. It may be physical in cause, an anxiety about the bodily well-being of a character—say, a girl being pursued by a grizzly suddenly reaches the brink of a cliff. Or the cause may be psychological, resulting in anxiety about the mental or spiritual well-being of a character—as, for instance, our solicitude for Othello made jealous by Iago's insinuations. Or, of course, the cause may suggest both physical and psychological disaster; any old melodrama will be rich in examples, but I like the type in which the villain binds our hero, prone and head-first, to a log in the sawmill, then turns to the heroine and showing his teeth, with his hand on the carriage lever, rasps out: "Now, my proud beauty, be mine or see Harold halved," etc.

But there is a better classification of suspense into two kinds, which might be called simple suspense and complex suspense, depending on from whom information is withheld. A diagram will help to explain what I mean:

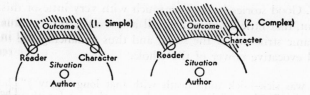

In simple suspense the character shares the reader's knowledge of the character's desperate situation (girl, bear, cliff's edge), and from them both is withheld merely the knowledge of the outcome (that stout sapling below the brink, just out of the bear's reach, and Gamaliel Truebody's saving shot that will echo across the canyon). The Oedipus story is an example of complex suspense; literature is full of others: Beowulf's men seeing, but mistaking, blood on the water while their leader fights the monster in the cave; the child Isaac in the miracle play cheerfully gathering faggots for what Abraham and the audience believe will be his funeral pyre; the mousetrap play in *Hamlet;* the bashful lover in *She Stoops to Conquer* misled by Tony Lumpkin. In complex suspense the reader shares the author's knowledge, withheld from the character, about the true nature of the character's desperate situation, besides being left in the dark about the outcome.

Complex suspense—on the stage called dramatic irony—is potentially the stronger because pity for the character in his blindness is added to anxiety about his fate. Perhaps the strongest management of this factor would combine the physical and psychological characteristics of disaster, and focus first on complex (the character unseeing), then on simple (the character at last seeing but by then helpless) suspense up to the point of climax and solution. But this is suggesting a formula. No writer is wise to sweep up his workshop floor for the last crumb of suspense; artifice and implausibility may be the result. Far better for him to manage skillfully, without over-playing, the kind and amount of suspense natural to his material. Good stories have done much with very little of this element, that little employed for all it is worth, integrated in the organic structure of the story, and thus enhancing the reality and evocative power of the whole.

> I was sick—sick unto death with that long agony ["The Pit and the Pendulum" begins]; and when they at length unbound me, and I was permitted to sit, I felt that my senses were leaving me. The sentence—the dread sentence of death—was the last of distinct accentuation which reached my ears. After that, the sound of the inquisitorial voices seemed merged in one dreamy indeterminate hum.

We have come a long way from this simple, though fundamental and universal suspense wrought by the bodily anguish of Poe's victim of the Inquisition. An able modern writer, familiar with Freud, not only sees a subtler relationship between body and mind than Poe saw—or, seeing, dared to represent—but he is equipped with an assortment of technical and conceptual devices unheard of in the nineteenth century. Franz Kafka's "In the Penal Colony" also deals, basically, with a human suffering in the toils of a human machine. But it begins in a peculiarly terrifying, dispassionate undertone:

> "It's a curious machine," said the officer to the explorer, and despite the fact that he was well acquainted with the apparatus, he nevertheless looked at it with a certain admiration, as it were. It was apparently merely out of courtesy that the explorer had accepted the invitation of the commanding officer to attend the execution of a private soldier condemned for disobedience and insulting a superior officer. Nor did there appear to be great interest in this execution in the penal colony. At any rate, here in the deep, sandy little valley shut in on every side by naked slopes, there were present, besides the officer and the explorer, only the condemned man—an obtuse, wide-mouthed fellow, with neglected face and hair—and a soldier acting as guard. The latter held the heavy chain to which were attached the little chains that fettered the offender's ankles and wrists as well as his neck, and which were themselves linked together by connecting chains. As a matter of

fact, however, the condemned man looked so doglike and sub-missive, one had the impression that he might be allowed to run freely about the slopes, and that, when the execution was about to begin, one would have only to whistle for him to come right back.[1]

The explorer, indifferent, paces back and forth while the officer first goes over the apparatus making last-minute ad-justments, then launches into an eager explanation of its func-tions—an explanation tantalizingly slow, cruelly suggestive with such hints as "Up till now it still had to be worked by hand; now it works entirely alone," "The apparatus has to run for twelve consecutive hours," and with common but grue-some words used for various parts, such as *bed, draughtsman,* and *harrow*—an explanation, in short, which does everything but explain. "The harrow?" asks the explorer with some faint interest. "Yes, harrow," the officer tells him. "It's a suitable name. The needles are arranged as in a harrow and the whole thing is worked like a harrow, although always on the same spot, and much more artistically." Meanwhile the guard has stood drooping, unhearing, callous to everything. The officer is speaking in French, which the soldier does not understand. Neither does the victim. But he, now—this doglike, "wide-mouthed fellow with neglected face and hair"—he now be-gins to make a pathetic effort to follow the explanations of the officer, his eyes following every pointing movement of the officer's hand. And the tardy revelation of the sort of execution this is going to be is synchronized precisely with our horrible realization that the condemned man—he is never called any-thing else, there is no bid for sentimental pity—the condemned man does not know yet what is about to happen to him; *his* enlightenment is to be slower, even, than was the reader's; *he* will know only . . . as . . . it . . . happens.

As examples of complex suspense we may examine two re-cent short stories with a common denominator: both treat the relationship between parents and children, and in both—

[1] From *Partisan Review,* 1941. Reprinted by permission of the publishers.

though in one far more successfully than in the other—dramatic irony is achieved by transmitting the main theme of the story to the reader over the head of the unaware child.

In Mary Porter Russell's "Arrival" a little girl accompanies her mother on a visit to her father, a patient in a tuberculosis sanitarium. Told through the child's stream of experience, the story makes clear very early Joan's ignorance of the nature of the visit and creates pathos, via this ignorance, as we slowly comprehend the desperate situation of her parents. They are deeply in love. The husband is incurably ill. Torn between desire to live together normally again and fear of the consequences, their brave attempts to make light of this crisis, set against Joan's innocently pointed comments and real light-heartedness, are often moving but never quite reach the stature of tragedy.

The situation should be rich in complex suspense, and only close study can reveal why the story does not realize its full possibilities. The child Joan, on whom the success of dramatic irony depends, is vague: apparently only in the second grade at school, she has on the one hand an uncanny ability to find things to say that will make her parents suffer, and on the other hand an astounding obtuseness not to see something, if not all, of her parents' distress and its cause. With Joan remaining ignorant to the end of the story, development of her character remains impossible (contrast the excellent change and growth in Nick Adams at the end of "The Killers" when he learns the truth), and the real story becomes, not hers, but her parents'—and remains untold. We feel that the author has manipulated a situation merely to twist our heartstrings, and as the effect becomes mawkish and unreal, those tough old lashings refuse to be twisted. Honest sentiment grows with overemphasis into sentimentality. The powers of implication are overplayed. The first time Joan didn't understand we got a sizable jolt, but with each succeeding time the jolt decreased in strength, our disappointment that nothing more was coming increased, and by the final paragraph our reaction is merely nausea:

Father was coming with Mother down the sunlit path. His arm was still around her shoulder. "Who lives here, little girl?" he called out, just as if he didn't know Joan at all. Father was great fun.

Now notice the differences in Edwin Granberry's "A Trip to Czardis." Two brothers, children of poor whites, waken at dawn of the great day on which they are to be allowed to visit their father. The author uses space at once to engage the reader's interest and strong sympathy, showing the boys' personalities through talk and the protective bearing of the older. They go downstairs to their mother and breakfast, dressed for the trip. Their uncle comes in, a timber man as their father had been. He asks the mother if she is going to take them "after all." She says yes, the father asked to see them. The boys consider what to take their father as gifts, decide on pomegranates, and climb the tree to get them. The mother says pomegranates won't be needed, and she cautions Jim, the elder, not to bother their father with questions "but speak when it behooves you and let him see you are upright."

Even at this early stage the withholding of information, exactly pacing the information withheld the boys, has created suspense so acute that to stop reading is impossible. The mother is keeping herself under control by sheer will. References to the father set up a strong implication of the truth while at the same time denying an explanation of where he is and what has happened to him: pomegranates not needed, the father absent for a year, some doubt about the boys' going at all; yet the father must be alive, he asked to see them, his word is still law, be careful not to talk too much—but talk, make him proud of you.

Two wagons are going, theirs and Uncle Holly's, but to the boys' questions about this the mother will not reply. On the highway they see other wagons, and many people on foot, all heading for the town; when questioned again, the mother tells the boys to be quiet. She looks straight ahead, speaks to nobody. On the edge of the town they pass along a high brick wall topped by a barbed-wire fence, and the boys see men in trees looking over the wall into a courtyard.

The reader has guessed the truth. Here the older boy, Jim, discovers it:

"We're not to talk today," said Jim. "Papa is sick and we're not to make him worse." But his high, thin voice made his mother turn cold. She looked back and saw that he had grown pale and still, staring at the iron-barred windows of the building. When he caught her gaze, his chin began to quiver and she turned back front to dodge the knowledge in his eyes.[2]

So Jim takes over the mother's task of hushing the younger boy's questions. The moment marks his growth. What was for a short space complex suspense (the reader knowing, both boys ignorant) has become simpler with reference to Jim but remains complex in the case of frail little Dan'l. Will he too, the baby, be made to know? There is no letdown; the tension is all but unbearable.

They go into the building and are led to the father.

His face was lean and gray, which made him look very tall. But his hair was black, and his eyes were blue and mild and strange as he stood up and held the two boys against his body while he stooped his head to kiss their mother.

They sit down together, the father's arms around his sons, the mother close beside him. They talk a little. The parents touch each other. Instead of the boys bringing gifts to their father, it seems he is to give things to them. His watch he gives to

---

[2] This and the quotations immediately preceding and following are from "A Trip to Czardis," by Edwin Granberry. First published in *Forum*. Reprinted by permission of the publishers of *Current History*.

Jim, the chain to Dan'l. Dan'l is shyly pleased. Marching is heard in the corridor, and men come for the father. Uncle Holly leads the boys and the mother away. The crowd outside presses forward to stare, and Jim cringes. The boys get into their mother's wagon.

Leaving their uncle and his wagon behind, they started off on the road that led out of town.

"Is papa coming home with Uncle Holly?" Jim asked in a still voice.

His mother nodded her head.

Reaching the woods once more and the silence he knew, Dan'l whispered to his brother: "We got a watch and chain instead, Jim."

But Jim neither answered nor turned his eyes.

Thus the end of the story is seen to be not only just but merciful. Jim's growth is confirmed by his adoption here of his mother's manner. We have been forced to witness his hard initiation but spared the pain of the revelation to Dan'l of things he could not possibly understand.

The telling is objective, more difficult than stream of experience for effecting dramatic irony (since the objective method denies itself access to characters' thoughts), yet wisely chosen here, I believe, in order to keep the narrative completely free from sentimentality. Though objective, "A Trip to Czardis" is told in language very close to the idiom of its chief characters—a restrained, grave, and quaintly formal prose that lingers like a child's cry in darkness. Note that the two children here, an older and stronger, a younger and weaker, not only give the chance for contrast between them, but the chance to let the older see the truth, his character develop in consequence. As compared with Miss Porter's, the end of this story is conclusive; we know what will happen, whereas the end of "Arrival" seemed only the beginning of something to which there might be several outcomes. Finally, reader reaction to "Arrival," whatever outcome is conjectured, can be only pitying distress; but Granberry's story provides as an end to its intense suffering that sense of relief, of calm, of personal dignity preserved in disaster, of something accomplished, that is at once the solace and the inspiration of high tragedy.

The innocence or naive precocity of children is an attractive field for dramatic irony, but it should be entered only with the greatest care. The ever-present danger of distortion, naturalness sacrificed for effect, can be seen in Jim's final question ("Is papa coming home with Uncle Holly?") in this otherwise grimly honest story. The firm implication has been that Jim knew his father was to be hanged. Knowing that, would he have put his question that way, which allows Dan'l to remain ignorant, or put it at all? One can't be quite sure. Wilbur Daniel Steele's "Bubbles," in which a child's stagey innocence effects the reconciliation of her parents, reveals the formidable mass of treacle always waiting here to bog the undisciplined, the sentimental, or the unwary author.

To the reader, surprise—plausible relief from the tension of suspense—is sheer delight. To him it has a magical quality, and as such is acceptable—that is, not implausible—only because as a rule he doesn't analyze and understand the workings of his own mind while reading. For any well-managed surprise has premonitory roots or leads far back in the story. They were unobtrusive there, the reader noting them but, as the author planned, in some other connection or reference. In O. Henry's "The Gift of the Magi," for instance: on the day before Christmas a young and poverty-stricken couple are concerned over the matter of gifts for each other. The reader notes that Jim lacks a suitable chain for his handsome, inherited watch as Della, who without Jim's knowledge has sold her hair to buy him a gift and got a chain for him, thinks:

With that chain on his watch Jim might be properly anxious about the time in any company. Grand as the watch was, he sometimes looked at it on the sly on account of the old leather strap that he used in place of a chain.

But the reader notes this watch-but-no-chain situation only as a detail of Jim's poverty. It is actually a strong lead toward the coming surprise: for meanwhile Jim has pawned the watch to buy a gift for Della. And the gift turns out to be combs for the hair she has sold to buy him the chain for the watch he has pawned. The surprise springs full-blown on the reader, an inevitable miracle, his subconscious now admitting the supporting presence of the leads, which he did not recognize as leads before.

To the writer, therefore, surprise must be merely the planned and prepared-for revelation of something that was true, or potentially true, from the start—but something that not until now, the moment of revelation, is to be recognized as true by the characters and the reader.

How, exactly, can a true thing go unrecognized as true without the loss of reality or illusion? W. S. Gilbert told us, as Buttercup sang in *HMS Pinafore:*

> Things are seldom what they seem,
> Skim milk masquerades as cream,
> High-lows pass as patent leathers,
> Jackdaws strut in peacock-feathers,
> Black sheep dwell in every fold,
> All that glitters is not gold.

The simple fact is that, because of the equivocality of men's behavior and their fallibility in interpretation of each other, surprise may be based, without the slightest impairment of plausibility, merely upon the difference between appearance and reality. The writer starts (thinking, not yet writing: see 1 in the diagram following), of course, with reality, which to him is not surprising at all. He then considers possible areas of fallacious but plausible appearances with which the story might deal, which seem to conceal, deny, or refute reality. (As in the case of a miser who appears only thrifty, a broad-minded person who appears immoral, or vice versa, depending on the convictions and prejudices of the people around them, through whom the story might be channeled.) Then, making the actually *un*true appearance, at the start of the story itself, as convincing as it seemed to those involved, he works slowly (see 2 in the diagram), and with reference to his own thought processes, backward, toward the area of truth that was his own, concealed starting point.

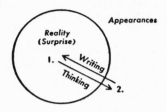

For instance, suppose A and B married, middle-aged, content. Assume that a writer can see both clearly enough, and make both appealing enough to the reader for their happiness in the face of adversity to be a matter of real concern to him, for him to like them in spite of their faults. Let A lose his job and not tell B because of his fear of what she will think of him. Let him continue the deception, leaving the house every day as usual but now to hunt for work, in the hope that he will find it before B knows he lost it. (This of course is simple suspense, and the telling method would be A's stream of experience.) The deception seems to work, but A is running short of funds, no job appears, the time of reckoning draws near, and B's unfailing cheer and her pride in A as a provider are a hollow mockery to him. Suddenly A learns, and without himself having to tell B his desperate situation, that she knew it all along, that she never worried or blamed him except in his imagination, that her good spirits were a spontaneous expression of her confidence in him plus her desire to keep *him* from worrying. Beside such a demonstration of faith, whether or not he got work at the end could be made to seem of little importance; but a carefully wrought story for the general market would see that he got work, and by his own efforts, also motivated far back.

Suddenly A learns . . . But just how? In small Maine-coast houses without central heating, there is often a grille or register in the floor of the bedroom directly above the kitchen, letting heat and the smell of good things cooking—and talk— come up through. In the story I have been describing, called "Don't Tell Your Mother," A learned by this means. Up there in the bedroom changing his clothes, he heard B casually tell their daughter what he had been at such great pains to keep B herself from knowing. The reader knew the grille was there because the story began with A waking up in that bedroom and B's singing and the smell of broiled bacon coming up from the kitchen. Thinking about the story long before it was written, I began with the fact, the reality, of the woman's great faith in and close knowledge of her husband—later to be the surprise. As the area of appearances seeming to deny reality, there was the man's anxiety about finances, his knowledge of his wife's naturally placid temperament, and the humdrum matter-of-factness of long-married relationship—all these allowing him (and the reader) to misinterpret the woman's behavior. The second use of the grille, near the end of the story, transmitted the surprise and reconciled appearances with reality.

It will be seen that up to the moment of revelation the writer must be convincing on two levels, a conscious and a subconscious: the immediate and temporary level of mere appearance that seems reality to the character and the reader (A's theory of successful deception keeping B cheerful); and the now subordinate but eventually dominant level of reality itself (B's deception of A) here made unobtrusive by apparently different reference (B's natural cheerfulness) but actually the motivating lead to the surprise, noted by the reader's subconscious and recalled at the moment of revelation when the two levels become one.

"It fell upon me," says Robert Louis Stevenson, "like a surprise that I had expected." The subconscious does the expecting.

Thus surprise is the supreme test of plausibility. If its motivating roots are allowed—by negligence, underestimation of the reader's perspicuity, or overconscientiousness—to show in their true reference, the revelation leaks out prematurely and the story falls flat. (This explains why writers will spend days on end sweating out the inclusion or deletion of a single word that may make or break surprise.) If, on the other hand, the necessity of motivating roots is ignored, revelation produces not so much surprise as shock—quickly followed by disbelief and perhaps derisive laughter. In short stories, no rabbits may be pulled out of hats. The motivating roots from which your surprise is to spring must be far enough back so that they do not appear to be lugged in as explanation near the moment of revelation, but not so far back that they are forgotten. Often they will be of two kinds: physical or mechanical, such as the grille, and psychological, that is, having to do with the personalities involved; and although the second kind is more important, neither should be neglected.

In general advice to writers it is easy to make too much of surprise, for the element was exaggerated by O. Henry and is still overworked by his followers and imitators in popular magazines. Surprise, like suspense, should not be cultivated for its own sake. It is a fundamental ingredient of the popular, oral source of the short story, the told anecdote. But the literary ancestor of the short story, suggesting stronger emphasis on individual character, less on manipulation of material, has bred stories of deeper emotional appeal to the discerning reader, stories that are, literally, truer to life. Slavish attention to surprise as a final twist or fillip will result in formularizing, which may be financially profitable in the general markets, but will win no prizes. On the other hand, scornful disregard of this factor of interest may result in the sort of photographic realism (as it does, for instance, in some of James Farrell's stories) which, though admired by a small group of literati, cannot in the long run prove emotionally stimulating or satisfying to many readers. The best plan is to steer a middle course between these extreme attitudes, using surprise where you can naturally, without going far out of your way to cultivate it as an end in itself. This was done by Katharine Brush in "Night Club" and "Good Wednesday," in both of which surprise was skillfully planned and executed and plays a small but important part. William Faulkner's "A Rose for Emily" is an example of expert motivation of a surprise so violent as to be almost incredible.

13

CHARACTERIZATION

N OBODY should generalize about ghosts walking and corpses coming alive in print. This is what happens, but nobody knows just how. Some writers seem to snatch their characters out of thin air, with no conscious reference to anybody they ever heard of; slap any old names to them, and by a few quick casual strokes that leave most of their personalities unexpressed, make them vivid and notable. Others must document, correlate, catalogue their fictional people, laboriously selecting externals indicative of needed traits, and if not literally transcribing living humans bodily to paper, at least building composites all of whose parts are drawn straight from life. Each writer must find his own method, and a good result will justify almost any means. Yet the apprentice will do well at least to begin thinking about characters in terms of the people he has known. He need not search for the quaint, the eccentric, or even the unusual figure. In fact, he had better not, for if he waits until he finds such characters he may never write stories. Better to start with anybody at all (the kid across the street that he grew up with, the girl across the car aisle that he never saw before today and will never see again), remembering and observing these individuals more closely. There may be the making of a short-story character in everybody that breathes.

Not that the character comes out on paper a facsimile of the person observed. And not that it doesn't take, usually, the hardest sort of work to create the finished article. But the prospects look brighter as soon as we view the range of material; and what a writer needs is bright prospects. I mean, it is the impression made on a creative mind by an observed human figure, rather than the details of the figure itself, that will be important in this business of ghost raising.

To make the prospects seem better yet, let us note a limitation—a specification, rather, of the short-story form, most attempts to pass which will prove futile. When we think of an outstanding novel, we think as a rule of its central human figure—Anna, Swann, Henchard, Jim, Heyst, Becky Sharp; it is the protagonist that somehow makes the book memorable. James Joyce applied a similar criterion to the short story, believing that the form should deal with a single figure and culminate in an epiphany, or revelation, of this person at a significant moment of his life. It is too soon to say surely, but Joyce's seems an esoteric view, rationalizing his own considerable achievement in *Dubliners,* at the same time confusing the short story with the larger composition and hobbling it. Barring the short-story character that has induced familiarity by repeated appearances, such as Sherlock Holmes, Jeff Peters, or Mr. Glencannon, what short-story protagonist epitomizes the narrative in which he appears, so that we think of it and of him as, virtually, one? Maupassant's "Tallow Ball," perhaps, and a few others. But who remembers even the name of the man who picked up a piece of string, of the wife who slaved for ten years to accumulate the "value" of a paste necklace? Who *is* the protagonist of "The Killers"? Is he the story? What personal characteristics of, say, the young "I" of Joyce's own "Araby" do you recall, besides his anger at the end? Is he the story? Is it not youth in general deluded by his dreams, rather than any particular individual, that we remember? Is there, anywhere in the whole of short-story literature, a single depiction of human nature bodied forth in a personality of stature comparable to the immortals of long narratives: Odysseus, Don Quixote, Robinson Crusoe, Macbeth?

The reasons for this difference are not sprung from the fact that, for the most part, we must compare the work of lesser with that of greater writers; or from the fact that the short story is young yet, while the novel, the epic, and the drama are old. The reasons are two, and neither disparages the short story. The less important is simply a matter of length and depth. No right-minded critic would look for a system of ethics in a sonnet, the sweep and action of a landscape in a miniature, counterpoint in a song. The feat of short art is that it can suggest so much by so little, that it can transcend space and time limitations and make every stroke tell—perhaps twice; and for what its product lacks in range and depth it may more than compensate in impact. It is a single blow, to achieve which—and here is the second and more important reason—the writer must assemble, integrate, and coördinate a group of forces in a manner, and toward an end, unknown to most of the tellers of long stories. Integration and coördination may level all members of the group to equivalent, or nearly equivalent, status; characterization taking its place merely as one unit in the team. The end is the sudden sharp conveyance of an idea. Properly timed and directed, no one factor dominant but all working as one, that stroke can touch the heart.

So we may leave the eccentrics to the cartoonists, the heroes to the poets, turning instead to all the plain everyday folk we happen to know.

But are they worth the trouble? And, once really observed and finally understood, what to do with them? Ghost raising needs breaking down into parts: conception and portrayal.

Nothing said above about the lack of great protagonists in short stories should be construed as minimizing the power of short-story characterization in general. To the reader, its characters are the story. Perhaps he will not admit this fact. He believes that stories are about events. If you ask him to retell one he has read or seen on the screen, he will begin "This girl falls in love with this boy, but he is in the Navy and gets sent to the South Pacific . . ." paraphrasing the incidents and ignoring the kind of personalities involved. But it is actually,

I believe, the lovely girl and the plucky, lonely boy that have kept him reading or watching, comparing their experience with and applying it to his own, and getting rest and refreshment, feeling pity and fear, thereby. And this is how we too should rate characterization. Fiction is primarily about people, human beings living out a sequence of action and reaction to illustrate a human idea, in compliance with readers' passionate and perennial curiosity about their fellow men. Editors, publishers, literary agents are agreed that if a story has vivid characters, lack of other merits will not prevent its being read with satisfaction. This truth was well stated by Wilkie Collins, who without any very profound understanding of character or very impelling or subtle portrayal, still succeeded in being a consistently good storyteller:

It may be possible to present character successfully without telling a story; but it is not possible to tell a story without presenting characters: their existence, as recognisable realities, being *the sole condition* on which the story can be effectively told. The only narrative which can hope to lay a strong hold on the attention of readers is a narrative which interests them about men and women —for the perfectly obvious reason that they are men and women themselves.

Now this is a point of some importance. Probably the greatest single cause of failure by the inexperienced to produce evocative stories is—not, of course, ignorance of rhetorical principles or technique, not lack of imagination in the usual sense of fancy, not difficulties with plotting (that colossal bugbear), not even imperfect powers of observation; the cause lies rather in the inability or unwillingness of a young writer to even try to satisfy this hunger in readers to read about people. Ability and willingness follow interest, which I suspect must be congenital—though weak interest can be stimulated. But this is the one area of creative writing that cannot be taught. A man uninterested in people can circle the globe without finding anything to write about; another, having that impetus, will produce book after readable book without leaving his home, his room, even his bed.

Here, in fact, a conscientious young would-be writer may reach an apparent dead end. He has, let us say, this itch to write, make words on paper, see the page fill with stuff that will mean to somebody else what he meant. And let us say he has this interest in people—even those, perhaps especially those, that he sees right around him. And he is not to be fooled by the false hopes held out by mere fancy, by escape into unknown and therefore more attractive life than his own; or by imitation of successful writers. But he wants above all *to be himself*. He frets at the notion of truckling to readers' tastes in characters. He sees a good many stories in print that have done that, and the characters seem to him rubber-stamped, custom-made. He wants to be himself, to express himself, portray people as they appear to him regardless of their appearance to readers. Yet when he tries to do so, an editor or instructor says his people lack "bite" or "snap" or appeal. There is something wrong, but he can't see what it is. He has worked hard, presented the truth as he sees it, than which nobody can do more. It is an impasse. And here he may conclude that editors buy only big names, instructors give high grades to those who pander to their prejudices or to those who got high grades last time; that nobody can really tell what readers want, and if you could it would be intellectual prostitution to let them have it; and the whole thing is a racket, etc.

I think he is right, up to a point, and then quite wrong.

Some authors, certainly, have held this view of the inviolate creative ego. Many have died inviolate, unprinted. Those with independent means manage to hold their own; and a few, particularly in our novelty-loving country, have set up as a coterie of intransigents and become a legend. Thomas Beer said of Stephen Crane that he died "without discovering that successful literature is mainly the conciliation of stupid people." This seems an overstatement of something very hard to put accurately. Crane is certainly "successful" now. Perhaps he had made a greater discovery than Beer suspected. Beer admired Crane the realist and was trying hard, if somewhat awkwardly, to praise him, a man who would never cater to readers' tastes at a time when O. Henry and Richard Harding Davis were doing that and making money. But Beer himself conciliated readers to the extent of a series of popular short stories. Is he any less of a craftsman for that? Is Bernard De Voto a poorer historian or critic because, now and then when he needs the money, he writes an able romance or mystery for popular consumption? Was Shakespeare a lesser playwright when, ready with the subtlest, most moving, loftiest themes in our literature, he held back on all that, making sure first with his ghosts and his witches that the drunks in the pit would not start throwing oranges?

Writing, I concede, must be satisfying to the writer. As Ernest Renan said, "We should never write save of that which we love." We must live our stories, believe them if we expect a reader to believe, and feel that we are ourselves and are giving our best. But Renan's statement might hold if it had been, "We should never write save *for* that which we love." The writer who deems financial profit his ultimate aim will achieve in himself an adaptability to readers' tastes amounting to what the less mercenary will call pandering—and will still preserve his self-respect. Even the man with the highest aesthetic ideals has a right to feel with Don Marquis that "money is pretty welcome if you can manage to connect with it," and feeling thus, be glad enough, not to pander, but to compromise This, surely, is what Shakespeare did and what others, less gifted but no less honest, have done or tried to do: giving in to readers here but requiring something in return there. Conciliation, appeasement, like pandering, imply surrender of integrity. A compromise is give and take, fifty-fifty. And if readers are "stupid," as Thomas Beer and the *avant garde* contend, those arrogant souls have cause therein for humility and gratitude: readers as wise and intelligent as they are would hardly bother to read them.

But where our conscientious, creative but inviolate young ego went chiefly wrong was in his failure to see the reader as an instrument essential to the expression of himself. Sound does not exist without an eardrum on which it may vibrate. So words have no meaning unless they are read. Obviously, then, they must be written to be read: the first compromise. The writer has rights, and he must guard them. A reader, who has paid for a story, has certain rights too. All he wants is his half of that compromise. A writer really interested in people will be willing to give him that half, if he can find out what it is. For readers are, after all, people.

The search, then, in conception of characters is for common ground. Not for any sort of dummy that will catch a reader's eye. Not, on the other hand, for any sort of person that may be literally true, or may seem literally true to the writer's ego on a certain day, or may merely catch his ego's eye. The search is for characters within the range of the writer's experience that the reader may find germane to his own experience. We might as well call this search what it is, a search for universality.

Extremes of character concepts can be represented on the one hand by a personified abstraction (a single trait exclusively epitomizing a person, who is usually so named: Sloth, Folly, Wit) in a morality play; and on the other hand by an exact transcript of a living individual, such as we are inclined to feel has been sometimes committed to paper by Dreiser, James Farrell, or Thomas Wolfe. By citing these examples out of five hundred years of story-writing I do not mean to imply any orderly historical progression from abstraction to transcript. On the English stage there was, perhaps, a slow and uneven development from abstraction to type or vocation (Peddlar, Palmer) to individual (Tamburlane, Falstaff) paralleling growth in technique and content; and this haphazard evolution may have been reflected to some extent in the kinds of people chosen to impersonate the ideas of prose fiction. But the Industrial Revolution, Darwin, Naturalism, and Freud exerted a push toward literal transcription in fiction unfelt by the drama. And we had characters as late as the nineteenth century such as Tiny Tim, Pearl of *The Scarlet Letter,* Simon Legree, who were little more than personified abstractions, just as we continue to have them (Snow White, Superman, The Lone Ranger, almost any detective) in various story forms today. I mean that both extremes are undesirable oversimplifications, the first oversimplifying the material itself, the second oversimplifying the creative function.

One or the other of these extreme concepts may look attractive, depending on the temperament of the young writer in need of a method. Either may give him the comforting assurance of definiteness, of specified limits. In the one case, he can resolve, just determine a single quality or trait that will stand roughly for the personality as a whole—a symbol, as it were; and lean hard on that. In the other, just photograph. It could be fun, as easy as that.

But of course both are dangerous, as almost any test of their products will show. The abstraction is too simple to be real, too good—or too bad—to be true. The transcript is actually too true to be true. Having inevitably many conflicting traits which often seem to hold it in a sort of implausible paralysis, it is, like its prototype, a unique individual—if not a monstrosity—too strange to draw reader sympathy and usually too complex to carry significance. Neither conceptual method promises to find common ground between the experience and ego of the writer and the experience and ego of the reader. The reader wants somebody a shade familiar, that is, understandable, yet fresh. The writer needs somebody he knows well enough to draw vividly, yet adaptable to his meaning. Both are agreed that whatever is created and presented must be done, here in the short story, quickly; and the writer knows besides that it may have to be done indirectly and subject to several considerations and conditions, of which the reader is ignorant and must be allowed to remain so.

Will not some mean between the two extremes, theoretically at least, suggest the solution? Instead of a complete transcript, a few details observed in some living person, or in two or more persons now fictitiously combined in one, may lend reality lacked by the mere abstraction; and a chief but not exclusively dominating trait, perhaps observed in still another living person, perhaps unobserved in real life but sprung from one's general knowledge of human nature, may give the reader something understandable with reference to his own experience, at the same time permitting the writer to establish his meaning.

This is a suggestion, by no means a law. It is synthetic, *ex post facto,* and in itself oversimplified. Conception of characters without any conscious analysis undoubtedly is better, if the product shows living details, some trait or faculty that the reader can grasp, and integration of these elements in the theme of the story. I believe—nobody can be sure—that many short-story characters have been conceived, deliberately or not, in this way. But let the suggestion be taken merely as a starting point based on essentials. People who are made to represent emotions shared by the writer and reader do make characters; characters, and only characters, will make story. They do not make all of story, but they start it and with help from other evocative factors they keep it going. The essentials that will launch us on our way are observed details and a human trait.

Each of us stands in daily living as if at the center of widening concentric circles of living people. Those radially nearest are of course our families and closest friends, while the others range out to remote limits of chance acquaintance or persons merely seen in passing. Composition of the intermediate circles is always changing as we lose track of old friends, meet new ones and come to know them. These concentric circles of human beings—plus some general knowledge of human nature drawn from reading and past experience—are our basic supply of characters in the rough; or, rather, our supply of the component parts of characters. Our subconscious may add to them, fixing certain types—from no known source—in our minds. Our heritage and environment may make some of them seem more important, more worth writing about, than others; may even make us ignore others and take on certain attitudes toward those we hold important that change them from what they are to what they only seem to be. Still, these shifting, widening circles of observed humanity can be our only primary and factual source of human material. Luckily it is inexhaustible.

The trouble with the outer circles is that we cannot see them very clearly. But effort may heighten clarity. Writers are confirmed and unashamed gossips, eavesdroppers, and kibitzers. The trouble with the inner circles, and particularly with the center (ourself), as material, is that familiarity has dulled perception while prejudice and mild complexes, often operating in us unknown to us, emotionally distort what should be positionally our clear view and impair our ability to portray character that will draw reader interest and sympathy. We may think we know all about ourselves and our nearest friends, but from the reader's point of view we do not. For what we know about this inner group is radically distorted by pride, ambition, fear, and a dozen other personal and special attributes that we ignore or take for granted but the reader knows nothing of. In short, perspective is here usually impossible, and perspective is necessary if a reader is to find in a character what he needs: enough of universal man to make a part or piece of that character recognizable as a part or piece of himself. Thus, as we should make a positive effort to see the remote circles more closely, in order to make characters drawn from those positions intelligible to a reader, so here in the nearer groups— and the nearer they are to us, the more need—we must exert negative pressure to delete bias and prejudice from our too-special knowledge, in order to make characters from this region appealing to the reader's sympathies.

Portrayal of character recalls us at once to technique. We know and should here remind ourselves of a general principle basic in narrative. First: least effective in revealing character, even though it saves space in the short story, will be a statement about a personality: such as, *John was stubborn*. This because, though narrative in form, being synoptic, being based on the authority of the author alone, who thus becomes visible and distracting, it is expository by intent and deprives the reader of his cherished right of inference and his pleasure in suspense. Second: more effective in revealing character will be an unassociative but detailed record (often as economical of space as the summary statement above) of talk or action: such as, *John stood up*. Because here the reader gets the feel of an immediate scene, as if on the stage, the stage of his imagination, and can identify himself with it undistracted by general statements or the presence of an author. Third: most effective in revealing character will be the not only detailed but associative record of talk or action implying the trait of character which the summary statement in the first example postulated, and which the unassociative though detailed action in the second example needed further space to make clear: such as, *John stood barring the door. "Okay," he said again. "Just try it."* Because, allowing inference, holding suspense, it conveys a trait of character (stubbornness) indirectly by integrating it in the continuing action.

But characterization is not something that can be sprinkled over human figures, bringing them to life. The thumbnail sketch or description upon first appearance of a character was never natural, never really integral, never anything but more exposition in disguise. It assaults the reader with a catalogue, all of which irritates him and most of which he forgets. Equally specious is the leitmotiv or descripto-characterizing tag lugged in whenever a certain person speaks or acts. The practice of the general principle noted above must become second nature. It will become so only when the writer has got to know his fictitious person so thoroughly that he could predicate convincingly the character's behavior and speech under any conceivable circumstances within or beyond the range of the story. That is, only when, to all story intent and purposes, the writer has imaginatively become the character.

The naming of characters should be done as early as possible and with some care. Obviously to be avoided are the easiest and commonest names: Tom Smith, Dick Brown, Harry Jones —because names can help to define personality and these have lost suggestiveness through overuse. Actual names, for equally obvious reasons, had better not be used. At the other extreme from the too ordinary, and also objectionable, is the sort of name so queer that it sounds like a character's name rather than a person's. The best source of names is a directory, polling list, graveyard, or roster of people at the scene of the story. Such names can be mixed or slightly changed, and they should be. The name chosen for a character should suggest the personality, if only in sound. "Soames Forsyte" is an instance of expert naming. "Becky Sharp" is perhaps too obvious for readers today. "Scattergood" is ridiculous.

Portrayal of character, again, in appearance and personality must be instrumented by the telling method of the story. Hence the kind of people to be presented is often one factor—the nature of the theme, the locale, the time span available are others—to be considered in choosing a telling method. For instance, any narrator—protagonist, participant, or mere witness—who has not only a seeing eye constantly trained on the story but the power to analyze what his eye sees and express it, will help greatly to interpret and clarify complex, introspective, low-toned or inarticulate people whose natures don't show on the surface; and the plausible but eventually wrong analyses of such people by a personal telling medium offer rich material for stories. Objective telling, on the other hand, will facilitate swiftness in presenting simpler types and individuals, those to whom action is more important than thought—the extroverts, the picturesque and readily pictured. It must be borne in mind here, too, that if there is a narrator he may see everybody but himself; of course he *may* see himself, but if he looks deliberately you may be doing something to his personality that you do not intend to do. He may analyze everybody, including himself, rightly or wrongly, within the limits of his plausible powers of analysis and the reader's willingness to read a dull sort of story. Interpretation by a character is only a little better, with reference to reader interest, than interpretation by the visible author. Objective telling has its limitations as well: if strictly consistent, it will see everything that a fly on the wall could see, but must select for record only what is revealing or helpful to its purpose; for it will neither record thoughts, analyze character, nor interpret behavior.

But just how, then, you have a right to ask, can a character be brought into a story and appear to the reader alive and convincing, yet remain amenable to the writer's needs of consistent technique, swiftness, and the demonstration of the story's meaning? You have the right to ask, but I haven't the right, much less the ability, to say. Presentation and integration of character in story could hardly be tabulated: personal qualities, details of behavior, themes to be dramatized, and methods of approach constitute such a vast diversity of material that the list would be as long as the total number of short-story characters and ideas it attempted by classification to reduce. Granting the possibility of such a list, the only effect on somebody who wants to write a story would be stupefaction or suggested imitation. The fact is, ghost raising, like the interest in humanity which inspires it and impels it, can only be talked about; it cannot be explicitly taught. As in choosing between writing blind and finding a method, here you have to travel alone. You have to try and try and try, and fail and fail and fail, and weep and pray and sweat, and then try again. When at last you succeed, you will know it long before some editor tells you so.

14

PLACE AND ATMOSPHERE

I never saw a moor,
I never saw the sea;
Yet I know how the heather looks,
And what a wave must be.[1]

EMILY DICKINSON's wistful surmise will not suffice the story-teller. A little poetry in his soul—enough to let him discover beauty in unlikely corners and work easily with images—is good for him; but he must try to be content with a little. For story settings he will do well to confine his efforts to places he has seen. It is only natural for him to want to do the opposite. Perhaps New York is more fun, in fancy, than his home town; and having read books, seen films, talked with those who have lived in the great city and know all about it, why shouldn't he try? But in so doing he is confusing his function as a writer with his pleasurable habits as witness or reader, he is trying to experience the reader's vicarious living while he, as a writer, should be providing it. He may have his stolen fun, but the New York that he creates second-hand will not usually give any to a reader. His home town may seem dull to him, not worth writing about. If it does, there may be something the matter with him as a writer; but this needn't be fatal. He can either look closer at the spot he really knows and persuade himself to see there things worth writing about that he never saw before, or perhaps he can go and try New York. Only if New York proves on acquaintance no better, is his trouble fatal. Then, impervious to place, he is incurable. There is little likelihood of his being able to make a reader see a locality which

---

[1] From *The Poems of Emily Dickinson*, edited by Martha Dickinson Bianchi and Alfred Leete Hampson. Reprinted by permission of Little, Brown & Company.

does not move himself enough to make him want to reproduce it.

Next in importance, in fact, to the sort of imagination that is really curiosity about and sympathy with people, comes this awareness of the emotional power of place, weather, atmosphere—we have no exact word—in a story. Satisfying characterization is largely a matter of the understanding. Convincing setting is almost wholly a matter of the senses—the result of acutely active observation of, or natural impressionability to, the sense stimuli, which identify localities and make them exist in the reader's mental senses as if he were there. It is the product of something approaching total recall, then of scrupulous selection.

Even assuming these requisites, because of space limitations and the necessary swiftness of the short story, getting place and atmosphere on paper may be the toughest sort of problem for the deliberate, careful writer. It requires first the creation of a real other-whereness at the start of the story, where much else more important must also appear, and then its maintenance throughout, despite increasing demands by those more important elements and despite accelerating pace. For setting, though subordinate, mere background, must be functionally clear; it must be authentic in the (perhaps) ignorant reader's view, not merely accurate in the general sense; and it must be integrated in the story.

Maupassant could begin "The Piece of String" with four hundred words of unassociative description of peasants arriving at a town on market day—with no central character named, with a sort of mass action but as yet no story motive, with apparently no story yet begun or even impending. As a rule we may not do this today. The reader expects both more and less than the bracketed setting with which "The Piece of String" begins. Such an opening in inexperienced hands usually means that no story existed, even in the writer's head, at that point; he began with description hoping that a story

220

would come. Professional writers sometimes begin that way, too, but when the story comes they push those opening pages off the worktable into the trash basket. Most readers today want, at once, at least one individual figure in a recognizable scene, either living as a part of it or at least observing it; and a motive for his presence or action. Having these they care nothing for descriptive completeness; lacking them, they will hardly be placated by anything else and are bewildered, bored, or irritated by attempted substitutions.

Of course this reader expectancy complicates the writer's task enormously. He has a part of the world (the smaller the better) to make clear and convincing without any apparent means of doing the job. He is aware that only the small appeal of his title has brought a reader to the point of scanning idly his opening sentence, and an equally small *un*favorable reaction may lose him; that this capricious reader is not only ignorant of all the facts of place, situation, and character necessary for an understanding of the story, but here at the beginning is emotionally cold, critically alert if not hostile; and that mere understanding of any facts will be futile unless *at the same time* his interest is awakened. Vagueness will irritate him, a mass of details will send him packing.

But if the writer will imagine himself a reader—he must be able to do that, for he cannot write any story without imagining himself another person, that is, a character—the situation will not prove so bad as it seems. Seeing what he would need as reader, as writer he may perceive ways of meeting these needs.

Let it be a recognizable place on earth, if he imagines himself representative of a great majority of readers; whether a place identified by name or not is not important. If it must be a dream place for, say, a fantasy—one hopes for the beginner it need not —let him at least force himself to know it as thoroughly as he knows his own bedroom and think of it always in terms of specific details—the very details that through familiarity he has perhaps lost touch with in his bedroom, but of which a reader would have to be apprised. Let it be a formal garden with peacocks, a marble hall, a baronial mansion, the Duchess's dinner table; or a tenement, the town dump, a sweat shop, a submarine in action—always provided he has been there and would know his way around even if he were blind, deaf, and dumb. Whether it be a fresh scene or not has no bearing, for the more unusual it is, the more need for establishment of some familiar basis, the greater the strain on his portrayal of it; and if it is well known he will have to make it seem fresh anyway. Let him live imaginatively in this place before beginning to write of it, knowing he will have to throw most of it aside. The little left, though, will be his setting.

This is as if to say that the choice of place in a short story is free. Of course it is not. Besides being dependent on the range of the writer's experience, choice is dependent on his own feeling. A man can no more pick a remembered spot out of the air and say "I will use that" than he can pick any person of his acquaintance to write about. The writing itself has got to be an emotional experience—fun, if you like. A writer has got to want to recreate a place, and enjoy the act of creation as he would enjoy living there if, after long absence, he returned to a favorite locality of his dreams. Most of us know well several places, enough for us to classify them as I classified in widening concentric circles the groups of known people. And what is true of our range of personal acquaintance may also be true here: the inner group of places, subject to prejudice, may seem too humdrum to afford the needed emotional stimulus; the distant groups too little known for us to bring them back to vivid being. Whereas some middle group—places once known well but from which time and space have removed us—may perhaps still be clear enough in our memory, give us the necessary perspective, and provide a sort of nostalgia, bitter or sweet, that will make writing of them a moving experience in itself. Thus the young writer, for instance, may find what he wants not in his present environment—the college he is attending, the job he now fills, the house and neighborhood he now lives in—but in the school he went to several years ago, the town from which he and his parents moved, or his summer home. Let him search and find such a place, and settle down there, comfortingly sure in detailed knowledge and a little excited by his return: he will be the better able to impart both information and excitement to his reader. Finally, choice of place depends usually on a previous interest in or choice of character. But this is no very serious restriction. A story idea may entail lifting somebody out of his natural environment and setting him down among contrasting conditions. And it seems unlikely that one should know a living person well enough to make a character out of him or part of him, without knowing also, through his senses, his environment.

Therefore, although choice of place is not quite so free as it might appear, there is room enough in anybody's experience for many scenes, many stories. We cannot, fortunately, stop living. With every day lived, experience grows. It grows faster by our deliberate effort, becomes more comprehensible as we reflect upon it; but it will grow anyway, whether we seek growth or not. Suppose we are standing on the observation platform at the tail of a moving train. We can't look ahead, don't want to, knowing that what lies ahead is coming into our sight soon enough. As what lay ahead comes first into sight, for a moment it is blurred by speed, dust, too-great proximity. Then for a moment, before being blurred again by distance and fading into oblivion—for an instant the shabby farmhouse with the new red truck in the yard, the grade crossing, the children pouring out of school, the chasm of a city street, the river crossed—in that blink of eternity what was unseen ahead, then blurred and soon to be gone, now stands magically, magnificently clear. Let us catch and hold it, if only we can, forever.

It won't be too hard. Portrayal of place, like that of character,

223

lies ready to be implemented by the telling method of the story. In a sense we do not have to consider ourselves concerned in this matter at all. If there is a personal telling medium, he would naturally say something of place as he felt it; all we need do is act as motor to make sure he says enough to make it clear to the ignorant reader, and as brake lest he become—since after all he is probably familiar with the spot—unnaturally informative. Use of the teller's emotional state, a quickener of all the senses, will help here; a man under stress will see as new and notable what before has been too familiar to be noticed. If we are in the protagonist's stream of experience, of course the same principle holds. And if the telling is objective, it is that figurative fly on the wall, that anonymous, surface observer, which is our channel; that and the bare facts carrying overtones of motive and meaning. But in whatever medium, the bare facts must be the few, chosen, sharp details—the distillation of our long meditative sojourn in that place: nothing general, nothing abstract, every least bit particular, concrete, under the circumstances of situation and character unique. For here we are using description by indirection, and description is by nature selective. What we omit about a place matters nothing so long as the minute amounts told are distinctive and functionally important to the story.

The beginning is the crucial spot. It is here that illusion can slowly, bit by bit, build up into solid other-whereness. Contrast these two beginnings:

She looked over the rail.

Within confines of grammatical form it could scarcely be worse. Who is she? How old? What direction do her eyes take? Is it a bridge, a ship, a race track, a theater balcony, an altar rail she looks over? What is she looking over any rail for? Is the look bored? Eager? Angry? Does she want help? Is she seasick? But no amount of explanation will do any good. It's all off. The beginning may tell only a little, as this does, but that little must either be very interesting or very clear. This is neither.

Everyone else in this dressing-room had gone. Linda sat down with a sigh and began to unwind the fake muscles from her legs.

Smell the grease paint? Feel tired, forlorn, wanting to be alone? Sick of pretense, of trying hard at something and seeing it flop? *Are* there such things as fake muscles? Want to read on and find out?

Both of these excerpts are from students' manuscripts. Investigate the beginning of every story you read; see whether or not it has this magic touch compounded of specific, concrete clarity of place in minute amounts, and a little interest. Here are a few openings of published stories:

He had been asleep! He had been asleep! And now maybe the Holy God had come. Maybe he had already come! But surely—For a moment he could not see down there, though he had his eyes already to the crack.[2]

Notice the vague "he," confusion resulting. Notice the repetition, taking badly needed space and impairing human interest. "The crack" is the only concrete detail, and it does not make the scene clear.

At least once in my life I have had the good fortune to board a deserted vessel at sea.[3]

There is more here than appears. "Vessel" seems general, but "deserted vessel" specifies. Human interest depends on "I," rather weak support. But "the good fortune to board a deserted vessel at sea" is irresistible.

It is likely that at some time in his extreme youth Junius Peabody was introduced to those single-minded creatures, the ant and the bee. Doubtless he was instructed in the highly moral lessons

[2] From "The Little Him," by Ernestine Magagna. First published in *American Prefaces,* June, 1940. Reprinted by permission of the author.

[3] From "The Yellow Cat," by Wilbur Daniel Steele, in *Land's End and Other Stories;* Harper & Brothers, publishers.

they are supposed to illustrate to the inquiring mind of childhood. But it is certain he never profited by the acquaintance—indeed the contemplation of such tenacious industry must have afflicted his infant consciousness with utter repugnance. By the time he was twenty-seven the only living thing that could be said to have served him as a model was the jellyfish.[4]

No scene, no character yet; mere chit-chat. Human interest must survive this garrulous storyteller's academic prose about abstract qualities in a person who seems unappealing. "The ant," "the bee," and "the jellyfish" as concrete details have only a rhetorical connection with the story.

I knew him from the days of my extreme youth, because he made my father's boots; inhabiting with his elder brother two little shops let into one, in a small by-street—now no more, but then most fashionably placed in the West End.[5]

It took skill to introduce four persons and two aspects of a specified place, all in one sentence that also arouses interest in the relationships between cobbler and customer.

During the day the Marne was green, but at twilight the soft haze of falling evening obscured its face with a film of blue, like smoke from an autumn bonfire.[6]

A very clear picture, but with nobody there to see it—except the author.

It's a story they tell in the border country, where Massachusetts joins Vermont and New Hampshire. Yes, Dan'l Webster's dead—or, at least, they buried him. But every time there's a thunderstorm around Mansfield, they say you can hear his rolling voice in the hollow of the sky.[7]

[4] From "Jetsam," by John Russell, in *Where the Pavement Ends*; Harper & Brothers, publishers.
[5] From "Quality," by John Galsworthy, in *The Inn of Tranquillity;* Charles Scribner's Sons, publishers.
[6] From "Responsibility," by Thomas Boyd, in *Points of Honor;* Charles Scribner's Sons, publishers.
[7] From "The Devil and Daniel Webster," by Stephen Vincent Benét, in *Thirteen o'Clock,* copyright, 1936, by Stephen Vincent Benét. From: *Selected Works of Stephen Vincent Benét,* published by Rinehart & Co., Inc.

This is explicit at once, and implicit too: the image connecting the voice of the dead orator with present thunder is exactly right for the story.

> "You ought to change your clothes, pa."
> "What you in such a hurry to get my clothes changed for?"
> "Well, you want to be ready when George comes in, don't you?"
> "Aw, he won't get in today. How can he get the car through all this snow?"
> "He will, too. Didn't they invite us out there?" [8]

By the most deft and yet natural dialogue imaginable Miss Suckow has indicated locality, the age of her characters, their relationship to each other and to other characters mentioned, and the situation impending.

> A drift of hard small leaves clicked from the live oak at the main gate of the penitentiary. The man Adams looked at the sky and turned up the collar of his coat. Then he turned it down again, with the uncertainty of a man for whom decisions have been made too long. The sky was gray, mottled with the harsh blue of November. [9]

The details are sharp here, but more numerous than necessary. After the title, the second sentence makes it clear that Adams is leaving, not entering the penitentiary; the third sentence is superfluous. Human appeal is strong. The two sense impressions, hearing the leaves and seeing the sky, are both what the man would notice and what the reader needs for picture.

> The fall had been dry and the giant milkweed pods broke early in September. Lean Neck Creek dried to a thread, and all the springs under the moss were damp pockets without a sound of water. Father had sent me over from Little Carr in April to help Grandma with the crop while Uncle Jolly laid out a spell in

[8] From "Golden Wedding," by Ruth Suckow, in *Iowa Interiors,* copyright, 1926, by Ruth Suckow, and reprinted by permission of Rinehart & Co., publishers.

[9] From "The Pardon," by Marjorie Kinnan Rawlings, in *When the Poor Whippoorwill;* Charles Scribner's Sons, publishers.

the county jail for dynamiting a mill dam. I was seven and Grandma was eighty-four, and we patched out two acres of corn.[10]

Concrete details are here expressed in language that creates unique atmosphere. The time element is uncertain, making us doubtful whether the story is going to happen in spring or fall. The child and the old woman planting corn pull hard at the reader's interest, while Uncle Jolly piques his curiosity.

"The Man That Corrupted Hadleyburg," one of the most ingenious and suspenseful of Mark Twain's short stories, begins poorly:

It was many years ago. Hadleyburg was the most honest and upright town in all the region around about. It had kept that reputation unsmirched during three generations, and was prouder of it than of any of its possessions. It was so proud of it, and so anxious to insure its perpetuation, that it began to teach the principles of honest dealing to its babies in the cradle, and made the like teachings the staple of their culture thenceforward through all the years devoted to their education.[11]

This is both general and abstract. No single figure is seen, and the town itself, unspecified and unlocated, as exponent of honesty and educator of its young is simply absurd. But the climactic scene in the town hall, which occupies more than the latter half of the whole story, is just the opposite: concrete, precise, full of particular detail and human interest:

The town hall had never looked finer. The platform at the end of it was backed by a showy draping of flags; at intervals along the walls were festoons of flags; the gallery fronts were clothed in flags . . . The house was full . . . the gold-sack stood on a little table at the front . . .

There is even a little dog that got in by mistake, scampering about and barking excitedly now and then.

[10] From "Job's Tears," by James Still. First published in *The Atlantic Monthly*, March, 1937.

[11] This and the extract immediately following are from *The Works of Mark Twain*, vol. 23, Harper & Brothers. Reprinted by permission of the publishers.

Flags, a packed house, a stray pup barking . . . Milkweed pods, a creek dried to a thread . . . Dan'l Webster, long buried, roaring through the hollows of the sky . . . The man who made my father's boots living on a small bystreet, now gone . . . The good fortune of boarding a deserted vessel at sea . . . In the end we return to Emily Dickinson's wistful surmise. For although the storyteller must know much more than a guess, only a poetic outreaching will seize for him the details that make a picture for the reader. The effort will be possible, it will come naturally and easily, if we keep our senses keen. Elizabeth Bowen has shown, with reference to the sense of light, this needed sort of sensitivity:

All day—speaking for these islands—our tone of living is conditioned for us: rainlight, sunlight, penetrating fogginess, or a metallic sunlessness that lets nothing through. . . . But past twilight we can create circumstance. . . . We can arrange our lighting. We work like sculptors upon these blocks of pregnant darkness rooms have become. We can control shadow, place, check, and tone light. The response from a light-switch, the bringing in of a candle is acute, personal as a perception. . . .

Who—since Da Vinci's note-books first made the thing explicit —first carried on to literature this exploitation of a particular sensitiveness? It was in *Madame Bovary* with its recurrent *crépuscule* that I had my first sense of the Vinci-esque chiaroscuro. The peculiar horror of Emma Bovary's fight for emotional survival is that it seems to be carried on in a succession of cold Norman half-lights . . . Conrad's chiaroscuro is remarkable: his chief power. In *Victory,* man and woman talk in a room "like a cage" from the shadows cast on the wall from a lantern set on the floor. The old merchant with his candle precedes Lord Jim down a chain of dark rooms stacked with polished furniture. Stevenson mastered the method: particularly, a moving candle tightens the mood of "Markheim." . . . Proust's pressure upon one's nerves of his super-reality—first pleasurable, then agonizing—works this way: that intolerable high-up Bulks bedroom is glazed with sea-reflections. . . .

Only in the remoter English provinces, in Irish cities where we are naive with dignity, does incandescence still blare unchecked and electricity frown boldly. And in the villa drawing-rooms of

North Oxford light comes down steep, distending intellectual eyeballs, outraging a sense kept delicate for the faint relief of façades and silver outlines on the Cherwell trees. Powerful minds interlock, and meanwhile light drifts and trickles down on the moiré wallpaper.[12]

But the sense of sight is only the commonest of five. The other four need this sensitivity even more, and will respond to it. Light alone is fascinating. But so is darkness. Once, to see if I could, I wrote a short story that took place entirely in the dark. An editor accepted it but returned the manuscript. "Put in a lantern or a flashlight or something," he wrote. "Our magazine is illustrated—or didn't you know?"

[12] From "Modern Lighting," by Elizabeth Bowen, in *The Saturday Review of Literature*, Oct. 27, 1928. Reprinted by permission.

15

PLOT versus THEME

PERHAPS plot could best be dealt with as Elbert Hubbard in his collected works discussed silence, in one blank page. The subject has been so overtreated, so maltreated by texts and lecturers and writers' magazines, that in amateurs' heads it has assumed the status of prime cause, *sine qua non,* be-all and end-all of short fiction. "I know I could write a story," students by the dozen have said wistfully, "if *only* I had a plot." If you are waiting for that, you will never write one. The statement is just as sensible as the act of a thirsty man who turns from a spring of water because he has no cup.

But it is not, as I say, wholly your fault. O. Henry's trick ending made a deep impression on us, which fades slowly. Ingenuity is a very strong characteristic of our nation: we are good at it, we admire it, and the shortness of the short story gives it a handsome chance to flourish here. Moreover, the plot fetish has been spread, usually to the detriment of good stories, by academic as well as by commercial influence. Literary reviews cannot avoid the word; we have no other in common currency; and with insistent repetition it becomes by implication isolated and independent, which it is not. Textbooks devote chapters to this potent ingredient, wrapping it in pretentious phraseology (situation, deadlock, denouement, rising action, catastrophe, falling action, etc.) and listing brilliant but to the novice discouraging plot turns of the past. Correspondence schools and some schools of journalism boldly reduce plot to a formula; writers' magazines coyly make it a sort of parlor game "that may reap rich profits." I have seen a plot chart to be used with a pencil, the eyes closed, leaving the whole matter up to God. There is, or was until recently, a diversion for manuscript clubs called "Plotto." And at five or ten dollars you can still buy a Plot Robot, a large cardboard figure of a man with a numbered dial in his stomach; spin the pointer, see where it stops, look up the number in a little book, and you have, all thought up for you: *a.* hero's name, *b.* heroine's name, *c.* conditions under which they meet, *d.* place of meeting, *e.* his reactions, *f.* hers, and so on to the end of "the story." (Of course you could do all this at no cost by playing Consequences, and by so doing get just as near to a short story as the Robot gets— nowhere near.) I have already mentioned the translation of Georges Polti's *Thirty-Six Dramatic Situations* and its deceptively encouraging effect on young writers. I once read an article by Harry S. Keeler called "The Mechanics and Kinematics of Web-Work Plot Construction," complete with two-page-spread diagram; this doubtless well-meant work simply put me off all writing for a week. The business has gone on for years and will probably go on forever, deluding people who want to write into believing that all they need is a plot.

Most writers of my acquaintance have nothing to do with such mumbo jumbo. Most writers pay little or no attention to plot in itself, having learned by hard experience that concentration on incidents distracts their attention from the characters who must plausibly enact them, with unconvincing results. The exception, of course, is the mystery or adventure story-writer, who is dealing with a highly specialized product requiring an unusually high percentage of suspense, surprise, and physical action, with correspondingly slight emphasis on character. Such stories must be carefully plotted. Numerous, highly popular, often extremely ingenious, these tend to become mere contests of wit, or guessing games, between the author and the reader, and reach a literary level only when other attributes creating a solid illusion of life (as in Conan Doyle, S. S. Van Dine, Dashiell Hammett) are at least as important functionally as is ingenuity. To most writers plot is merely an end product visible to critics and readers; they themselves must concern themselves with the means to achieve the end: human nature manifest in characterization.

This is not to say that a storyteller will discard a plot germ—some small, usually concrete fact or circumstance both plausible and surprising, on which a story outcome could be based—that happens to infect his head. Maupassant's "The Necklace," O. Henry's "The Gift of the Magi," and hundreds of delightfully surprising yet logical stories are proof of alertness in this respect. Melville Davisson Post solved a murder by pointing out that the shape of drops of blood fallen on the floor from a running man's body will show in which direction he ran. Wilbur Daniel Steele hid a man where nobody, not even the reader, thought to look, in the pursed topsail of a schooner; and the man became wonderfully both a cat and a ghost. G. K. Chesterton, among many feats of ingenuity, built a story on man's universal disregard of the letter carrier as a human being. But these are largely authors' windfalls. No storyteller can afford to stop telling stories if they do not occur to him. Once conceived, the plot germ is useless without all the rest of story, by which it is absorbed, in which it is integrated. It is at best a device, not a plot.

There is no short cut, then. You must usually do it the hard way: you must feel, fall in love with, get mad at and desperate over, suffer through—in short, you must *live* a story, in order to write it. It must become more real to you than daily living. No plot externally suggested, not even a plot germ that wriggles into your head will of itself really help. "Writing, like birthing and dying," somebody has said, "must be done alone."

The area to brood in is not plot, the events, but idea or theme, the meaning. The questions to be asked yourself are: What one thing is this story going to mean? What will in the end distinguish it from a mere list of details about people, their talk, a sequence of facts and acts? Or, if you haven't even got that far (you are perhaps better off if you have not)—what, exactly, *is* a theme suitable for elucidation in a short story?

How can it be got at in the mind, then how bodied forth in fiction?

Theme is only another word for the point of the story, which both ancestors of the short story possessed. The literary ancestor of the short story, you remember, stated its point explicitly in an appended moral. The popular ancestor carefully prepared the hearer's mind for the point, but left it only implied, for his wit to pick up. Thus "The Fox and the Grapes" told its story and then added in a separate paragraph, "It is easy to despise what you cannot get." This observation, not generally thought much about in the daily course of our lives, becomes instantly acceptable because true to human nature (that is, plausible) as soon as we see a dramatic application of it to a hungry fox and something he wanted to eat and couldn't get. In the sense, then, that it is plausible upon recognition, but until that moment unthought of, it is both plausible and surprising; therefore a kind of plot germ. But it was reached by the author through brooding over human nature, not over plot.

Now by the time that Stevenson came to write "The Two Matches," implication from the popular source of the short story had long since worked its way into the written form, permitting him to elucidate much the same idea without a stated moral:

One day there was a traveller in the woods in California, in the dry season when the Trades were blowing strong. He had ridden a long way, and he was tired and hungry, and dismounted to smoke a pipe. But when he felt in his pocket, he found but two matches. He struck the first, and it wouldn't light.

"Here's a pretty state of things," said the traveller. "Dying for a smoke; only one match left; and that certain to miss fire! Was there ever a creature so unfortunate? And yet," thought the traveller, "suppose I light this match, and smoke my pipe, and shake out the dottle here in the grass—the grass might catch on fire, for it is dry as tinder; and while I snatch out the flames in front, they might evade and run behind me, and seize upon that bush of poison oak; before I could reach it, that would have blazed up; over the bush is a pine tree hung with moss; that too would fly in fire on the instant to its topmost bough; and the flame of that long torch—how the tradewind would take and brandish that through the inflammable forest! I hear this dell roar in a moment with the joint voice of wind and fire, I see myself gallop for my life, and the conflagration chase and outflank me through the hills; I see this pleasant valley burn for days, and the cattle roasted, and the springs dried up, and the farmer ruined, and his children cast upon the world. What a world hangs upon this moment!"

With that he struck the match, and it missed fire.

"Thank God!" said the traveller, and put his pipe in his pocket.

Aesop's explicit moral has become an idea unstated but implied by dramatic representation: the illogicality rooted in all of us by which a thing wanted may become a thing unwanted, without in itself changing. Or, as Hamlet put it, "There is nothing either good or bad, but thinking makes it so." If readers' wits had been as sharp in Aesop's day, and if the beginnings of fiction had not labored under the burden of didactic intent, Aesop could have lopped off his moral and been just as clear and far more effective.

In both fables there is a point, a theme: that is, the events of both are unified by an attempt to illustrate dramatically a truth in human nature. In both the illustration is presented through a pattern of problem and its solution: in "The Fox and the Grapes" the fox wants grapes but can't reach them (the problem), and calls them bad to save his pride (the solution); in "The Two Matches" the traveler wants to smoke but has only one match which will probably not light (the problem), but imagining the consequences of carelessness if it does light, puts his pipe away content (the solution). The pattern is the same, but Stevenson's illustration of the theme is better, not alone in technique, using implication instead of expository statement; it is better in substance, for the traveler is more worth reading about than the fox-with-a-subhuman-quality.

235

The traveler has closer contact with humanity in the large. Like most of us, he can be and here is two men: the tired extrovert who wants to rest and smoke, the tired introvert who must worry. The introvert was the stronger.

And, strangely enough, both fables have plot, in that, in each there is suddenly presented an idea about human nature that is both surprising, or not recently thought about, and acceptable, that is, plausible, admitted as true. Stevenson's plot is enhanced by his better technique and characterization, and by his longer suspense. But both plots are the direct result of natural action, which itself resulted from a human desire opposed by difficulty and needing solution. Two forces in combat produce outcome.

Plot, if you must, therefore, always happens, and *of its own accord,* when two human forces are brought plausibly into conflict. Not only is there no need to hunt for it, you cannot escape it; all you need do is sit tight and watch closely while it occurs. The two forces should appear equal to the reader, or nearly equal (actually, of course, one proves the stronger or there could be no outcome); or the force with which the reader is in sympathy should appear the weaker and prove the stronger, or appear the stronger and prove the weaker. Both forces need not be individuals, but one, I believe, must be, for dramatic concreteness. The reader's sympathy, I also believe (but naturalistic storytellers do not), should be allied with one or the other, and the outcome must make sense in human terms. Perhaps this outcome can be shaped to our advantage while we sit and watch. Stevenson undoubtedly shaped his. If the second match had lighted and the traveler had smoked in apprehensive misery; or if the second match, missing fire, had thrown the traveler back into the petulant state of the beginning, the reader's grant of sympathy would have been insulted and the story wouldn't have seemed to get anywhere; as it is we can laugh at the traveler and like him too. But the point is that this shaping and devising (plotting, if you will) will come easy and sound plausible only *after* the task of characterization has been done, a theme conceived for illustration, and the two forces arrayed against each other—not before.

As in the case of human traits available for characterization, here, I suppose, it would seem convenient to list all, or nearly all, possible themes for short-story illustration. But to do so would certainly not further the writing of good short stories. Discovery of a theme, inextricably linked with knowledge of character that will convey it, must result from the writer's perception and interpretation of his own experience in actual life, of which his story is to create an illusion. It is the great moment of a writer's life. To enumerate themes would be only to invent a Super-Plotto, and to take that moment from him.

But stories, published or in manuscript, or as yet unwritten, can be tested for theme, and with good result. A short story that can be summarized sensibly in a sentence has a theme. Compression of time and space will provide unity that will make the theme more easily demonstrable. And never mind how proverbial, or even trite, the sentence summary of your story sounds. Make sure the theme behind it is not too large, and that it is true. The Worm Turns has made hundreds of stories, How Have the Mighty Fallen hundreds more; and Things Are Not What They Seem has worked for thousands. So long as you start with characterization, then proceed to live the story (with some part of you always on the alert for ways of shaping material, the elucidation of your theme always uppermost in this watchman of your creative mind), the result will not sound trite in the least degree. It will appear as fresh and original as did Stevenson's "The Two Matches" even to readers who knew Aesop's "The Fox and the Grapes" by heart.

Theme is perhaps a matter of relatively small importance to our modern short-story writer, contributor to three-million-circulation magazines who has an eye on Hollywood, our man with a big stake and a fat living to make. To the young unpublished storyteller dead set on doing his best at every lick, and hoping for adequate reward, however, it should bear this considerable weight: in short-story writing, theme could be called the factor of permanent impression. Place may fade, details of character and action become lost; but if the story was a good one we remember what it means.

16

INDIRECTION AND RESTRAINT

To convey an idea, not by expressing it directly, but by devising a character or characters to represent it and demonstrate its application by speech and action, is to practice indirection. This is the high purpose of all forms of narrative, requiring a maximum effort by the writer and a maximum coöperation on the part of the reader or hearer. The ancient poets and dramatists of Greece and Rome knew the principle; as best they could, the Renaissance writers caught it from them and passed it on down; but the prose story, at least, had to survive the Romantic Movement, feel the impact of Darwin and Freud, and shake off didacticism before indirection could be fully developed and fully recognized.

It now pervades and controls the whole of story-writing, technique and content. We can hardly begin to conceive a workable idea without snatching at a notion as to how, indirectly, to convey it. Whenever we get into a character, use him as an objective correlative to our experience—that is, whenever we begin to think in narrative rather than autobiographical terms—we practice indirection. The choice of any kind of telling method only carries on the principle, by its refusal to reveal the author, or rely on his authority, or display omniscience—or even to employ exposition that tells all, from any source, at any time. Within the story, whenever we withhold information for the purposes of suspense, or prepare the reader by unobtrusive reference for the purposes of surprise; whenever by selection of characteristic traits of personality or of physical conditions or circumstances of place, or of limits of time, or of details of episode and action—whenever we motivate for the purposes of plausibility, again we are but following this basic law of our craft. And the law reaches down into the smallest devices of our prose. A bit of action or behavior recorded contiguously to words spoken, connoting the identity of the speaker without the necessity of stating his name with a verb of saying, is one instance. Interruptions, or action speaking louder than words, what would have been said being clear without quotation, are another. Apt and appropriate figures of speech, by implication telling a whole through vivid imagery of one part, or by agreed association, are still another. Indeed, any bi-functional utterance carrying an overtone of emotional or behavioristic significance as well as its literal clarity—the mainstay of objective writing—falls within the scope of the principle. And I mean any concise record, such as *Sam looked at him,* unembellished by stage directions or descriptive qualifications, but packed with contextual implication—anger, doubt, fear, hope, relief. Here in the regions of rhetoric and general narrative technique, indirection and successfully channeled suggestion are attributable to the same motive, employ similar methods, and produce the same result.

Originally this way of writing, resulting in all such concepts and devices, was inspired by a single, classic precept: that of descriptive selection, by which the significant or striking or salient nature of a thing is revealed, not through complete elucidation, but through disregard of some of its aspects with consequent stress, with overemphasis amounting to expository inaccuracy, on a chosen one or two others. Herein lies the source of graphic power: force replacing complete meaning. For the image left with us by this selection and exaggeration, though sometimes sharper than truth and sometimes duller, by fixing a single attribute on our minds sets it up as a symbol of the whole that can work more quickly and remain longer—a flash, a mere image, compelling but wordless, thought-less, in the memory.

Space is saved, a memorable quality supplied: sufficient

reasons in themselves for the adaptability of this classic precept to the short story. But there is another reason, stronger yet. Indirection in all its forms, implication, and descriptive selection exert a never-ceasing stimulus, they extend an almost constant challenge to the reader's intelligence. This challenge, the psychologists tell us, rouses him, tickles his ego minutely but perceptibly; as all of us are put on the alert during the telling of a funny story, look for the point in the telling where our wits must bridge the gap between what is told and what is not going to be told, and when the gap appears make the jump —and laugh, as much with delight at our own agility as at the point of the story. Just so the reader. He accepts with pleasure an offer that actually enlists him in the work of creation. He gets the point of implication or suggestion, and perhaps subconsciously pats himself on the back for his keen perception, while consciously admiring the storyteller (who let him do part of his own work). In short, the reader coöperates unwittingly with the writer.

Now this contribution by the reader to the art of narrative is a very precious asset. But we must not overcapitalize. To write by indirection, which as storytellers we must do, is to play with fire. Squib in hand, we light the match and hand it to the reader; but without care the thing will explode in our faces. Subtlety striven for as an end in itself may defeat itself in a variety of ways: loss of interest, preciousness, distraction of attention, obscurity. Indirection may easily go wrong, may run wild into the absurdities of euphemism, Dadaism, non-objectivism, disestablished symbols, the arcana fetish, and so on down, ultimately, to gibberish. This is the risk we take. This is the stake we put up, prepared to lose but determined to win. All writing plays with fire anyway. And it is only human to feel that the light and warmth of the blaze, under control, are worth the risk of burned fingers. Indirection, though powerful and pervasive, must be but a means to an end: *rapprochement* between writer and reader, irresistible evocation of the reader into the world of the story, and his complete surrender to its intellectual and emotional demands. Achievement of this end requires a constantly watchful eye on the reader as guest, sharer in daydreams, or willing victim.

"The reader," here, includes of course his representative, the editor. If we could only study and come to know a composite personality so thoroughly that its every reaction were predictable in quantity and kind, our watchful eye would be really potent and story-writing would perhaps be easier, if less interesting. But no reader is exactly predictable. Readers, editors too, are of widely variant degrees of mentality. They have all sorts, and all combinations of sorts, of interests; they are infected with all sorts of whims and prejudices; and, being human, will jump sometimes in no direction or in all directions at once. To follow them around taking notes as Boswell followed Dr. Johnson might eventually produce complete understanding, but it would not produce stories. With the generality, the average, we must be content. This has been indicated by the reading habits of different kinds of readers and the establishment of different kinds of magazines to satisfy various tastes. Without suggesting any preference one can very easily trace a rough line from the experimental journal, requiring much intellectual effort on the reader's part, through the literary monthlies, still making considerable demands of this sort, through the popular monthlies and weeklies, demanding less, to the pulps and juveniles, asking little effort if any at all. Thus one arrives at the generality, to be modified by specific knowledge gained from experience with individual editors and readers, yet in the main holding true: the greater the reader's intelligence and sophistication, the readier will be his acceptance of planned omission and the substitution of implication for statement; the heartier, in short, will be his coöperation with indirection. If this seems vague, perhaps a closer calculation can be got at by appraising one's own tastes and capabilities in this respect—strictly as reader, of course. Writers should write for, and generally they do, barring accident, write for, readers a good deal like themselves.

Restraint, if not a part of indirection, is at least an important corollary. It exerts a similar force, in a slightly different way. The force is condensation effected for emotional impact, a primary need of the short story. But before indirection can exert this force by selection, withholding, and translation of material, restraint must begin to exert it by working on the writer himself, suppressing, playing down, deleting his own excess of emotion about the story, which would otherwise make indirection impossible and reduce everything he wrote to a reflection, even an exposé, of his quivering self. For there are limits to a reader's ability to absorb and share emotion. The emotion to be shared must be the character's, not the writer's. A writer must acquire detachment by restraint in order to see these limits and not overstep them.

It took fiction a long time to discover and master this lesson. Some eighteenth and nineteenth-century novels are soggy with characters whose overemotionalism is but a reflex of the authors' lack of restraint. Pamela swoons, methodically as a puppet, whenever Squire B. makes amorous advances, in themselves probably the least seductive in all literature. Roderick Random, doughty adventurer, gushes tears whenever he meets or parts with an old friend; once at least his nose spouts blood. Marianne Dashwood, forced by her father's death to leave the family estate, addresses the house (and grounds) in these feverish terms:

"Dear, dear Norland! . . . when shall I cease to regret you? when learn to feel at home elsewhere? O happy house! could you know what I suffer in now viewing you from this spot, from whence perhaps I may view you no more! and you, ye well-known trees! but you will continue the same. No leaf will decay because we are removed, nor any branch become motionless although we can observe you no longer! No; you will continue the same; unconscious of the pleasure or the regret you occasion, and insensible of any change in those who walk under your shade! But who will remain to enjoy you?"

And Lady Deadlock, confronted by evidence that Esther Summerson is really her daughter, Esther Hawdon, falls upon her knees in a kind of anecdotal anguish to soliloquize:

"O my child, my child! Not dead in the first hours of her life, as my cruel sister told me; but sternly nurtured by her, after she had renounced me and my name! O my child, O my child!"

Regardless of the language used—for Richardson, Smollett, Jane Austen, and Dickens labored under a burden of convention too severe for their product to bear criticism by modern standards; and relying on the printed word alone we can't, now, be certain just how people spoke in those distant days— the language aside, consider the amount and quality of emotion displayed, in comparison with amount and quality that would normally be displayed by persons of similar temperaments today. Were people so different a hundred, two hundred years ago? Have Freud, a mechanized civilization, and two world wars buried our feelings under a mask of diffidence or apathy; or perhaps destroyed them? I do not think so. Speech changes, but thoughts and emotions remain. More likely the novelists mentioned, naturally excited themselves and wanting to express emotion, took the easiest way with an audience they were none too sure of: that is, overexpressed it. As writers learned very slowly to demonstrate or exemplify instead of preach, so they had to learn subtler, truer-to-life ways than gushing tears, swoons, tearing hair, and bended knees to manifest emotion. A parallel, not so inexact as it might appear, lies in the development from crude registration of emotion by actors in the old silent movies to more natural and more moving, less violent exhibition through the added medium of speech.

For the purpose of illustration, let us assume that the figure 10 represents the precise quantity and quality of emotion felt by a living person under given circumstances at some moment in his life. Overstatement of the emotion by only one or two points above actuality fixed at 10 will hardly be serious and might provide useful flexibility for needed factors in a story. Overstatement to the extent of five points, however, will at first confuse and then repel a reader, and ultimately make him laugh—as we laugh today at swoons and heartsick nosebleeds. *Under*statement by a point or two, generating excitement in the reader by playing it down in the character or situation, is the goal for the novice to aim at. He will need detachment, complete knowledge of his material, and above all, absolute control of language. Most young writers go astray here not through excessive emotion themselves, but by trying too hard to express, and thus overexpressing, something for which they lack utterance to convey exactly. And they can nearly always tell when this is happening by noting a rash of superlatives and exclamation points in their prose.

Restraint is particularly valuable in view of the very wide range of subject matter available to the story-writer today. By delicate, implicit treatment of physical and psychological matters long denied expression, it is helping to break down the last remnants of prejudice against fiction as a wicked escape from life. In "Honey, We'll Be Brave" James Farrell brings inherited syphilis between a young, happily married couple with a dramatic pathos the more appalling for his compassionate but cool detachment from the whole affair. In "Hills Like White Elephants" and "The Sea Change" Hemingway writes of an abortion and of homosexuality, respectively, in an undertone that not only forestalls any charge of giving offence but divests those long-tabooed matters of everything but reality, calling forth from us nothing but sympathy and pity.

The most difficult part of a short story, again in this matter of indirection and restraint, is the beginning. Here it is the coldness of the reader that must be taken into account. His coldness is of course the result of his ignorance. He must be informed, but at the same time he must be—slowly—excited. Let first his curiosity be piqued, then his interest or sympathy be aroused, before bringing any big guns to bear on him. In these opening lines let him be given only what is, first, perfectly clear—no matter how little; and, second, emotionally shareable—no matter along what broad lines. Only indirection and restraint—together they are a soft pedal—will do this double, delicate task. The next most difficult place in the story is, naturally, the end. Here restraint should be exercised in direct ratio to the depth and violence of the emotion represented. If the author has practiced indirection faithfully, there is small danger of straight intrusion of his emotion (like Irving's essay on love, Hawthorne's "Blessed be all simple emotions!") repelling the reader. But he must guard against oblique intrusion, such as exaggeration of his characters' feelings or behavior, or any implicative comment by so much as an unintegrated adverb.

17

BEGINNING

BEFORE he begins, a writer should know his purpose in writing, the motive that drives him and the reward he hopes to get for his work. The knowledge will be more valuable to him than a study of markets or critical appraisal of good stories in print. His purpose may change as he goes on; but if he faces and admits it squarely now, he will be ready to recognize change when the time comes, and thus will spare himself wasted effort and know at all times where he stands.

Conceivable impelling purposes are four: briefly stated they are money, vanity, altruism, and communication. Don Marquis defined the lot in a paragraph:

I think it was Dr. Johnson who said that [1] *nobody would write at all, except for money* The Doctor could be an awful old ass at times; and yet, of course, professional writers know what he was driving at when he made that ill-considered remark. I have just been reading the Bible again, and have run onto some good stuff that probably never made a cent for the authors. . . . It isn't the money that makes people start writing, and stick to it; [2] *it is the hope of publication.* The exhibition of the ego in public places means more to us writers than money. . . . In its highest phase the writing mania proceeds from the wish [4] *to break down, somehow, that awful barrier which exists between soul and soul,* and share even bitterness, if there is neither [3] *knowledge nor joy to be shared;* in its lower manifestations it may be merely exhibitionism, and yet, there, too, is the wistful hope of being better understood. Those who write only for money, and who would cease to write if they had enough money without it, I don't consider writers at all. The money is pretty welcome, of course, if you can manage to connect with it. Those lonely, timid, fine souls who write and never show it to any human being at all, show it to God; they are the supreme egoists. They think nobody else could appreciate it.[1]

(Italics and numbers indicate the defining phrases.)

But hasn't Don Marquis done more than define those four motives? Has he not acknowledged by implication the presence of all four in a creed of honest craftsmanship; and shown how the domination of either of two, at least, the money motive and vanity, can be aesthetically dishonest? I believe he meant to say that all four motives are legitimate, at least in the sense that all four are essentially human desires, but that they will work best as a team, in something like equilibrium, not when one or another excludes the others. With such an estimate of motive, certainly, most professional authors could agree.

Yet for themselves they are inclined to make exceptions, and the novice will wish to do that too. Let him, by all means; but let him see what he is doing in the light of others' past performance, and admit the doing to his faith, instead of professing one aim and reaching toward another, or not having any. Recognition of a guiding, if not exclusive or dominant motive, will to some extent determine the nature of his product, as it has shaped others'. Under the guidance of the money motive he will see the writing businessmen—from Trollope to Louis Bromfield—working hard, producing too much for all of it to be their best, but getting well paid for the pleasure they give to many readers by a representation of life not as it is but as those readers wish it could be. Carrying his ego on his sleeve he will find, for instance, William Saroyan. Under the aegis of altruism he will discover Samuel Butler, much of Dickens and Charles Reade, the proletarians and propagandists, the social novelists, the crusaders, and all worthy souls whose birthright seems to have been, as Douglas Bush wittily told us, "a pot of message"—who write for what they think will be the betterment of mankind. And for sheer communication he will find

[1] Reprinted by permission of *The Saturday Review of Literature.*

248

Ruth Suckow as good as saying: "I will write of life exactly as I see it, for it excites me and I can't help trying to pass the excitement on." Let him learn from these others how best to shape his product to his aim.

The shaping will demand certain requisites in himself. If he has or can acquire them, well and good; if not, there is still time—in a writer's life, nothing should happen in a hurry—for frank acknowledgment and a wise change of purpose.

The man who writes chiefly for money must possess a high degree of adaptability to mass reader taste. He must be willing to go for the big markets even if at times the going seems likely to finish him. Timeliness must become his law. He must keep his ear to the ground, and always write what it hears instead of what he may want to hear. Possession of the money motive is so general that it is worth careful investigation; for it can go tragically wrong.

Every so often a student comes to me and says: "I have the Great American Novel in my system, no fooling, but of course I have to live while writing it. Here's what I thought. You know how to hit the *Post;* please show me. I want to do eight or ten short stories for the *hoi-polloi,* and then settle down to the real job." This man, I have bitterly learned, is not worth any effort. Probably he will never write anything publishable. Without any of the requisites, he wants to be a writing businessman in order to support himself as an exhibitionist.

But the fallacy is not confined to the young. Years ago a New England schoolmaster complained in the columns of *The Saturday Review of Literature:*

I have been writing stories and articles for twenty years, and have sold about one a year. . . . I know well two phases of life [schoolteaching and Central America] which have in them elements of popular interest. I cannot write the accepted tale about either; believing in Dr. Johnson's dictum, I have tried to, shamelessly. I cannot sell a story which delineates a new type of teacher —Ichabod Crane set that fashion for all time!—or Central American—[Richard Harding Davis set that one!] Yet it seems to me important that the truth about these two aspects of life should be told.[2]

Here is the same sort of confusion of aims that blocked the Great American Novelist. "The truth" about life, anywhere, assuming that he saw and could express it, would not be an asset of great importance in dealing successfully with the popular magazines. Without seeing this man's product we can surmise his trouble. Obviously inadaptable in a field where adaptability is imperative, he must have written down to his readers (just what the G.A.N. wanted to do), and occasionally sold a story but usually, lacking conviction himself in his work, failed to create conviction in his readers. His frank commercial motive sent him to the highest-paying markets without the requisites for success there; and while he mourned their stupidity in rejecting him, Thornton Wilder's *The Bridge of San Luis Rey* and James Hilton's *Goodbye, Mr. Chips* achieved the creation of those new types of Central American and schoolmaster that he said couldn't be done.

Arthur Train pointed out this fallacy even in a man who had reached fame and adequate monetary reward in other lines:

John Jay Chapman, whose essays on the Greek poets had made him famous, told me he'd give anything to write for the *Saturday Evening Post*. I told him it was merely a matter of selecting some topic of general interest. "That's what troubles me," he said. "What interests me doesn't always seem to interest other people." "Why not be interested in what does?" I asked. He nodded, and about a month later he sent me his idea of a popular article. It had to do with social service work in the slums. It was jejune, solemn, didactic. Gifted though he was, Chapman was not enough of an artist to alter his personality to suit his readers.[3]

[2] Gerald Chittenden, "Sour Grapes," Dec. 8, 1928. Reprinted by permission of *The Saturday Review of Literature*.

[3] *The Saturday Review of Literature*, Nov. 5, 1928. Reprinted by permission.

Aesthetes, perhaps, will quarrel with Train's wording, but I will let it stand.

The money-writer, of course, if too adaptable must usually be content with money for reward; he will get no *succés d'estime*. As Henry Seidel Canby has written:

> The price of popularity is high. Some of our very best writers have paid too much for it. . . . Readers in the mass have their stock reactions, and once the writer begins to play upon these he is weakening. The poor boy making good, the roughneck revealing a heart of gold, the lone woman fighting for independence and safety, the inhibited when they break through inhibitions—[may be mentioned as sure of stock reactions]. These are very human. It is impossible to write much without touching them off. But when a writer begins to *try* to touch them off, his decline begins.[4]

This is strictly a critic's point of view, generalizing and over-simplifying a standard that is variable when specific writers and stories are considered. How is anybody going to know when a writer tries to do something for itself and when he tries to do it for an ulterior motive? And is the ulterior motive always bad? Some very highly respected writers have professed it. But it is not too much to say that the money motive, and its essential adjunct, adaptability, may not safely encroach on aesthetic integrity. It is usually impossible to write anything successfully without, at least, the conviction that it is the best you can do.

As for the man who writes largely to gratify his ego, without an independent income he is very likely to starve. If he wins a hearing, as Saroyan has done for instance, he may attain great popularity briefly, perhaps through some medium that keeps his ego in eclipse. Saroyan's real success came via the stage, on which he cannot easily appear in person. But of course something depends, too, on the kind of ego involved. Saroyan's is childlike and refreshing. His belief in the writer's experience as the basis of writing, his resentment at slavery to

[4] Reprinted by permission of *The Saturday Review of Literature*.

form, and his determination to write whether he is read or not—all aspects of his ego—outweigh his prolixity, his sentimentalism, and his usual lack of objectivity. One cannot say that his kind of ego doesn't deserve to be gratified in print.

He who writes to improve mankind also needs, as a rule, financial backing from other sources than his stories. Magazines willing to print propaganda disguised as fiction pay little, because they have relatively few readers and advertisers; and the public is pretty cold to this kind of fiction. It is only rarely that an *Uncle Tom's Cabin,* a *Looking Backward,* or a *Native Son* becomes widely read through the greater freedom that book publishers enjoy over magazine circulation. And the public taste and distaste are not far wrong. As a general rule, story values decline with the rise of the propagandist's temper. Particularity of attack, with respect to time and place, is another deterrent here. Even now it is hard to remember the circumstances that made *The Grapes of Wrath* seem poignant. It is true of short stories as it is of novels, that the really great ones of the past had no local or temporal message.

One hesitates to cramp a storyteller's notions, but it must be said that No Propaganda seems a wise creed for the young writer. He won't like it. He wants to be up and doing, he longs to hit somebody and see him bleed. Whether or not this hitting and bleeding business improves mankind remains a question. Perhaps improvement will follow in due course. But certainly most propagandist fiction stirs up rather than builds up. In his attempt to relieve the sufferings of the underdog, too often the fictional propagandist loses sight of his aim in a free-for-all with the dog on top. Propagandists need logic, straight rhetoric, and a soapbox to get what they want, political action; the ways of storytelling are neither logical nor straight, and a soapbox for the teller will only make his sad discrepancies in the other respects more visible. Compassion not only for the Negro, the Jews, henpecked husbands, parent-suppressed children, but for the whole pitiably brave human race—compassion with or without a sense of humor for edge—is the artist's weapon. Daudet's "The Last Class," Crane's "The Red Badge of Courage" cut deep with it, but the wound healed and the patient as a whole, not merely some organ or member, is the better for the operation.

He who writes chiefly to communicate and preserve human experience—unless, as in the case of Thomas Wolfe, for instance, the only experience that moves him has himself as subject and predicate—possesses at least the prime merits of sincerity and objectivity. I believe this to have been the basic motive behind most work judged by time better than good. I do not mean that it is a sure key to success, there is no such thing; I mean simply that this motive seems likelier than the others to drive a writer to achieve his best, at whatever level that best must be.

Ruth Suckow—not yet a very famous or highly paid writer, but a very honest one—has discussed all four motives and acknowledged this last as hers, in a passage worth the young writer's close attention. Though she speaks here of the novelist, what she says applies to the storyteller in general:

The reasons behind writing are multitudinous and complex. There is Dr. Freud's by now very well-known reason: to permit the writer an imaginary substitution for whatever he has lacked in real life. I consider this a frequent but on the whole pretty rudimentary reason, negative rather than positive in quality. There is the amateur's reason, displayed in an overwhelmingly large number of first novels: to rush out with a highly personalized account of what he has learned from life so far (usually up to the age of twenty-six) including his findings about women. Another reason, related to this one of the amateur, but much less to be respected, is exceedingly frequent also: to justify and glorify the writer and at the same time confound his enemies. . . . Then there is the reason of the thinker on general questions—he it is who "casts his book in the form of fiction." His reason is worthy, from some standpoints; but his impulse is not that of the artist. . . .

Perhaps several of these reasons enter into the writing of any novel, although the less that some of them do so, the better. But

253

they are not fundamental. A better reason . . . [is] an impelling desire to preserve what has been seen and felt, not of course in terms of historical reality but translated into that imaginative form [the story] which is the most evocative and enduring. [This] is an ambitious desire, but it seems to me the only one worth the attempt.[5]

Whatever his motive, as he begins the novice will need some advice on the practical matters of human relationships. What to do about literary agents, for instance. That question is difficult, and no general answer to it can be conclusive. Many amateurs feel that all they need for success is a good agent behind them; once he is secured, they are sure, they can simply lie back and let him make them rich and famous. On the other hand some inexperienced writers, brilliant and promising, feel that business relationships with editors and readers are hard enough, to set up with an agent would be the last stage of artistic degradation. Both absurdities aside, the question should be carefully considered *pro* and *con* the individual writer's best good, and, as in the case of motive, an answer should be found and faced.

A good agent is one who makes his living by commissions (usually 10 per cent), not by reading fees. He is a member of the Incorporated Society of Authors' Representatives. He will not take more clients than he, or some responsible member of his firm, can handle personally. He does not advertise. He forwards net sales on the day the gross amount is received. He does not expect to be asked to teach clients how to write, or to keep clients writing. He does expect, once a working agreement with a client is reached, to handle all of that client's output. There are none too many really good agents, and far too many bad ones. No author should shop around among agents, trying one out for a while and holding others in reserve in case the first does not sell his stuff at once. Choice, even among

[5] From *Wings*, The Literary Guild of America. Reprinted by permission of Rinehart & Co., Inc.

254

good agents, is important enough to suggest the advantage of personal acquaintance before the deal is closed. This is a kind of partnership, the future success of which depends not only on whether you like and have faith in your agent but whether he likes and has faith in you.

Having an agent is a physical advantage if the writer lives far from New York or some other publication center, or if he travels to get material. The personal contact that every good agent maintains with many editors permits ideas to pass quickly from a man who wants something to a man who may supply it. Although he may deny this, the expert agent is a critic in the sense that he knows, he cannot help knowing, what is wanted and what is not. The magazine field is so huge and so complex, at times so transitory, that a writer unassisted may spend valuable time and energy merely trying to keep up with it. Most magazines have a few specific taboos, to discover which, alone, may be a long and bitter business. The agent has a clear head and an objective view. He knows when it is time the writer's rate should be raised. He has always in mind the possibility of multiple sales—foreign, dramatic, movie, second-serial rights; and knows how to go about putting them through. He is a legal authority in the matter of contract wording and copyright assignment.

But a good agent can be much more than an expert clerk. He can be an accessory before the fact of writing; in an indirect and subtle way he can help to create. I know of one who, in an hour's talk with a client, changed the man's conception of an unsalable story into one that sold at once. A writing friend of mine once felt suddenly empty, written out. He was surprised and pleased to be told by his agent to take a vacation. The agent and an editor, to my friend's further surprise, went along too, in the agent's car. The three of them loafed through Pennsylvania, Maryland, and Virginia, and the eventual result was a series of admirable short stories of the War Between the States. Such an experience is of course very rare, but smaller instances of the same sort of judgment and insight are too numerous to mention. At the very least, the agent's greatest merit lies in the relief he provides us from the dreary business of peddling our wares in the public streets. That blank hostile void that surrounds the workroom can be a big obstacle to production. The agent breaks that down; he establishes a friendly atmosphere, first between himself and client, then between client and editor. There is comfort, even inspiration, in the knowledge that one has such a champion out there on the firing line. I know no greater stimulant to good work than this assurance that someone is expecting it. To experience the full benefit of an agent you must, if he will have you, spend a week end in his home; play bridge or chess or ping-pong with him, meet and know his wife and kids, talk long about other things than writing, forget all that for a time while you discover the boon of a professional friendship.

On the other hand it must be said that the agent is, economically speaking, merely another middleman—another apparent short cut that may be the longest way round or no thoroughfare. Our intricate civilization seems to demand him. But before we manufacturers accept him in the field of literary production, we must consider whether there is justification behind his offer to create and span still another step (for the publisher, the editor, the printer, the jobber, the news dealer have already made a flight of steps) between our commodity and its consumer. Our motive in writing may decide the question very quickly. But suppose we want something more than money. Is the creation of literature aided by coöperation, or must the artist struggle alone? How many really great works are the result of collaboration? What has multiple production done to the movies? The weakening effect of creative props is very familiar; perhaps, after all, this is a phase of the problem to which there can be no categorical answer. But it can be said with certainty that in the case of the unsalable story mentioned above, which became salable after an hour's talk with an expert agent, the effect was weakening. For I was the author. The incident made me grateful, but it did not make me want to conceive another story; it made me want to run down to New York again and receive another.

Again, although the good agent is in a sense a critic, like that of other critics his judgment is fallible. It may be more fallible than that of the poor writer who knows nothing of market conditions. The agent's view is bound to be colored by what has succeeded recently, whereas the author is guided only by the radiant beacon of what he can do. Editors are often timid about novelty. A timid editor plus a timid agent equals something pretty cut-and-dried, pretty thin and formula-ridden by way of story. You cannot blame an agent for being an opportunist, playing the main chance, for he has a living to make now, not in the next century; the creation of literature must be subordinate with him, if he considers it at all. I was once amazed to find that a man whose agent had placed seventy-five short stories of his with a certain magazine had a selling ratio of less than two in five, an attic crammed with unsold manuscripts, and a bad name with other magazines, which assumed that if his agent and the periodical in which he had appeared so often gave them the chance to read something, there must be something wrong with it. Years ago one of my students had the good luck, as she thought then, to be taken on by a good agent. In the following twelve years he sold virtually every manuscript she sent him, to a single market. At the end of that period the editor tired of her product and asked for something very different. By that time it couldn't be done. She had tried repeatedly, during those twelve years of success, to persuade her agent to spread the market, to make new outlets, to stop playing the main chance to death. Naturally this was futile. Her stories had improved too. It was simply that too much of any one writer was enough. If you will read thirty-five to fifty short stories by any one hand, no matter how great, at the rate of one every two or three weeks, you will see that the editor was right. From his point of view, the agent was also right. Between them, however, by this intensive culture they had reduced the potentiality of the short story as a work of art just as certainly as they shortened the writing life of one writer to those twelve splendid years.

I have tried to be fair to both sides in an attempt to show that a good agent may be, but is not necessarily, good for a good writer. Remembering your chief motive in writing, you must use your own judgment here. You will have time to reach a sound decision, for a good agent will probably not take you as client until you have shown promise by selling something, somewhere, direct. When you have done that, if you decide that you want to work with agents, get in touch with their organization and talk, if you can, with several before you make your choice. Then be an applicant, not a donor. And expect to work harder, in partnership, than you ever worked before alone.

A few other matters having to do with ways and means to authorship may be worth mention here. I believe that joining manuscript-reading clubs is usually unwise. The membership of such organizations often includes dilettantes and incurable amateurs who sublimate their longing to appear in print by this activity, and whose critical opinions are prejudiced and arbitrary. To read a story of your own before such an audience may give you a disproportionate idea of its worth. I would not even talk about a story you plan to write or are writing or have written, with a friend. In the same class of inadvisable literary activity I would place subscribing to so-called writers' magazines. Not that some of them are not good, not that there isn't some good in the worst, and not that an intelligent subscriber cannot winnow the good from the bad. But these magazines, like writers' sewing-circles, are camp followers of authorship; they live chiefly on subscriptions of would-be writers, not of professionals. A similar argument operates against your taking courses in writing, or at most more than one course. There is a natural feeling that some superimposed schedule is bound to keep you at it and make something of you. It won't, of itself. To take on one is to sidestep the real test. You must be able to set your own schedule and stick to it. All these activities are substitutes; they will delude you into thinking you are a writer long before you can be one. To be one you must push off by yourself, get lost in the deep woods, and find your way out alone.

There is no short cut, no royal road, no easiest way. If you bought this book hoping to find one, you have been cheated. Keep to the one purpose of writing the best story that is in you and let it be a story to be printed and read in a magazine. "Some writers, would-be or arrived," a good agent has said, "seem to have the idea that you can hit the movies by writing essentially a film story for the magazines. The result, invariably, is a piece that is no good for the magazines and too full of cliché situations or ideas, or both, to appeal to the movie producers. The way to hit the movies is to succeed as a short-story writer or novelist." Equally fallacious is the belief that you can write original scripts for films, wherever you are, whatever your knowledge of what an original must have to sell is, or is not. Those who succeed at movie originals live in Hollywood and know the technique of that kind of writing from experience gained on the lots. Neither this book nor any other will give you that technique or any substitute for the essential necessity of your presence at the place where films are produced.

We come to the end, which I hope is a beginning. Writing short stories is an art, a craft, and a business if not a racket. Here I have told what I know of the craft, which perhaps can reach without presumption a little way into the higher realm of art, and without indignity look down also into the practical aspects of the business.

One thing more:

Suppose you began to think in story terms of somebody you know well, or of a combination of known figures and personalities fused into organic unity. What would happen? You might, quite naturally, conceive of this person as representative of some universal human attribute—say, stubbornness, our imperishable will to stick with a thing wanted until we get it, even at the risk of its getting us. You might think up this wanted thing for him, and continue thinking. Just the individual and the wanted thing—probably you would leave in abeyance all the rest, but focus on that.

His wanting, his struggle, would have to happen somewhere. A place that you know well, very likely, since by now you know him well. In terms of eternity it would happen quickly if you caught him an hour, two hours, before the outcome of his struggle and followed it just from there on. But two hours can seem a very long time if you live it under pressure, and that is what you would be doing, living through it with him; and in two hours of slow motion like that you know how the past flashes into sight, on and off, and the future too; some of that would have to be there too. And the person or persons who stand in the way of his getting what he wants; they would bear a lot of thinking. By the time you see them clearly, perhaps you would begin to know whether your man is going to get what he wants and be happy, or get what he wants and find it not worth getting, or be got by it—or end in some other way. Whatever the outcome, you would think of an opposite possibility as seeming likely, even inevitable, at the start; but you would plant small true signs of the coming actual turn of affairs early, much earlier than the point at which actuality appears as such. And all this time you would be sorting out and testing for accuracy small matters of fact that might make this business of the man and what he wants convincing. And all this time you would still be only thinking.

For the question of how all this could be got across to somebody who knows nothing about it—that would come up and have to be decided. You would probably imagine several ways. You might go back to the beginning of your thinking and see whether the man himself had better do it, or one of those others who are trying to stop him, or perhaps some new person you hadn't thought of before, who sees the whole thing but isn't seen and doesn't take sides; or you might decide the best way would be not through any person, yourself included, but by some articulate but impersonal vehicle offering so much interest that nobody would bother or stop to think what it was or how it functioned. All this would take time and long thought. Following the business through by one way, you might almost reach the end and be blocked, and have to go back and try another. Two ways might seem equally good, and there you would be at a desperate pass. You might have to forget, for the time being, all you had learned about the whole affair—drop it clean out of yourself while you imagine yourself somebody else and see how he would like to learn of it—and not your way of learning either, his would be for fun. But eventually you would either go mad or make a decision.

What would happen? You would have a short story—all but the shortest though not the easiest part, the actual writing; all but the talk and the action. But by this time, after all that toil and broil, you could hardly bear not to have something to show for it, and something would pull you ahead anyway. You might give yourself fifteen pages for the whole, and no harm if it runs a page or two more; and you might set off certain page-points by which certain things must be accomplished. Somewhere along the line of all this planning you would call the thing something, in three to seven words. You would make very sure that the man, what he wants, whoever is likely to stop him from getting it, and the place where this happens—that all of these without exception are clear by the bottom of page two; and you would probably spend more time on that part than you spend on all the rest of the pages put together. Once that was done, you could let yourself go for a while, holding the lines of your tandem or four-in-hand carefully, however, and keeping an eye out for the turns ahead. When you drew near the end you might want to quit and go to church or take a walk. Whether in church or not you would be praying—asking, searching, groping for some way of saying what you chiefly want to say here, without saying it. Making somebody do it, or leaving it unsaid but there, somehow, for the reader to say to himself. That would turn up, too.

You would have, then, actually a story. And you would be so tired and flat and disgusted you would want to haul off and spit in its face. But proud of it too. For maybe it is a poor thing, but it is your own, the best you can do. And you would make a clean copy, on white paper, leaving wide margins and improving bits here and there, and when that was done you would read it over for typographical errors. Then you would write your name and address on the smaller of your two large manuscript envelopes, put on return postage, and slip the manuscript and this smaller envelope into the larger. You would send the thing off, first-class, to the magazine whose stories you like best to read. And you would have a drink on that—with somebody, I hope—but not talk or even think about the story if you could help it. And next morning, if you knew what's good for you, you would start another.

It's all there, inside of you. This is only the beginning. It won't be easy, but it may be good. Let it all out.

18

LIST OF SHORT STORIES

Most of the stories discussed in this volume appear in one or more of the books listed below under Collections. When one of these collections is a source in the Short Stories list, it is referred to simply by the name of its editor or editors. Original magazine publication of short stories is cited only when no other source is available.

COLLECTIONS—

Harold Blodgett, ed. *The Story Survey;* J. B. Lippincott Company.

Dorothy Brewster, ed. *A Book of Modern Short Stories;* The Macmillan Company.

Cleanth Brooks, Jr., and Robert Penn Warren. *Understanding Fiction;* F. S. Crofts & Company.

Leonard Brown, ed. *Modern American and British Short Stories;* Harcourt, Brace and Company.

Gordon Hall Gerould and Charles Bayly, Jr., eds. *Contemporary Types of the Short Story;* Harper & Brothers.

Henry Goodman, ed. *Creating the Short Story;* Harcourt, Brace and Company.

Frank Luther Mott, ed. *Good Stories;* The Macmillan Company.

Frank Luther Mott [and Bennett Alfred Cerf] eds. *The Bedside Book of Famous American Stories* (college edition); Random House.

Cynthia Ann Pugh, ed. *A Book of Short Stories;* The Macmillan Company.

——. *Ibid.* (revised edition).

Harry Shaw and Douglas Bement, eds. *Reading the Short Story;* Harper & Brothers.

SHORT STORIES—

Anderson, Sherwood. "I Want to Know Why," from *The Triumph of the Egg;* The Viking Press. Also in Brewster, Brooks and Warren, Gerould and Bayly, Mott-Cerf.

Benét, Stephen Vincent. "The Devil and Daniel Webster," from *Thirteen O'Clock;* Farrar and Rinehart. Also in Shaw and Bement.

Boyd, Thomas. "Responsibility," from *Points of Honor;* Charles Scribner's Sons. Also in Gerould and Bayly, Shaw and Bement.

Brush, Katharine. "Night Club," from *O. Henry Memorial Award Prize Stories of 1927;* Doubleday, Doran & Company. Also in Brewster, Mott, Mott-Cerf, Pugh I, Pugh II.

——. "Good Wednesday," from *O. Henry Memorial Award Prize Stories of 1931;* Doubleday, Doran & Company. Also in Shaw and Bement.

Caldwell, Erskine. "Kneel to the Rising Sun," in Mott-Cerf.

Clemens, Samuel L. [Mark Twain]. "The Celebrated Jumping Frog of Calaveras County." In Mott-Cerf.

——. "The Man That Corrupted Hadleyburg." In Mott-Cerf.

Collier, John. *"De Mortuis . . . ," The New Yorker,* July 18, 1942.

Conrad, Joseph. "Heart of Darkness," from *Youth;* Doubleday, Doran & Company, Inc.

Ervine, St. John G. "The Conjuror," from *The Mountain and Other Stories;* The Macmillan Company. Also in Mott.

Farrell, James T. "Honey, We'll Be Brave," from *Calico Shoes and Other Stories;* The Vanguard Press.

Faulkner, William. "A Rose for Emily," from *These 13;* Random House. Also in Brooks and Warren, Mott-Cerf.

——. "That Evening Sun," *ibid.* Also in Blodgett.

Galsworthy, John. "Quality," from *The Inn of Tranquillity;* Charles Scribner's Sons. Also in Shaw and Bement.

Garland, Hamlin. "Mrs. Ripley's Trip," from *Main-Travelled Roads;* Harper & Brothers. Also in Blodgett.

Glaspell, Susan. "A Jury of Her Peers," in Mott-Cerf, Pugh I, Pugh II.

Granberry, Edwin. "A Trip to Czardis," from *O. Henry Memorial Award Prize Stories of 1932;* Doubleday, Doran & Company, Inc. Also in Blodgett, Shaw and Bement.

Green, Eleanor. "The Dear Little Doves," from *O. Henry Memorial Award Prize Stories of 1942;* Doubleday, Doran & Company, Inc.

Hawthorne, Nathaniel. "The Birthmark," from *Mosses from an Old Manse.* In Brooks and Warren, Pugh I.

——. "Rappaccini's Daughter," *ibid.* In Mott-Cerf.

——. "Mr. Higginbotham's Catastrophe," from *Twice-Told Tales.* In Blodgett.

Hemingway, Ernest. "Hills Like White Elephants," from *The Fifth Column and the First Forty-Nine Stories;* Charles Scribner's Sons.

——. "The Killers," from *Men Without Women;* Charles Scribner's Sons. Also in Brewster, Brooks and Warren, Brown, Goodman, Mott-Cerf.

——. "The Sea Change," from *The Short Stories of Ernest Hemingway;* The Modern Library.

Irving, Washington, "The Legend of Sleepy Hollow," from *The Sketch Book.* In Mott-Cerf.

James, Henry. "Paste," in Blodgett.

——. "The Turn of the Screw," from *The Novels and Tales of Henry James,* Vol. XII; Charles Scribner's Sons.

Joyce, James. "Araby," from *Dubliners;* The Viking Press. Also in Brewster.

Kafka, Franz. "In the Penal Colony," in Brooks and Warren.

Kempton, Kenneth Payson. "Don't Tell Your Mother," *The Saturday Evening Post,* July 13, 1940.

Kipling, Rudyard. "Bitters Neat," from *Plain Tales from the Hills.*

——. "In Error," *ibid.*

——. "Without Benefit of Clergy," from *The Courting of Dinah Shadd, and Other Stories.* In Pugh II.

Lardner, Ring. "Haircut," from *The Love Nest and Other Stories;* Charles Scribner's Sons. Also in Brewster, Gerould and Bayly.

Magagna, Ernestine. "The Little Him," in Shaw and Bement.

Mansfield, Katherine. "Marriage à la Mode," from *The Garden Party and Other Stories;* Alfred A. Knopf. Also in Brown, Mott, Pugh I, Pugh II.

Maupassant, Guy de. "The Necklace," from *The Odd Number;* Harper & Brothers. Also in Brooks and Warren, Pugh I, Pugh II.

——. "The Piece of String," *ibid.* Also in Pugh I.

——. "Tallow Ball," in Brooks and Warren.

Poe, Edgar Allan. "The Cask of Amontillado," from *Tales.* In Blodgett, Pugh I, Pugh II.

——. "The Fall of the House of Usher," *ibid.* In Brooks and Warren.

——. "The Pit and the Pendulum," *ibid.* In Mott-Cerf.

Porter, William Sydney [O. Henry]. "The Gift of the Magi," from *The Four Million.*

——. "A Municipal Report," from *Strictly Business.* In Mott-Cerf, Pugh I, Pugh II.

Rawlings, Marjorie Kinnan. "The Pardon," in Blodgett.

Russell, John. "Jetsam," from *Where the Pavement Ends;* Harper & Brothers. Also in Gerould and Bayly, Shaw and Bement.

Russell, Mary Porter. "Arrival," in Shaw and Bement.

Saroyan, William. "Myself Upon the Earth," from *The Daring Young Man on the Flying Trapeze and Other Stories;* Random House.

Steele, Wilbur Daniel. "Bubbles," from *The Man Who Saw Through Heaven and Other Stories;* Harper & Brothers.

———. "The Yellow Cat," from *Land's End;* Harper & Brothers. Also in Shaw and Bement.

Stevenson, Robert Louis. "Markheim," from *The Merry Men and Other Tales and Fables.* In Pugh I, Pugh II.

Still, James. "Job's Tears," in Blodgett.

Suckow, Ruth. "Golden Wedding," from *Iowa Interiors;* Alfred A. Knopf. Also in Blodgett, Brown.

Wister, Owen. "Safe in the Arms of Croesus," *Harper's Magazine,* October, 1927.

Zugsmith, Leane. "Back to Work," in Mott-Cerf.

NOTE FOR THE 4TH PRINTING. The Mott-Cerf *Bedside Book of Famous American Stories* (Random House) went out of print in 1953. All but the last of the stories cited above from that collection appear in *An Anthology of Famous American Stories,* edited by Angus Burrell and Bennett Cerf for The Modern Library (Random House).

ACKNOWLEDGMENTS

FOR gracious, often generous permission to reprint material, my sincere thanks are due the authors, publishers, representatives, or holders of copyrights listed below:

The Atlantic Monthly
Ed Bell
Sally Benson
The Bobbs-Merrill Company
Brandt & Brandt
Current History
Bernard De Voto
Duell, Sloan & Pearce, Inc.
Doubleday & Company, Inc.
Susan Glaspell
Harper & Brothers
Houghton Mifflin Company
Alfred A. Knopf, Inc.
Little, Brown & Company

The Literary Guild of America
Longmans, Green & Co., Inc.
The Macmillan Company
Ernestine Magagna
The New Yorker
W. W. Norton & Company, Inc.
Partisan Review
Random House, Inc.
Rinehart & Company, Inc.
The Saturday Review of Literature
Mark Schorer
Charles Scribner's Sons
Mrs. Walter Stokes
Jerome Weidman
Owen J. Wister

I want especially to thank the Editorial Department of the Harvard University Press for expert and patient help in preparing this book for the printer.